D1533136

77 Miles
of
Jewish Stories

History, Anecdotes & Tales of Travel Along I-8

7 February 2018
For Bob & Helaine
Friends and
Shipmates !

Donald H. Harrison

By Donald H. Harrison

Donald H. Harrison

Copyright 2017 Donald H. Harrison
All rights reserved

ISBN-13: 978-1977676801
ISBN-10: 1977676804

Table of Contents

Foreword

Donald H. Harrison

Publishing an on-line daily news publication with the bold motto "There Is A Jewish Story Everywhere," I often feel compelled to demonstrate the thesis. In this book as well as one written before it -- *Schlepping Through the American West* -- I have tried to demonstrate that our motto is not hype: that a combination of factors support this belief in the ubiquity and benefit of the Jewish presence, now and throughout history.

I will name three major factors among a myriad.

First, the Hebrew Bible underpins at least three major western religions – Judaism, Christianity and Islam – and references to these Scriptures permeate the cultures of a large portion of the world.

Second, throughout history Jews have been peripatetic. Sometimes, because of anti-Semitism, we have been expelled from our native countries to other countries. Other times, Jewish individuals have struck out on their own to find new markets, new ideas, and new stimuli. This is especially true in the American West.

Third, every country in the world either has a relationship with Israel, or because of ideology, refuses to do so. Either way, therein lies a Jewish story.

To bring this global idea to the local San Diego County stage, I decided to drive along the Interstate 8 Highway and seek a Jewish story in the vicinity of every exit as the freeway followed a course from its western terminus at the Jack G. Robb Memorial Field in San Diego's Ocean Beach neighborhood to the boundary line separating San Diego County from its eastern neighbor, Imperial County. From origin to that destination, the Interstate 8 Highway covers 77 miles – thus the title of this book, *77 Miles of Jewish Stories*. If you wonder who Robb was, as I did, he served as the supervisor of boys' and men's recreation for the City of San Diego between 1927 and 1944.

It's important to note that freeway exits are numbered by their distance from the freeway's point of origin, and not consecutively. For example, when I went from Exit 54 to Exit 61, I wasn't skipping seven exits. There actually were no other exits between them.

I was surprised and pleased by the diversity of stories that I found and published on *San Diego Jewish World* between April, 2015 and August, 2016. By no means is this only about synagogues and other Jewish communal places. It is also about Jewish men and women who work in a variety of professions and enjoy a wide range of hobbies and past times. This has been an exciting journey for me, and I suspect it will alert many readers to the richness of Jewish pursuits in San Diego County.

Acknowledgments are due to many people, especially those who agreed to be interviewed for this enterprise, and those who wrote articles, books, and memoirs from which some of the material herein is drawn. Their names are included in the individual articles.

Members of my family have been very helpful, particularly my wife Nancy, to whom I dedicate this book. She puts up with my excursions without complaint. My grandson Shor accompanied me to numerous venues, often taking photographs, and always asking intelligent questions. Daughter Sandi designed the cover and helped with the layout, and grandniece Jessica designed the map. Family friend Bob Lauritzen also has been helpful, often permitting me during our travels to tap into a non-Jewish perspective. John Finley diligently proofread the book, and if there are any errors left, they're my fault not his. Other people like Olga Worm, formerly of Alpine, have led me to Jewish stories in San Diego's back country, while librarians and archivists like Jane Kenealy, formerly of the San Diego History Center, and Richard Crawford of the San Diego Central Library have unerringly directed me to sources.

– Donald H. Harrison, San Diego, California

1. Exit 0

Point Loma Peninsula

The Western terminus of Interstate 8

SAN DIEGO — Nimitz Boulevard at the western terminus of Interstate 8 is named for Fleet Admiral Chester Nimitz, who commanded the Pacific Fleet against the Japanese in World War II, and was the man who signed for the United States in the ceremony aboard the U.S.S. *Missouri* accepting the Japanese surrender.

Following the war, he was appointed by President Harry S. Truman as Chief of Naval Operations (CNO), and in that position, he supported the proposal of then Captain, and later Admiral, Hyman Rickover, a Jewish officer, to convert the submarine fleet from diesel to nuclear power. Future U.S. President Jimmy Carter, who served under Rickover, considered the admiral an inspiration and a mentor.

From Nimitz Boulevard, one may follow "Cabrillo National Monument" directional signs to navigate up the western side of the Point Loma Peninsula. Along the way, on the left of Catalina Boulevard, is the top side of a naval submarine base. Down below at the bay shore is where submarines are repaired at a place known as Ballast Point, so called because it was there that sailing ships discarded rocks or picked them up for ballast. Among famous 19th Century sailors who visited Ballast Point was Richard Henry Dana, the author of the classic *Two Years Before the Mast.* In more recent times, Ballast Point has been the home of Submarine Squadron 11, which includes four nuclear-powered submarines and a floating drydock for their repair. Rickover was considered the "father of the nuclear Navy," which began in 1954 with the launching of the U.S.S. *Nautilus*. The skipper of that vessel, Eugene Wilkinson, much later in his career would retire as a vice admiral and is buried near the submarine base at Fort Rosecrans National Cemetery.

Located at the tip of Point Loma above the junction of San Diego Bay and the Pacific Ocean, Cabrillo National Monument celebrates the European discovery of San Diego by explorer Juan Rodriguez Cabrillo, then in the employ of Spain. However, Rodriguez did not name this area "San Diego."

Juan Cabrillo Statue and Lighthouse at Cabrillo National Monument

As was the custom of Catholic explorers, Cabrillo checked his calendar of the saints' feast days, and found that the one closest to the date of discovery -- September 28th, 1542 -- was that of Saint Michael the Archangel. Accordingly, Cabrillo named the place "San Miguel." The explorer died later on his voyage, and Sebastian Vizcaino, who "re-discovered" the area for Spain in 1602, named it "San Diego," for a recently named saint so honored for medical miracles, including the saving of the life of a child of the King of Spain.

The Archangel Michael is honored in Judaism because in the Book of Daniel (10:13), Daniel has a vision of an unnamed angel who describes the Archangel Michael as "one of the foremost (heavenly) princes" and further (12:1-3) describes what Michael's role will be at the End of Days. In a way, it is too bad that "San Diego" didn't stay named "San Miguel," because the angel's description of the End of Days might have taken on far more immediacy at Fort Rosecrans National Cemetery, through which one passes *en route* to Cabrillo National Monument.

The Scripture reads as follows:

Daniel 12:1. At that time Michael will stand, the great (heavenly) prince who stands in support of the members of your people, and there will be a time of trouble such as there had never been since there was a nation until that time. But at that time your people will escape; everything that is found written in this book (will occur). 12:2 Many of those who sleep in the dusty earth will awaken: these for everlasting life and these for shame, for everlasting abhorrence. 12:3 The wise will shine like the radiance of the firmament, and those who teach righteousness to the multitudes (will shine) like the stars, forever and ever.

Gravestones at Fort Rosecrans National Cemetery

On the uniform gravestones spread across hillsides overlooking the Pacific Ocean and San Diego Bay, there are markings of various religions, depending on the preference expressed by the deceased's written request, or that of his survivors. Throughout Rosecrans National Cemetery one can find Stars of David on the gravestones of Jewish personnel as well as the symbols of other religions.

One of the features of the Cabrillo National Monument is a lighthouse that was built in 1855, more than 300 years after Cabrillo's voyage of discovery. The original lighthouse keeper was named Robert Israel and because of his surname, curators of the small museum at the lighthouse once thought that he might have been Jewish. They even put a tallit, long since removed, in one of the rooms. Genealogical records showed that notwithstanding his Hebraic-sounding name and possible Jewish ancestors somewhere in his father's line, Israel was a Christian whose father was Pennsylvania Dutch and mother was Scotch-Irish. When he was married in 1852 to Maria Arcadia Alipas, a priest officiated at the ceremony. Among Israel's four children was Robert Decatur Israel, whose burial service in 1908 was officiated by an Episcopal priest. The younger Israel's stone is marked with a Christian cross at Fort Rosecrans National Cemetery.

Retracing one's drive through the federal installation atop Pt. Loma, one soon comes to Talbot Street, which heads east toward San Diego Bay. Turn right, and just before where that street intersects with Rosecrans Avenue (named for U.S. Civil War General William Rosecrans) stands Cabrillo Elementary School, which has some interesting connections to San Diego's early Jewish history.

Cabrillo Elementary School has a 'sister' relationship with a school in a German town where Louis Rose, San Diego's first Jewish settler, was born in 1807.

Just north of Talbot Street lies Roseville, a 30-block section that Rose founded in 1869 that today is incorporated into the Point Loma community. In 1895, seven years after Louis Rose's death, his daughter Henrietta was appointed by the San Diego School Board as the first teacher at Roseville Elementary School, a position she kept for a year before being transferred to the Middletown Elementary School. Too small to accommodate Pt. Loma's growing population, Roseville Elementary School eventually was torn down and replaced by Cabrillo Elementary School.

Cabrillo Elementary School, Point Loma
(Photo: Shor M. Masori)

The school's geographic and genealogical connections to Louis Rose led to the creation of a Sister School relationship between Cabrillo Elementary School and the Grundschule in Neuhaus-an-der-Oste, Germany, where Louis Rose grew up. Coincidentally, both schools serve pupils in kindergarten through 4th grade, and both schools are in communities built in the vicinity of ocean-going vessels. Students have exchanged letters and drawings, and teachers and administrators of the two schools have exchanged visits.

....

To return to Interstate 8, one may continue to the first street beyond the school, which is Rosecrans Avenue, and turn left.
Follow Rosecrans Avenue several miles to where it branches into the entrances of Interstate 8 East and Interstate 5 North.

....

-San Diego Jewish World, April 23, 2015

2. Exit 0

Bahia Hotel

Richard Nixon's post 1968 GOP convention getaway

SAN DIEGO — In August 1968, right after Republicans nominated him for the presidency of the United States, Richard M. Nixon traveled from Miami Beach to San Diego after a stopover in Texas where he was briefed by vacationing U.S. President Lyndon B. Johnson about the progress of the Vietnam War.

Following his meeting with Johnson, candidate Nixon said that he would refrain from making political comments about the war while there was a chance that the Paris Peace Talks with representatives of North Vietnam might bear fruit.

So what would Nixon and his vice presidential running mate, the relatively unknown governor of Maryland, Spiro Agnew, emphasize in their joint campaign against a Democratic nominee who was soon to be selected?

Hoping to find out, news reporters and pundits accompanied Nixon to the Bahia Hotel on Mission Bay where he and his family and staff had set aside one week, August 11-17, to discuss strategy and to vacation following the grueling primary campaign in which Nixon had outmaneuvered New York Gov. Nelson Rockefeller on his left and California Gov. Ronald Reagan on his right.

Block of rooms where Richard Nixon stayed with his family and aides after receiving 1968 GOP nomination.

Nixon, his family, and his closest staff stayed in a block of 40 bayside rooms of the Bahia Hotel, while news media and lower ranking staff members stayed at the Catamaran Hotel several blocks away on Mission Boulevard. Both hotels were owned by William and Anne Evans, loyal San Diego Republicans. Located on a 14-acre peninsula, the then 15-year-old Bahia Hotel satisfied the Secret Service's security requirements, although its presidential suite did not. That suite was deemed too close to the public view to be adequate for security purposes. The Nixons were put up in a room near the end of the peninsula.

While at the Bahia, Agnew and high-ranking campaign officials made it known that the Nixon campaign planned to stress the need to quell the violence and civil unrest that had erupted across America earlier that year in the wake of the assassinations of civil rights leader Rev. Martin Luther King, Jr. and Bobby Kennedy. They also opposed anti-Vietnam War violence.

During the week he stayed at the Bahia, Nixon did not yet know that Johnson's Vice President, Hubert Humphrey, would emerge from the Aug. 26-29 Democratic National Convention as the presidential nominee and that U.S. Senator Edmund Muskie of Maine would be the Democrats' choice to occupy the vice presidential position that both Nixon and Humphrey had held. Nor did Nixon know that violence between police and protestors outside the Chicago convention hall would become as big a story as Humphrey's nomination.

While preparing for his campaign against whatever Democratic rival might emerge, Nixon spent much of his time in San Diego on the telephone mending fences with the liberal Republican leaders who had supported Rockefeller's failed presidential bid, and with conservatives who had backed Reagan.

After winning public endorsements from Rockefeller and New York Mayor John Lindsay, Nixon announced at the Bahia that he would soon travel to New York City for personal meetings with the two leaders.

Whereas Rockefeller and Lindsay were quick to pledge their support for their party nominee, another important New York Republican — U.S. Senator Jacob Javits — was playing his cards closer to his vest. The Jewish Republican was considered by many to be one of the most liberal members of the Senate as well as an outspoken opponent of the war in Vietnam. Before he would climb aboard his party leader's campaign band wagon, Javits wanted to hear for himself exactly how Nixon viewed the Vietnam problem. From his room in the Bahia, Nixon made an appointment to meet Javits–an appointment that ultimately resulted in Javits' endorsement.

During the week-long working vacation, Nixon met at the Bahia Hotel with at least two other well-known Jewish political figures. Arthur Burns had served as chairman of the Council of Economic Advisors during the administration of Dwight D. Eisenhower at the same time as Nixon was the nation's vice president. Burns subsequently would be named by Nixon as a Cabinet-level counselor to the President and, later, as chairman of the Federal Reserve Bank — their conversation at the Bahia a step toward those appointments.

One of Burns' former students at Rutgers University, who had made quite a name for himself as a conservative economist, Milton Friedman, also met with Nixon at the Bahia. Although Friedman would be called upon by Nixon for advice now and then, it was not until the Reagan administration began in 1981 that Friedman would become widely recognized as a shaper of American economic policy.

A highlight of Nixon's stay was his meeting at the Bahia with California Governor Ronald Reagan, who himself would be destined to win the presidency in 1980. In a joint news conference, Nixon and Reagan told the media that Reagan would campaign for Nixon in California, and from time to time would go out on the national campaign trail as his responsibilities as governor permitted.

Besides wanting to unify the Republican party behind him, Nixon in the words of Press Secretary Herb Klein wanted to lay out with Agnew what they hoped would be "the most coordinated dual campaign in American political history."

In his book, *The Selling of the President 1968,* Joe McGinnis reported that such a campaign was easier announced than accomplished. One of Nixon's Jewish advisors, attorney Leonard Garment, was tasked with looking over documentary film footage about Agnew that had been shot on the Bahia grounds by a hapless and unnamed interviewer. Besides being often out of focus, the film was rendered unusable by boring questions and answers. For example, the interviewer asked whether Agnew was happy to be chosen as the vice presidential nominee.

As McGinnis reported it: "'The ability to be happy is directly proportional to the ability to suffer,' Agnew said. His tone indicated he might doze before finishing the sentence, 'and as you grow older you feel everything less.' He stopped. There was silence on the film. Then the voice of the interviewer: 'I see.'"

Garment commented about the film: "It looks like you're looking through a Coke bottle."

And about Agnew's on-camera performance, Garment added sadly: "He is rather nondynamic."

There is a Jewish story everywhere. As was the case with Javits, Burns, Friedman and Garment, sometimes "Jewish stories" constitute strands in the tapestry of a much larger tale.

···

*From the West Mission Bay Boulevard exit of westbound I-8:
Follow West Mission Bay Drive signs through the interchange,
and watch for the Bahia Hotel on the right. If you get to Mission
Boulevard, you have just passed it.*

···

-San Diego Jewish World, April 30, 2015

3. Exit 1

Valley View Casino Center

Originally known as the San Diego Sports Arena, today this building is called the Valley View Casino Center

SAN DIEGO — The International Sports Arena, today known as the Valley View Casino Center, was largely the dream of one Jewish San Diegan: Robert Breitbard.

Breitbard loved football, he loved playing it, and he loved coaching it, both at San Diego State College (now University) and at Hoover High School. In truth, he loved all sports and his collection of their memorabilia became the nucleus of the San Diego Hall of Champions in Balboa Park. The collection was enhanced with replicas of the awards bestowed by the Breitbard Athletic Foundation upon star athletes who either resided in San Diego, or played outstandingly for its sports teams. The Hall of Champions has been a feature of Balboa Park since 1961.

Breitbard's incredible enthusiasm for sports prompted him in 1963 to propose to the Western Hockey League (WHL) that San Diego be granted a franchise.

Fine, the WHL owners, in essence, told Breitbard, you can have one so long as you pay $75,000 to the league and provide your team an arena capable of seating 11,000 people at hockey games. The terms were steep, but Breitbard accepted.

Robert Breitbard

Next, he persuaded the City of San Diego to provide a 50-year master lease on an 80-acre site in what was then known as the Midway-Frontier area of the city. In return, he promised to build with private capital the International Sports Arena on 38 of those acres. The other 42 acres he proposed for commercial development. Breitbard then formed the San Diego Arena Lease Co., which, as a non-profit organization with the City of San Diego's blessing, could issue tax-exempt bonds to finance the construction of the arena. Additionally, he created Sports Enterprises, a for-profit company which became the lessee.

Ground was broken on November 18, 1965 by crews working for San Diego general contractor Gene Trepte, who had to import 40,000 cubic yards of dirt to firm up a base near an old river bed for the 121-million-pound sports arena, according to biographer Dan Fulop, who wote *Bob Breitbard: San Diego's Sports Keeper*. (That biography was published in 2012, two years after Breitbard died at the age of 91.)

Breitbard hired Mike McNab, who had been general manager of the Vancouver Canucks, to be the first head coach and general manager of San Diego's new hockey team, which, as the result of a name-the-team contest, was called the San Diego Gulls.

The $6.4 million arena was finished in time for the Gulls' inaugural game against the Seattle Totems which, surprisingly, the Gulls won -- surprisingly, because over the rest of the season, the team's record was 22 wins, 47 losses and 3 ties. Notwithstanding this last-place finish, the Gulls created hockey-mania in San Diego, averaging in their first season 8,751 paid spectators per game. The season total of 315,201 paid admissions set a WHL record, according to biographer Fulop.

The success of the Gulls made owners in the National Basketball Association (NBA) wonder whether San Diego fans might be just as excited and loyal to a professional basketball team. Breitbard thought they would, and this led to an announcement in January 1967 that the following season San Diego would have its own NBA team. Fulop reported that with San Diego's motto then being "A City in Motion" and with Convair building Atlas rockets for the National Aeronautics and Space Administration, the name San Diego Rockets was chosen from among numerous entries in another name-the-team contest. Jack McMahon was named the first head coach.

Like the Gulls, the Rockets had a dismal first season, winning only 15 of their 82 games in 1967-68–the most losses any NBA team had suffered in a single season. But unlike the Gulls, the Rockets did not excite the imagination of the fans. Average attendance was only 4,606 per game, far less than that of the Gulls. But Breitbard thought he had a way to fix that. For the next season, he was able to obtain as a draft pick a star player from the University of Houston, Elvin Hayes, nicknamed the "Big E." What a difference Hayes made! He helped the Rockets in their second season to compile a 37-45 record and win a playoff berth. At the same time, average attendance climbed to 6,054.

With Hayes starring for the Rockets, and Willie O'Ree playing for the Gulls, Breitbard could count on the celebrity of these players to stoke the fans' enthusiasm. O'Ree previously had played for the Boston Bruins of the National Hockey League, and because he was the first African-American to play in that league, he was sometimes honored as "The Jackie Robinson of the NHL."

Despite the presence of these celebrities on his teams, Breitbard's sports empire was headed for trouble. While Hayes boosted attendance for the Rockets, paid admissions still did not climb to the level of attendance enjoyed by the Gulls. The 42 acres of land surrounding the Sports Arena never attracted a sustainable commercial development, and overdue payments mounted up to the NBA for its franchise, as well as to the City of San Diego for bond payments and interest.

Momentary diversion from Breitbard's financial troubles came in 1971 when his International Sports Arena hosted the NBA's 21st Annual All Star Game, at which 14,378 people enjoyed the playing of Kareem Abdul Jabbar (then still named Lew Alcindor), Wilt Chamberlain, Willis Reed, Oscar Robinson, and Jerry West, among others.

Unable to pay his mounting debts, Breitbard sold the Rockets in June 1971 to a partnership in Houston, Texas, where the team still plays today. A month later, he forfeited ownership of the International Sports Arena through sale of its lease to Canadian entrepreneur Peter Graham.

For a while at least, Breitbard still had the popular Gulls. He hoped that the team could be elevated into an NHL franchise, but he didn't reckon on the fact that Graham wanted his own hockey team in the arena. And Graham was known as a tough businessman. When the national Republican party failed to agree to his terms for leasing the International Sports Arena in 1972, he told the GOP to take its national convention elsewhere.

Prompted also by the controversy engendered by the International Telephone & Telegraph (ITT) affair, in which the Nixon administration was accused of favoring ITT in an anti-trust investigation in return for financial backing for the GOP convention, the Republicans relocated their convention to Miami, much to the great consternation of the City of San Diego and its then mayor Pete Wilson.

Graham was just as tough on Breitbard, reportedly requiring the highest rent in the Western Hockey League, and this, along with higher player salaries, resulted in Breitbard losing money on what previously had been a successful franchise, according to biographer Fulop.

Eventually Graham decided to grant a World Hockey Association team -- the New Jersey Knights -- an exclusive five-year lease at the International Sports Arena, leaving the Gulls with nowhere to play. Breitbard and the Gulls formally were evicted on June 2, 1974, leading the Gulls to fold and the Western Hockey League to disband. Renamed as the San Diego Mariners, the Jersey Knights never caught on as the Gulls before them had. They played only three years before they too were folded.

Dr. Leonard Bloom, an orthodontist, obtained a franchise from the American Basketball Association for the San Diego Conquistadors in 1972, and unable to work out an arrangement with Graham, had his team play at San Diego State University and the San Diego Convention Center in 1973 and 1974. The ABA purchased the team from Bloom, and, playing at the Sports Arena, it became the San Diego Sails. But it failed by 1976.

Another NBA team, the San Diego Clippers, came to San Diego in 1978 and despite losing season after losing season, lasted until 1984, when their second owner, Los Angeles attorney and real estate man Donald Sterling moved them to Los Angeles, where they became the L.A. Clippers. Like the Gulls and Rockets before them, they had been named the Clippers in a name-the-team contest conducted among San Diegans by the first owners, Irv Levin and Harold Lipton. While in San Diego, the Clippers had been head coached by Gene Shue, Paul Silas, and Jimmy Lynam. Some of their best-known players were Randy Smith, Bill Walton, and Swen Nater. Walton, a local favorite, was forced to miss numerous games because of a stress fracture in his foot.

All in all, there were a number of Jewish owners of a succession of basketball teams in San Diego—Breitbard, Bloom, the partnership of Levin and Lipton, and Sterling—and all of them had bad luck here.

In May 1985, Graham was replaced by Vincent Ciruzzi as operator of the International Sports Arena, marking the end of a stormy 14-year tenure. After Ciruzzi came Ernie Hahn II, the current general manager of the Valley View Casino Center.

Breitbart spent much of the remainder of his life in his office at the Hall of Champions in Balboa Park, greeting visitors and reminiscing with sports celebrities about his one-time Hoover High School classmate Ted Williams of Boston Red Sox fame and other star athletes who had made San Diegans very proud.

Near the end of his life, Breitbard moved to Seacrest Village Retirement Home in Encinitas, California, which is operated by a non-profit arm of the local Jewish community. He died there in his sleep in May of 2010 at the age of 91.

At the funeral service at Tifereth Israel Synagogue in San Diego, Rabbi Leonard Rosenthal said: "Bob Breitbard never cared about a person's station in life, or their background, or religion, or ethnicity, or the color of their skin, or what they could do for him. He had a gift for making anyone he met and spoke with feel they were the center of his universe and that no matter who they were or their station in life, they were a unique and valuable human being. He would just as warmly embrace the woman who cleaned his house as he would a captain of industry."

Five years after Breitbard's death, a new hockey team, also named the San Diego Gulls, began playing at the Valley View Casino Center in the American Hockey League. The new Gulls were a farm team for the National Hockey League's Anaheim Ducks. Surely, Bob Breitbard would have been pleased.

··

Sports Arena Boulevard has a westbound Exit 1, and eastbound entrance to the Interstate 8 and is located about 1/2 mile east of the I-8 terminus. To reach the Valley View Casino Center, known formerly as the San Diego Sports Arena, follow signs through the interchange to Sports Arena Boulevard and then turn left into Valley View Casino Center parking lot. Sponsored by the Valley View Casino located in northern San Diego County for advertising purposes, the Arena does not offer on-site gambling.

··

-*San Diego Jewish World, May 7, 2015*

4. Exit 2

Roseville Section of Point Loma

Setting for Louis Rose Monument
(Photo: Shor M. Masori)

SAN DIEGO — The Rosecrans Street exit from Interstate 8 leads to Loma Portal, Roseville, and La Playa, three neighborhoods of the larger Point Loma community of San Diego. To the west of Rosecrans Avenue is a high bluff leading through a United States government reservation to the Cabrillo National Monument, which commemorates the "discovery" of San Diego in 1542 by navigator Juan Rodriguez Cabrillo, who was sailing in the service of Spain. As previously reported in this series, Cabrillo National Monument also can be approached from the Nimitz Boulevard exit of Interstate 8.

That "Roseville" and "Rosecrans" sound so similar is just a floral coincidence. William Rosecrans, for whom the street was named, was a gentile Civil War general who, following service in the Union Army, came to California with the idea of creating a San Diego terminus for a transcontinental railroad that would sweep across the southern states. However, Los Angeles, not San Diego, became the terminus.

The community of Roseville, on the other hand, was named for a visionary entrepreneur, Louis Rose, who in 1850 was the first Jew to settle in San Diego. Rose had grown up in the little town of Neuhaus-an-der-Oste in modern-day Germany, near the confluence of the Oste and Elbe Rivers close to the North Sea. He immigrated to the United States in 1840 settling first in New Orleans, and later making his way to Texas. Following news of the California gold discovery, he like many other merchants, continued westward to what became the Golden State. San Diego had just 650 residents when he settled here.

Then located under the Presidio hilltop, where Spanish soldiers in 1769 had built a mission and a fort, Old Town made no commercial sense from Rose's standpoint. From his experiences on the Elbe River in Germany and the Mississippi River in the United States, Rose knew that ships and their cargo could mean trade and riches for any city.

Shaking his head over the fact that Old Town was located a couple of miles from the bay, instead of being situated alongside it, Rose decided to accumulate as much bayside property as possible between Old Town and the entrance to San Diego Bay to build a new town. Having accomplished that by 1869, he began selling lots in Roseville, an area 30 blocks long and stretching 8 blocks inland from the bay. The thoroughfare that today is named Rosecrans Street, Rose had named Main Street. Cross streets that today are mostly named in alphabetical order for authors, he named more prosaically as 1st through 30th Streets.

In memory of Rose's efforts to move San Diego's location to the Bay from Old Town, a plaque has been placed at Louis Rose Point at a point where Roseville meets the Boat Channel leading into San Diego Bay.

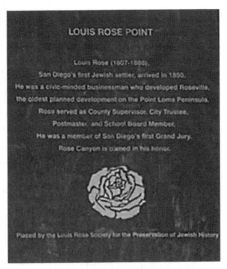

Louis Rose plaque.
(Photo: Shor M. Masori)

Despite the magnificent views offered from the lots he carved out on the Pt. Loma hillside, Roseville was slow to develop. Investors preferred the New Town location across the bay that was chosen by private developer Alonzo Horton. Today, Horton's Addition is the heart of San Diego's downtown.

From his Roseville holdings, Rose sold for a nominal fee to the Jewish community its first cemetery (later moved to another part of the city), and gallantly presented residential lots to some of the women of San Diego with whose families he had dined during his bachelorhood.

Roseville was not the only geographic location where Rose left his name. In an area that once was known as *La Cañada de las Lleguas*, or the Canyon of the Mares, between Old Town and modern day La Jolla, Rose purchased property for San Diego's first tannery. The area that came to be called "Rose Canyon" is known especially to geologists because a well-known fault line runs through it. The small stream that runs through the canyon bears the name Rose Creek.

Trappers brought many animals with furs for tanning, sometimes paying money, and more often offering goods or livestock in trade. This was how Rose acquired his beloved Galapagos tortoise Chili, who was so big children could ride on its back. Rose and Chili and a small dog named Pat would take walks together, and Pat sometimes would bark seemingly ferociously at passing animals or humans. But when anyone approached Pat, the dog showed its true colors, skittering between the legs of Chili for protection.

Not wanting to waste any part of the cattle whose hides he tanned, Rose opened a butcher shop in Old Town, only one of his many enterprises. He also owned a small hotel, saloon, and a general store, and served as an officer of the would-be San Diego and Gila Railroad Company which hoped in vain to link up someday with a transcontinental line.

In Old Town San Diego State Historic Park, the two-story Robinson-Rose Building on the Plaza recalls Rose's memory and that of James W. Robinson, a Texas politician whom he met on the wagon train to San Diego. Together, Rose and Robinson became powerful members of the San Diego City Board of Trustees as well as the first county Board of Supervisors.

Rose also served on San Diego's first grand jury, and was an early member of the San Diego School Board. He was a member of the San Diego Masonic Lodge No. 35, F & M.

After his close friend Robinson died in 1857, Rose purchased the home from the widow Sarah Robinson. Today that building serves as the State Park's visitor center.

Besides providing upstairs living quarters for Rose and Mathilde Newman Rose, whom he married in 1869 when he was 62 years old, the building also provided offices for the Masons, for the railroad, and one year was used by Rose and his fellow Jews to conduct High Holy Day services.

It was there that Henrietta Rose, his spinster daughter, was born. Seven years after her father's 1888 death she became a school teacher, serving the San Diego Unified School District for 45 years. In 1901, she was elected president of the Southern Star Chapter 9 of the Eastern Star Masonic organization.

....

Rosecrans Street is westbound, Exit 2, and eastbound entrance of Interstate 8. Rosecrans Street through the Point Loma Peninsula formerly was designated as State Route 209 South. To get to Louis Rose Point from the Rosecrans Street exit, continue straight and turn left onto Womble Street and follow it through the parking lot to the turnaround, and park. The marker honoring Rose is alongside a walkway adjacent to the boat channel.

....

-San Diego Jewish World, May 14, 2015

5. Exit 2

University of San Diego Law School

Herbert Lazerow in his office at USD Law School

SAN DIEGO — In the news and in movie theaters that show such films as *The Lady in Gold*, perplexing questions continue to arise about who is the rightful owner of art works seized by the Nazis before and during World War II.

Atop the hill guarding the northwestern entrance to Mission Valley -- and easily reached via Interstate 8's Morena Boulevard exit -- is the Catholic-run University of San Diego, where Herbert Lazerow, a Jew who holds the distinction of being USD's longest-serving faculty member, teaches courses in international law and other legal subjects.

One of his areas of specialty is the law of art, and another is the art of the law. In the latter, employing the Socratic method of asking questions, rather than lecturing, Lazerow familiarizes his students with the kinds of questions to ask as they frame their approach to a law case; how to anticipate counter-arguments from legal adversaries; and what kinds of approaches may help them debunk those arguments.

In his office brightened with paintings by his wife Jane, Lazerow keeps on a shelf *Mastering Art Law*, a book he authored that, among other topics, explains the complicated law concerning the recovery of art objects once seized by the Nazis. In an interview, he was kind enough to walk me through five legal classifications for art that had been confiscated from its previous owners.

First, governments, however heinous they may be, have the right under their police power to decide what kinds of art are morally acceptable and what kinds are beyond the pale. These definitions will vary from country to country. For example, said the law professor, "In the United States, we draw a line between 'obscene things' that are basically contraband and 'erotic art' that is okay." During the time of the Nazis, he added, "the German government confiscated what they considered to be 'degenerate art,' (also 'decadent art') and they confiscated it from Jews, other Germans, state-owned museums, and that was all perfectly legal."

Courts are unlikely to return to their previous owners any art found to meet this description.

Second, the Nazis needed money to finance their war machine, and accordingly it commissioned agents to sell some so-called 'decadent art' to collectors in other countries. As Germany owned the 'decadent art' under its police power, said Lazerow, it also had the right under international law to sell it. So museums, galleries, collectors, or any other party that purchased the 'decadent art' purchased it from a party that had the legal right to sell it.

Therefore, courts would not require those purchasers or their heirs to return the art, according to Lazerow.

Third, in some situations, the law professor said, dealers who were selling art on Nazi Germany's behalf were unable to locate buyers, so ended up storing the art on premises under their control. Inasmuch as such a dealer was an agent of the government of Germany, Lazerow said, the art remains the property of that nation if the art was legally acquired.

Fourth, Hitler's government not only seized art, it also purchased art at market prices for what the Nazi *fuehrer* intended to become the largest and greatest art museum in the world – to be located in Hitler's hometown of Linz, Austria. That art also remains the property of Germany, because it was legally obtained, said Lazerow.

Fifth, many art pieces were confiscated from Jews for no other reason than that they were Jews—and such a discriminatory policy was clearly illegal under international law, according to Lazerow. But that doesn't mean that to prevail in court all a Jewish family has to do is prove that the art was previously under its ownership—and that it was not so called 'decadent art,' Lazerow said.

"A major problem that you are going to run into over the next ten years is the question of whether a particular piece of art was stolen from a Jewish family or not. Obviously anybody who sells art, sells it because they would rather have the money than the art, but sometimes you sell it with a gun to your head. 'I'm not sure we can issue this exit visa unless you sell this art to the state for $1.' Those are the easy cases — those were sales that were not really sales but thefts."

"But," continued Lazerow, "consider a situation where a Jewish manufacturer of underwear is on vacation in Switzerland at his summer home, and gets a call from a friend in Germany who says, 'the SS is in your house! Don't come home!' Unlike other people, he took the advice, and didn't come home. There he is in Switzerland, his factory in Germany seized, and he had relatively little to support himself. He had a few paintings in his Swiss summer home, which he sends to an auction house in The Netherlands, which was not then under German control. Now, were those paintings stolen? They were sold under duress, but is it enough duress that we in the United States would consider it stolen art — especially when the people who purchased at the auction were not the people who applied duress?"

The professor explained that there is a conflict between common law systems, such as are practiced in the United States and Great Britain, and the civil legal systems derived from Roman law that prevail through much of the European continent.

"In the common law system, art that is stolen remains stolen; there is nothing that anyone can do to wash the title clean," Lazerow said. "In legal systems that follow Roman law, they favor the 'security of commerce' over the 'security of ownership,' so that if an item is stolen and then sold to a purchaser who doesn't know anything about the theft, either immediately or within a very short period of time, that art becomes the property of the purchaser. So, it depends on whether you are going to apply, for example, American law or French law."

I asked the professor whether that meant that a museum owning a piece of art stolen from a Jewish family may or may not have to return it depending on the country where the museum is located?

Lazerow responded: "You tend to find this problem less with museums than with individual purchasers although it certainly can occur with museums. I think the problem tends to arise less with museums because museums are so dependent on public good will; they are disposed to do the right thing, although in the past they haven't always. Whereas a private individual may have a collection of 30-40 pieces of art and to give one back is significant. But a museum which has 20,000-30,000 pieces — most of which are in storage — it is not such a big deal to give one back, and you get a lot of good will out of that.

"That is one of the reasons why museums have fared relatively well in the litigation," Lazerow added. "They have given back a lot of the meritorious claims. But there again, there is general agreement in international circles that a country can restrict the export of art in order to maintain national treasures. In Austria, for instance, after the war, a lot of art was restored to Jewish owners but they were not allowed to take the art out of the country. And one of the questions the courts have dodged is under the European Convention of Human Rights, you have the right to travel, the right to leave any country including your own, and you have the right to enjoy your personal property. But the courts have refused to put those rights together and say if you move out of the country, you have the right to take your art with you!"

Having served on the USD faculty for 47 years at the time of our interview in 2015, Lazerow was the "dean" of the faculty in the usage of the word meaning "longest serving." Because of his tenure, which he said is one year greater than that of History Prof. Iris Engstrand, at any graduation ceremony that he attends, he carries the ceremonial mace and precedes the President in the academic procession. There are ceremonies for undergraduates, law school students, and graduate students in other fields of studies. Lazerow said for him it is sufficient to carry the mace in the law school ceremony. He yields that honor to other faculty members at the other ceremonies.

The origins of the ceremonial mace go back to the days when it was used as a weapon by a knight to bludgeon any enemies who might attack the king. "Since I have carried the mace no one has even attempted to harm the president at graduation," Lazerow deadpanned.

While Lazerow has taught at the law school, there have been seven academic deans–three of them Catholic, two of them Protestant, and two Jewish.

The first Jewish dean, now deceased, was Don Weckstein, who was followed by the second Jewish dean, Sheldon Krantz. Weckstein served in the 1970. His particular specialties were labor law and professional responsibility, meaning the rules of ethics and conduct for lawyers. "He was very successful in building a law school. He believed in planting a thousand flowers," Lazerow said. "You would go to him with an idea and he would say 'let's run with it.' He wasn't always as generous with funding!"

Weckstein enjoyed repartee—particularly in the form of the mock insults that one associates with the comedian Don Rickles. "He was an equal opportunity insulter. Nobody around escaped some sort of insult, but nobody took it too seriously."

Krantz, who was dean during the 1980s, was considered an authority in criminal law, particularly the ins and outs of sentencing. Additionally, "Sheldon was very good at the outside aspects of being a dean. He established a rapport with the practicing bar, he established a community mediation service in conjunction with the city to try to get minor disputes like landlord-tenant disputes, or disputes between neighbors out of the courts and into a mediation setting," Lazerow reminisced.

"He developed relatively close ties with the Hebrew University of Jerusalem and we have profited by that enormously. We have had a number of faculty members from Hebrew University come here; I hired a number of them to teach in the summer and they were so successful that they were brought back as visitors during the academic year."

Currently, he added, "we have someone on our faculty who is tenured for one semester, the spring semester, and the fall semester he is on the faculty at Bar-Ilan University."

Lazerow said that Israeli law professors often have law degrees both from Israel and the United States, and are therefore conversant and able to compare the law of both countries. He added that as a country that became independent only in 1948, Israel developed a unique legal system which looked not only at precedents from Great Britain—which administered Israel under a League of Nations mandate—but also precedents from other countries, including the United States.

As for Lazerow's own academic background, he graduated from Harvard Law School in 1963, and worked subsequently in the international division of the Internal Revenue Service, before accepting a professorship at the University of Louisville's Law School, which today is named for Supreme Court Justice Louis D. Brandeis. The Justice had grown up in Louisville, and today his body is buried under the portico of the law school. Lazerow joined the USD faculty in 1967.

Was it strange being a Jew on a Catholic campus? I asked Lazerow, who is a member of Congregation Beth Israel, which is part of the Reform movement. "You never had any sense that there was a problem," he answered. "I don't know whether that was because I was clearly what Catholics would regard as an observant Jew. That is one of the strange things, I probably know more about our religion than 99 percent of Jews, and yet what I know is so small compared to what there is to know. Several thousand years of very smart people thinking about a religion produces a wonderful literature, full of interesting ideas."

Mock Supreme Court at USD Law School

From Exit 2 C (westbound), the University of San Diego is reached by merging onto Morena Boulevard, then making a slight right onto Linda Vista Road, and a left at Alcala Park Way into the campus. Eastbound traffic should take I-8 to Taylor Street, turn right to Morena Blvd, and then a slight right on Linda Vista Road, to a left onto Alcala Park Way into the campus.

-San Diego Jewish World, May 21, 2015

6. Exit 2

A Ceremony at the Immaculata

David Stutz and Papal Sword

SAN DIEGO — That such a man should be knighted by the Pope was not surprising. The retired colonel had donated substantial sums of money not only to the Catholic-run University of San Diego, but also to other universities founded under religious auspices, including Cal Western on Point Loma, which since has become Point Loma Nazarene University.

At USD, a lecture hall is named for him; on the Point Loma Nazarene campus, there is a theatre named in his honor. He also served on the boards of Georgetown University, Brandeis University, Atlanta University, Pepperdine University, and the Claremont School of Theology.

A benefactor who had a love for students from preschool through college, this man also had donated sufficient money to the church for the construction of a school at the Pala Mission, and to the City of San Diego for a playground along the Sixth Avenue side of Balboa Park.

And, having been appointed in 1953 by President Dwight D. Eisenhower as a U.S. delegate to the United Nations General Assembly, he also provided the funds for a community center in San Ysidro, which is Mexico's next-door neighbor.

At USD, this man wearing top hat, tuxedo and white gloves was honored with a procession that included San Diego Mayor Pete Wilson, Rabbi Joel Goor of Congregation Beth Israel, many priests, and other faculty, as well as Knights and Ladies of the Holy Sepulcher and fellow Knights of St. Gregory wearing their ceremonial green uniforms and plumed hats. When the procession reached the Immaculata, this man was welcomed and respectfully ushered through the solid brass front door of that church.

When USD President Author Hughes and Monsignor I. Brent Eagan, the diocesan chancellor, watched this man kneel on August 24, 1974 at a prayer desk known as *prie-dieu* at the large Immaculata Church on the University of San Diego campus to be dubbed by Bishop Leo Maher as a Knight of St. Gregory, the only thing that may have been surprising was that this man was not a Catholic.

Sir Knight, Colonel Irving Salomon, was a Jew.

So far as Bishop Maher or anyone else knew, Salomon was the first Jewish layperson ever to be so honored. According to the Catholic newspaper *Southern Cross,* Cardinal Sergio Pignedoli had been in San Diego to attend a Diocesan Pastoral Congress when he met and was impressed by Salomon's open-heartedness. The cardinal asked the bishop if there were not some way to recognize Salomon, and the two clergymen decided to quietly nominate Salomon for the honor. Salomon was unaware of what was coming until he attended a birthday party for Bishop Maher, at which time the bishop said he planned to have a birthday ceremony for Salomon too. Then he explained that Pope Paul VI personally had approved Salomon's investiture in a knighthood that had been established in 1831, perhaps recognizing in Salomon a man who mirrored his own goodwill outreach to many parts of the world. Salomon was active in the United Nations Education, Scientific and Cultural Organization (UNESCO), as well as the local World Affairs Council.

When Salomon received the news from Maher, he responded: "I recognize how important this honor is, but to be recognized in this way is stupefying." At the ceremony itself, Salamon said similarly: "Many words could be said on this occasion. But I am so grateful for this honor and privilege, and thank everyone, especially the Holy Father. I am so very humbled that I hope you forgive me if I don't say any more."

Saint Gregory, the man for whom the knighthood order had been named, had preferred the monastic life and was reluctant to become Pope in the 6th century. Once in the high office, however, he purged the Catholic Church of many pagan

Roman elements that had crept into its worship and instituted new styles of prayer. Gregorian chants are associated with his reign, and today he is honored as a patron saint of music and art. One supposes he would have been pleased that Salomon's largesse also extended to the arts, in particular the San Diego Ballet and the Old Globe Theatre.

The Immaculata is a large church that dominates the northern hillside as one enters Mission Valley from the west on Interstate 8. It has a colorful dome bearing an 8,500 pound statue of Our Lady of Immaculate Conception, as well as a bell tower with a 300-pound cross. From the ground to the top of the cross is a distance of 169 feet.

Other Jews might have felt uncomfortable in this Roman Catholic edifice — when does one stand? when does one sit? — but the urbane Salomon glided through the ceremony in which he heard himself praised by Maher for his "generous service to humanity (and) his long years of continual and devoted good works for the betterment of mankind."

In the community of Valley Center, near Escondido, Salomon for many years had made his home on the 2,300-acre Rancho Lilac, where he raised livestock and quarter horses, and entertained the elite of the world of politics and entertainment. He and his wife Cecile–and their daughter Abbe, who would grow up to become an attorney and a San Diego City Councilwoman–hosted the likes of former First Lady Eleanor Roosevelt, who wrote a column praising the rancho; UN Undersecretary and Nobel Peace Prize Winner Ralph Bunche; and film stars Myrna Loy, Ramon Navarro, and Jack Haley. Several years after he left office, President Eisenhower, who had appointed Salomon as a delegate to the U.N. General Assembly, visited the ranch on July 14, 1964.

Here is an excerpt from a "My Day" column by Eleanor Roosevelt that was published in 1960 by the *Evening Tribune* of San Diego.

> Salomon is raising pedigreed Herefords for breeding purposes, and they were grazing in the hills, for California has had more rain than usual recently, and the cattle looked very attractive as we drove around a part of the ranch. He used to raise hogs, but he has decided that they lose too much money. He has olive trees, but he can buy olives more cheaply than he can pick them.
>
> He takes keen pleasure in the fact that the milk and cream and butter and cottage cheese come from the ranch. All of these products are certainly very good, but I surmise also that they cost more than if he bought them outside.
>
> The ranch house itself is charming and the trees around it are the most beautiful old live oaks, with acacia and pepper trees here and there. I can well understand why Mr. and Mrs. Salomon love their ranch, and I can also understand that Mrs. Salomon is happy that she can have a delightful penthouse in San Diego too.

The penthouse, incidentally, was on Sixth Avenue, right across from that playground in Balboa Park.

You might think that this man who moved so easily through the top tiers of religious, political and entertainment accomplishment was, so to speak, born to the ranch. But you would be wrong. He actually grew up quite poor, and considered himself lucky as a youth in Chicago to be hired as an office boy at Royal Metal Manufacturing Company that made the steel chairs and desks that became standard equipment at schools, military bases, and government offices.

Eventually, through hard work and enterprise, he became the president of that company. A patriot, who had served as a Marine private in World War I, his knowledge of business and manufacture made him attractive to the Pentagon during World War II. He was assigned the rank of lieutenant colonel, and he worked in Washington, D.C.

After the war, he traveled frequently, and had several different U.S. passports, as well as one from the United Nations. He had become involved with the U.N. even before his appointment to the U.S. delegation by President Eisenhower, and after his appointment expired, he continued to take on U.N. responsibilities. His daughter, Abbe (Salomon) (Wolfsheimer) Stutz and her husband David Stutz, a former deputy district attorney in San Diego, suspected that some of his travel, be it on a U.S. or U.N. passport, may have been conducted as cover for secret missions for the U.S. Central Intelligence Agency.

If so, that was not the only secret that he kept. Many years after Salomon died in 1979 at age 82, his daughter learned that her father, the philanthropist, also was a philanderer. She discovered, to her shock, that she had a DNA-tested half-brother, Derek Taylor, who had been born to Ethel Mortenson Taylor, an American mistress Abbe's father had once ensconced for seven months in France and Switzerland. Neither of his families knew about the other, but Salomon's two children by different mothers–in the brief time before Abbe died of cancer in 2014–connected and became friends.

In 2009, Abbe Wolfsheimer Stutz and her former husband Louis Wolfsheimer donated some of Salomon's papers to the Valley Center History Museum, which six years earlier they had funded with a $250,000 donation. David Stutz retained at the ocean view La Jolla home he and Abbe had shared as well as other artifacts of Salomon's life, among them the sword used in Salomon's knighthood ceremony.

Salomon, who had been an active member and donor for the American Jewish Committee and a major contributor to Temple Emanu-El, is buried alongside his wife Cecile, who outlived him by 20 years, in the Home of Peace Cemetery, at rest with other Jews of San Diego.

*Papal Knighthood ceremony for Irving Salomon
(Historic photo courtesy of Dave Stutz.)*

From Exit 2 C (westbound), the University of San Diego is reached by merging onto Morena Boulevard, then making a slight right onto Linda Vista Road, and a left at Alcala Park Way into the campus. Eastbound traffic should take I-8 to Taylor Street, turn right to Morena Blvd., and then a slight right on Linda Vista Road, to a left onto Alcala Park Way into the campus.

-San Diego Jewish World, May 28, 2015

7. Exit 2

The Rabbi and the Monsignor

Rabbi Wayne Dosick

SAN DIEGO — Rabbi Wayne Dosick received a telephone call in 1988 from Richard Stern, an activist in the Jewish Chautauqua Society, which was formed in the previous century to spread among diverse audiences knowledge about the Jewish religion. Stern wanted to know whether Dosick would like to teach a course at the Catholic-run University of San Diego that would be underwritten by his society.

Dosick, then the spiritual leader of Congregation Beth Am, agreed to teach one course on the hilltop campus, and after it was completed, he was invited back year after year for a total of 17 years.

He recalled that on one occasion, Monsignor I. Brent Eagen, chancellor of the San Diego Diocese, told him he would like to start a new tradition, an All-Faith Service to be held at the beginning of every spring semester at which representatives of "every faith we could find" would pray together.

That first year, "We had Catholics, Jews, Buddhists, Baptists, Episcopalians ... and each year had a theme," recalled Rabbi Dosick, an author of many books who today leads the Elijah Minyan in suburban Carlsbad, California. "The first year it was peace and everybody chanted, danced, meditated, ohmmed, in his or her tradition. Another year, I preached."

He said in a subsequent year there was "an All-Faith Service that filled the Immaculata with about 1,000 people, and there were Native Americans in loin cloths and head dresses dancing up and down the aisles of the Immaculata."

Eagen also appointed Dosick to the campus ministry which "led to my leading for a couple of years a model Passover seder for the Catholic community at USD. We put together a beautiful model seder every year, with the entire ritual and liturgy left to me."

Msgr. Eagen and Rabbi Dosick became such close friends that "when he died (in 1997), he left in his will instructions that there be only two scriptural readings at his funeral mass—one from the New Testament to be read by the president of the university, Alice Hayes, and one from Hebrew scripture to be read by me," Dosick said.

Dosick contrasted his interfaith experience at USD with his earlier participation in the San Diego Ecumenical Council. Most of the times the meetings were "all very collegial and lovely, and they never needed a vote for anything," said the rabbi. "But one time an issue came up and they needed to take a vote, so I voted, and they said 'Rabbi, you can't vote. 'Ecumenical' is between Christians and Christians.'"

In October 1996, the 8,600-acre Harmony Grove Fire destroyed 100 homes in the northern part of San Diego County. Rabbi Dosick's home, including his extensive Judaic library, was among 100 homes that were destroyed.

"My house burned down on a Monday and unbeknownst to us, at a mass at the Founders Chapel, they took up a collection for the rabbi and his wife (Ellen Kaufman) and they came to me with a check for between $300 and $400 from the students. USD President Author Hughes and his wife wrote us a personal check. And regarding returning to teaching, they told me to 'take as much time as you need.' They were incredibly kind to us."

Dosick's busy schedule writing and lecturing on his books led to his departure from USD. "I wrote a book about Indigo children and I had to travel a lot around the country," he said. "The commute got worse and worse. They were understanding when I couldn't do a class at the time of the High Holidays, but book promotions was another matter."

The tradition of having a rabbi or knowledgeable Jewish layman teach a course on "Jewish Faith and Practice" became well established. The position has been filled in the years since Dosick by different Jewish spiritual leaders.

From Exit 2 C (westbound), the University of San Diego is reached by merging onto Morena Boulevard, then making a slight right onto Linda Vista Road, and a left at Alcala Park Way into the campus. Eastbound traffic should take I-8 to Taylor Street, turn right to Morena Blvd, and then a slight right on Linda Vista Road, to a left onto Alcala Park Way into the campus.

- San Diego Jewish World, June 4, 2015

8. Exit 3

CalTrans District 11

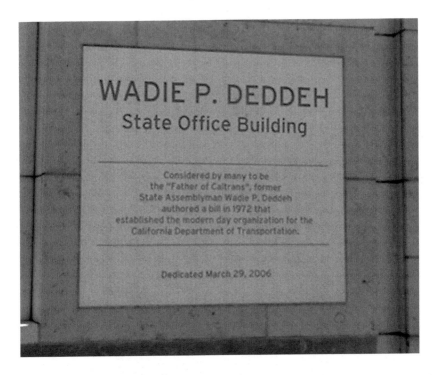

SAN DIEGO — No, Wadie P. Deddeh isn't Jewish. He's an Iraqi Christian, whose success in San Diego County rising from a professor at Southwestern Community College to a state Assemblyman and eventually to a state Senator was an inspiration to numerous refugees from Iraq who felt, rightly, that San Diego County was a place where people could rise on the basis of merit.

Today, San Diego County ranks only behind Detroit as a U.S. population center for Iraqi Christians, also known as Chaldeans. During his political career, Deddeh counted many friends in the Jewish community, including his longtime chief of staff Love Sachs, and he also had Jewish adversaries. In 1992, Deddeh fought and lost a bruising Democratic primary for a congressional seat against Bob Filner, who went on to serve 10 terms before being elected as San Diego's 35th mayor. The year following his mayoral election, Filner resigned amid charges of sexual harassment. The Deddeh family meanwhile continued to cover its name in honor, with the former legislator's son, Peter Deddeh, serving on the San Diego County Superior Court bench.

A plaque near the entrance of this three-building complex dedicated in March 2006 at 4050 Taylor Street explains why it is named for Deddeh: "Considered by many to be the 'Father of CalTrans', former state Assemblyman Wadie P. Deddeh authored a bill in 1972 that established the modern-day organization for the California Department of Transportation."

Stepping inside the courtyard of the CalTrans complex one may see various artistic renderings of San Diego County's freeway system. Hanging overhead, for example, is what the uninitiated might think is a representation of a tree grown wild, or perhaps a willy-nilly explosion of vines, but in fact, if one imagines oneself standing in Tijuana, Mexico, the trunk is the road leading from the south to the branching of Interstate 805 from the Interstate 5. The sculpture shows the two freeways joining again in the Sorrento Valley area, and depicts other freeways with which the two intersect. On a gate between the courtyard and Taylor Street is a sculptor's look at the interchange of Interstate 8 and Interstate 805.

Laurie Berman, District 11 CalTrans director

Approximately 1,200 state employees plan, build, and maintain the freeway system in San Diego and neighboring Imperial County–the border portion of California through which Interstate 8 passes. Leading them is a Jewish woman,

District 11 Director Laurie Berman. She is a Michigan State University engineering graduate whose first job out of college was in CalTrans' bridge-building department. She stayed with the state agency, moving from job to job, until 2009 when she was named district director.

Among Berman's lieutenants is Mark Phelan, a senior transportation supervisor, who, in an interview for this book, pointed out some features of the freeway system that motorists might give only passing notice to, but which are important in CalTrans' quest to provide the means for motorists not only to get where they want to go, but to do so safely.

Freeway Numbering: Odd number freeways, be they Interstate Highways or California State Highways, generally go north and south. Even-numbered freeways go east and west. The national Interstate freeway system was laid out as a grid with one- and two-digit numbered highways ending in "5" running between the northern and southern borders of the continental United States (excluding Hawaii and Alaska). Two-digit Interstate freeways ending in "0" run across the continent between the east and west coasts (again excluding Hawaii and Alaska). Interstate Freeways with other numbers (such as I-8, and I-805) parallel only a fraction of those routes and are considered secondary portions of the Interstate Highway System. Whereas Interstate 10, starting in the Los Angeles area, stretches all the way to the East Coast; Interstate 8 goes only as far east as Casa Grande, Arizona.

Types of Freeway Signs: Six colors predominate in freeway signage, according to Phelan. These are:

— **Green** signs with white letters provide guidance to destinations. They tell the distance to upcoming exits and towns, and identify the exits. The exits are numbered according to their distance in miles from the beginning of the freeway. In the case of Interstate 8, the measurement is from the freeway's onset at Robb Field in Ocean Beach. Green and white signs also identify honorific portions of the freeway, so designated by the state Legislature, such as, on Interstate 8, the "Kumeyaay Highway," named for the indigenous people of San Diego County. Currently, the white letters on the overhead signs are made with reflective materials which are activated by your car's headlights. There are plans to convert an estimated 37,000 such signs in District 11 so that both the green and the white tiles will be lit by a car's headlights. That will enable the district to reduce electricity use and also to remove the catwalks in front of the signs which attract spray-painting vandals.

— **Yellow** signs with black letters are intended to warn motorists about road conditions ahead, such as onramps where traffic may be merging; or a bridge where the number of lanes are reduced; or a tricky curve. They warn motorists to exercise caution.

— **Orange** signs are similar to yellow signs, but they are temporary, and are used in construction zones.

— **Brown** signs are used for state-designated points of interest such as historical landmarks or national and state parks.

— **Black and White** signs are used for traffic laws, especially to announce speed limits, anti-litter regulations, carpool lane restrictions, and other rules of the road. Phelan says the federal government allows states to decide on speed limits up to 80 miles per hour on Interstates. In California, where 65 is the standard freeway speed, 70 sometimes is allowed in rural areas. According to Phelan, speed limits are determined according to "road geometry, the curves in the hill, and also they are tied into population. The higher the population, the lower speeds. It gets up to 70 outside the metropolitan area."

— **Blue** signs assist motorists, telling, for example what offramp to take for a hospital, gas, food, or lodging, and where emergency phones are located alongside the freeway.

Additionally, there are electronic signs suspended over freeways on which are flashed safety messages and occasionally "amber alerts," in which the description and license plate of a car is given of a motorist suspected of abducting a child. The amber alert was named for 9-year-old Amber Hagerman of Arlington, Texas, who was abducted and murdered in 1996. Her given name was later formed into an acronym for America's Mission: Broadcast Emergency Responses.

A relatively new type of signage on the Interstate 8 are large road decals, helping motorists decide what lane they need to line themselves up on for interchanges. Director Berman said the I-8 and I-5 decals on the surface of Interstate 8 in the Hotel Circle area (Exit 4) were installed because Hotel Circle caters particularly to tourists, who may be unfamiliar with San Diego's road system. When going west, which lane do they want to continue to the beach? What about to go to Los Angeles? Or to head to Mexico?

Digital and broadcast messaging: At various freeway locales, AM radios may be tuned to 5-1-1 for the latest traffic information. CalTrans regularly posts traffic conditions on Twitter, with such messages often being the basis for news stations' traffic reports. This information also can be accessed by various in-car navigation systems.

Freeway Surfaces: Concrete is the standard surface for Interstate freeways, but sometimes a less rigid, more flexible surface like asphalt is used over land where there is subsidence. Unless it is broken by too heavy truck loads, concrete will last longer than asphalt, but it is far more expensive to replace. Whereas it once was standard procedure to utilize concrete for the freeways and asphalt for the shoulders, federal guidelines for future construction require, under most circumstances, concrete to also be used for the shoulders.

In Southern California, with its arid and temperate climate, bridges generally are constructed of concrete, rather than steel which is used throughout much of the country. However, steel was utilized for the San Diego-Coronado Bay Bridge, requiring constant painting and maintenance to guard against moisture-driven rusting.

Onramps and offramps: Whether ramps are one lane or two lanes at the time of construction depends on population projections made by such planning agencies as the San Diego Association of Governments (SANDAG). In building freeways and their ramps, CalTrans seeks to accommodate populations projected 20 years into the future by these agencies.

Retaining walls, landscaping and themes: Sometimes the retaining walls adjoining freeways are textured with simple designs that complement the freeway's theme and also make it more difficult for vandals to cover them with graffiti. The theme builds on the characteristics of the terrain through which the freeway passes. Interstate 5, for example, is "coastal," whereas Interstate 8 is "rural." Abutment designs might roughly parallel the shape of nearby landforms, whereas landscaping, to the extent possible, utilizes native trees and plants.

"One of the advantageous things about native plants," comments Phelan, "is that they generally require less maintenance."

Environmental stewarding: Whereas freeways once were built to get motorists from one place to another as quickly as possible, today they are constructed with far more attention to their effect on the environment. Below the road surface, there may be passageways, such as large pipes, through which animals may pass to get from one place to another.

Archaeologists monitor road construction projects for evidence of ancient human settlements or prehistoric animal life. Recently, on California State Route 76, near the northern border of San Diego County, the skeletal remains of an ancient bison was discovered. Having lived between 100,000 to 200,000 years ago, according to scientific estimates, it was the first creature of its kind known to have traveled so far south as San Diego County.

In other environmental developments, there are plans to have charging stations for electric cars to enable their drivers to feel secure on longer trips. Greater use of solar panels, such as may be seen above roadside telephones, is a constant consideration. Ramp metering to allow cars to join the freeway at certain intervals may ease congestion and concomitant air pollution.

The orange bags that CalTrans workers and volunteers carry to pick up litter may be turned inside out, and the blue bag that results is fit for carrying and instantly recognizing recyclable material.

Citizen participation: As state budgets decline while costs and miles of freeways go up, CalTrans looks increasingly to businesses and citizen groups to help maintain the freeways. Under the "Adopt a Highway" program, private companies or citizens may themselves pick up the litter off the freeway (after suitable training from CalTrans) or hire a private contractor to do so. In return, the company or individual receives recognition on freeway signs located within the stretch of freeway under their care. The program, according to Director Berman, is being expanded to also take in Park-and-Ride facilities, and onramps and offramps. Because it is a form of advertising which is seen by a relatively high volume of motorists, with regular frequency, there is a waiting list for some highway locations, while less traveled locations may meanwhile remain available.

Roadside Rest: For the sake of safety–as well as pride in the beautiful landforms of California–CalTrans provides rest stops (with bathroom facilities) and viewpoints (without such facilities). Phelan said that the stops are intended to encourage drowsy drivers to pull over, stretch their legs, and take a needed break before returning to the road.

···

From Westbound Interstate 8: Take Exit 3 at Taylor Street and turn left to the overpass. On other side of bridge, turn right onto Taylor Street. Eastbound traffic: turn right from exit onto Taylor Street. The Deddeh Building is at 4050 Taylor Street. It is at the top of the T-intersection with Juan Street.

···

-San Diego Jewish World, June 11, 2015

9. Exit 3

Robinson and Rose

Portrait of Louis Rose at Robinson-Rose House,
Old Town San Diego State Historic Park

SAN DIEGO — The visitor information center on the plaza of Old Town San Diego State Historic Park is located within the two-story Robinson-Rose House, named for attorney James W. Robinson and businessman Louis Rose. Robinson lived in the house first, and after he died, Rose purchased it from Robinson's widow, Sarah.

Rose had met the Robinsons in El Paso, Texas, when they joined the same wagon train *en route* to San Diego. They had to pass over the New Mexico, Arizona and California deserts, then navigate the Cuyamaca Mountains, before finally reaching San Diego County's inland valleys and the small village of San Diego. Upon their arrival in 1850, San Diego had a population estimated at 650.

Robinson had served as lieutenant governor and as the disputed acting governor of the Provisional Government of Texas, created in 1835 when some Texans favored independence from Mexico, and others believed Texas should remain part of Mexico if the dictator Antonio Lopez de Santa Anna would restore constitutional protections that he abolished shortly after taking office.

In balloting, delegates to the Texas Consultation of 1835 elected Henry Smith as their provisional governor, and Robinson as their provisional lieutenant governor. However, Smith and the new Legislative Council didn't get along, and before long the Legislative Council impeached Smith, while Smith meanwhile dissolved the Legislative Council. To replace Smith, the legislature picked Robinson to serve as the acting provisional governor. The net effect was that at a time when Texas was in mortal danger -- for example, when Mexican troops had the Alamo under siege -- the politicians of the Texas government were divided and fighting among themselves rather than rallying to the aid of Alamo's defenders, who had to fight vainly against overwhelming odds. The Provisional Government's term of office expired on March 1, 1836 when a Constitutional Convention met and decided to vote for independence, thereby creating the Republic of Texas.

When his term of office ended, Robinson enlisted as a private in the Texas Army that was being led by General Sam Houston. The general was impressed by Robinson's willingness to fight as a common private, notwithstanding the high office he formerly had held. After Houston became Texas's President, he named Robinson as a district court judge, a disastrous appointment. In one instance, Robinson ordered a defendant whipped before his lawyer could hear the verdict. In another case, the judge heard that friends of a defendant who was convicted in a capital case were planning to break him out of jail on the morning he was to be executed. So, Robinson ordered the sheriff to hang the defendant that very night.

Robinson was persuaded to leave the bench, and to resume the private practice of law. He was at the courthouse in San Antonio during the Consultation of 1842, when Texas politicians tried to reach an accord with Comanche Indians. There was a war whoop and then arrows began to fly — one of them penetrating Robinson in the buttocks. Two years later, in 1844, Robinson was again at the courthouse when the Mexican General Adrian Wall captured him along with other lawyers and judges who were there to conduct legal business.

Wall had them all marched to the Perote Prison in Vera Cruz, Mexico, where they were incarcerated. Robinson petitioned Santa Anna for a meeting, at which he offered to carry back to Sam Houston a proposal that Mexico would grant Texas autonomy if Texas would give up its independence and return to nominal Mexican nationality. Santa Anna apparently figured he had nothing to lose, so sent Robinson back to Texas. The wily Houston wasn't interested at all in giving up Texas's independence, but used the proposal to begin negotiations with the Mexicans. He did so, believing correctly that the United States, which thus far had rejected Texas's bid for admission as a new state, might be persuaded to act upon the petition rather than see Texas lost to Mexico.

While Houston was thankful for the opportunity to engage Mexico and the United States in negotiations, the populace of Texas turned against Robinson. Why was he free while his fellow captives continued to waste away in Perote Prison? Why would Robinson even discuss bargaining away Texas's hard-fought independence? Although Robinson tried to resume his career as an attorney in Texas, his business dropped precipitously. He and his red-headed wife Sarah decided to move to California, where Robinson's expertise in Mexican land law might be put to good use and the controversy put behind him.

Rose had grown up in the German river town of Neuhaus-an-der-Oste, near where the Oste River and the mighty Elbe River flow into the North Sea. When he immigrated to the United States in 1840, he found in New Orleans another important city dependent on river commerce. He was married in New Orleans, but his initial business efforts were failures. Alone, he moved to Texas to try to make a fortune selling real estate. When he heard of the gold strike in California, and the many business opportunities there, he pushed on, writing to his wife that he would send for her when his financial situation allowed. His wife, the former Carolyn Marx, either did not receive the letter or chose to ignore it. When Rose, in fact, sent for his wife some years later, she had taken up with another man, and a divorce was arranged.

When the Robinsons met Rose on the wagon train, they saw him as a man who, though politically naive, had become astute in business. They had many discussions as the wagon train proceeded to San Diego. They enjoyed each other's company. When the wagon train arrived in San Diego, word spread that three interesting personages had come to stay: Robinson, who had been a high official in Texas; his wife, Sarah, who was the first red-head many local residents had ever seen, and Rose, the first Jew to settle in San Diego. So whom do you think created the greatest stir? Sarah, hands down. Men and women all wanted to touch her long red hair.

Robinson went about practicing land law, and eventually built himself the house on the Plaza. It was very different from the Mexican era dwellings in Old Town, such as the Casa de Estudillo on the other end of the Plaza. Whereas Robinson's home was two stories, with windows looking out onto the Plaza and inviting people outside to look in, the Casa de Estudillo had walls protecting itself from the intrusive view of outsiders. Rooms were all accessed from an interior courtyard. Privacy and serenity were highly valued. Robinsons' home on the other hand served both as a residence and a place of business. The downstairs was divided into areas for small businesses. Here were held meetings of the board of directors of the prospective San Diego and Gila Railroad, as well as of the membership of San Diego's first Masonic Lodge. The Robinsons lived upstairs. There was a second-floor terrace from which Mrs. Robinson could view and converse with passersby below.

Rose meanwhile rented the Casa de Reyes-Ybanez to serve as his Commercial Hotel and Saloon, it being located along present-day Juan Street. While the hotel was far from luxurious, it was one of the first places that weary travelers from Los Angeles would notice as they rode into town. Robinson and Rose both joined the Masons.

The brand-new City of San Diego almost immediately got itself into financial trouble. It decided to build a jail and asked for bids on the project. Agostin Haraszthy, the sheriff, whose father was a member of the Common Council, won the bidding, even though his bid was not the lowest. The jail he built became laughingly known as the "Swiss Cheese Jail of the West." Almost anyone could get out of it. One of its early prisoners was Phantley Roy Bean, younger brother of San Diego's first mayor Joshua Bean. Accused of arranging a duel, which was illegal in California, Bean did not wait around to be tried. He dug his way out of the jail, some say with a pocket knife, others say with a spoon. (Roy Bean later became a saloon-owner and justice of the peace in Langtry, Texas, where he styled himself "The Law West of the Pecos.")

The embarrassed Sheriff Haraszthy said the condition of San Diego's jail really was not his fault; he didn't have the right building materials. But if the Common Council would vote him more money to make the repairs, he was certain he could obtain the necessary materials to make it better. The Council went along with the sheriff's request, but didn't have sufficient money to pay him. So, it issued IOU's in the form of $100 denomination bond notes. Anyone who purchased such a note would receive 8 percent interest a month! Unable to pay the bonds off, the Council's inaction resulted in the bonds compounding each month, until the debt was so high there was no imaginable way for the Council to pay it off. At that point, the State of California revoked the city's charter, and dissolved its Council. It then created a three-member Board of Trustees which, under the state's authority, was given responsibility for governing the town and finding ways to pay off the bond debt.

A first Board of Trustees was elected but was unable to come up with solutions, so its members resigned. Robinson and Rose decided to run for the second Board of Trustees, and were elected along with William Ferrell. Robinson and Rose always voted together, and one might refer to their years in office as the Robinson-Rose era of San Diego politics. They first refused to pay the 8 percent interest on the bonds, and after the owners of the bonds sued them, an out-of-court settlement was reached that only 4 percent interest would be paid.

Thereafter, the trustees arranged for the City to auction off the Pueblo lands it had inherited from Mexico. Most people at the auction purchased lots in Old Town itself, but Robinson and Rose successfully bid for bayside land lying between Old Town and the entrance to San Diego Bay. Additionally, Rose purchased land in a canyon through which travelers from Los Angeles ordinarily would pass. Here, in what became known as Rose Canyon, he built a tannery, which served as a complementary business to the butcher shop he opened in Old Town. Rose also operated a general store in San Diego. The bayside property Rose developed later as the town of Roseville, today part of the Point Loma community.

As members of the Board of Trustees, Rose and Robinson automatically became members of the first county Board of Supervisors organized in 1853. They laid out roads from San Diego to other cities, thereby affecting the area's pattern of development for years to come. Rose also served as a volunteer in a U.S. military unit that sought to track down Antonio Garra, who led an Indian revolt against the new San Diego County government. (Another unit found Garra and brought him back to San Diego for trial and execution.) Rose also served on the county's first grand jury, and was a member of the school board.

Robinson died in 1857 and some years later Rose purchased the home from Sarah. Not only was it a residence for Rose, but it also was the venue for Jewish High Holy Day services and the formation of a Hebrew Benevolent Society. Among Rose's deeds for the Jewish community was the transfer of land, at a nominal $5 price, for use as a Hebrew Cemetery. As a layman, he officiated at a Jewish wedding between Hyman Mannasse and Hannah Schiller.

A divorced man, Rose did not remarry until 1867, after friends promoted a union with the Jewish widow Mathilde Newman, whose husband Jacob had been a merchant. The couple had two daughters, one of whom died in infancy, and the other of whom became a spinster school teacher and a president in 1901 of the local Eastern Star Masonic organization. Mathilde died while Henrietta was still a child, and Rose, aging and blinding, entrusted her care to neighbors.

In commemoration of Rose's ownership of the building -- and to illustrate the religious diversity of San Diego's pioneers -- the administration of Old Town San Diego State Historic Park has hung a mezuzah on the inside door post of the auxiliary room of the Robinson-Rose House, a room that often had been used as a general store. Additionally, on Chanukah, Jewish volunteers light the menorah at the home.

Robinson-Rose Building
(Photo: Shor M. Masori)

··

From Exit 3, follow Taylor Street to Juan Street and turn left, park in one of the peripheral parking lots of Old Town San Diego State Historic Park and walk to the central plaza.

··

-San Diego Jewish World, June 18, 2015

10. Exit 3
Mannasse and Schiller

Joseph S. Mannnasse

SAN DIEGO — Inside the false-front Colorado House, one may get the false impression that Joseph S. Mannasse spent most of his life as an agent for the Wells Fargo Company. In fact, that was but a sidelight of the Jewish merchant's career as a businessman and civic leader.

Today, we associate the Colorado House with Mannasse because his photograph hangs inside, but in fact, his thriving Joseph Mannasse & Co. general store had been situated on the other side of Old Town facing Juan Street and backing on the small street that was called Camino de los Judios (Jews' Street). The back doors of the stores of several (but not all) Jewish merchants could be accessed from it. Depending on which side of the Camino the stores were situated, they fronted either on the Plaza or Juan Street.

Joseph Mannasse and his partner Marcus Schiller imported their supply of goods from the import-export warehouses of San Francisco, to which merchandise was brought by ship from the East Coast of the United States, Latin America, and Asia. Gathering goods of every description—ranging from clothing to tools to foods and perfumes—Mannasse and Schiller crammed into their store everything that pioneer families needed or wanted. Its bulging shelves represented the department store of its day, and here customers not only shopped, but traded gossip and news.

In the West of the mid-19th Century, very few people had money. So, to pay for these goods, ranchers would pledge to Mannasse and Schiller a share of their profits when the cattle was driven to market, or, failing that, a percentage of their herds. In time, the merchants had so many cattle, the livestock pens adjacent to their store could no longer keep them all. So, they decided to purchase two ranchos where the cattle could roam freely – Rancho Los Encinitos and Rancho San Dieguito. Had their families held onto that land, they would own most of the areas that today are known as Solana Beach, Rancho Santa Fe, Encinitas, and Carlsbad. Today anyone who owned that much land would be a multi-billionaire, but back in those days open ranch land was fairly inexpensive. One could buy it cheaply, and unfortunately, later one could sell it just as cheaply.

The business partners were responsible for creating a stage coach line that ran between San Diego and Los Angeles, and a remnant of one of the intermediate stage houses -- a crumbling wall of adobe -- can still be seen today at Stagecoach Park in Carlsbad, California.

Like many merchants, Mannasse and Schiller took an interest in civic affairs. The City Board of Trustees had remained dormant in the years following the United States Civil War. When entrepreneur Alonzo Horton came to San Diego, he liked what he saw and decided he wanted to buy some land along a middle portion of the bay, in the area that we today call downtown San Diego. When he inquired how he could do this, he was told that he would need to first arrange an election for a new City Board of Trustees, and then ask the trustees to agree to an auction of public land.

Horton persuaded Ephraim Morse, Thomas Bush, and Joseph S. Mannasse to run for the positions, which, unopposed, they all won. Then at his request, they scheduled an auction of public land. He purchased 960 acres for $2,165, which amounted to 27 ½ cents per acre.

A year later, Marcus Schiller replaced his partner Joe Mannasse on the Board of Trustees. His was the board that voted in 1868 to set aside 1,400 acres for a city park. Many years later, in anticipation of the 1915 opening of the Panama Canal, San Diego held a contest to name the park, and the winning entry was "Balboa Park." The Spanish explorer Vasco Nuñez de Balboa had been the first European to cross the Isthmus of Panama from the Atlantic Ocean to the Pacific Ocean, so the name was *apropos*, although Balboa never himself saw San Diego.

Today, the Cabrillo Bridge entrance to Balboa Park has a plaque on the gateway on which the mythical personages Atlantic and Pacific are depicted nearly touching hands. The plaque celebrates the foresight of Schiller and his fellow trustees Jose Guadalupe Estudillo and Joshua Sloane in setting aside the land.

Plaque on Cabrillo Bridge entrance to Balboa Park
(Photo: Shor M. Masori)

Mannasse and Schiller purchased a share in a ship that traveled up and down the coast between San Diego and San Francisco, their intention to assure favorable delivery for their goods and to cut costs. Additionally, they built a wharf in Horton's Addition, as downtown San Diego then was known.

In addition to their partnership in business, Mannasse and Schiller had an interesting family connection. Schiller's sister, Hannah, married Hyman Mannasse, who was Joseph's brother. Hyman moved to Arizona, where he was later killed in a holdup. Subsequently, Joseph Mannasse married Hannah, thus becoming his partner's brother-in-law.

Although Schiller was the junior partner in their business, he was the senior official in San Diego's budding Jewish community. He served as president of Adath Jeshurun (Gathering of the Faithful), which is what the congregation was called when it had no permanent place of worship. When the Jewish community had grown sufficiently to warrant the construction of a temple at which High Holy Day services were conducted in 1889, the congregation changed its name to Beth Israel (House of Israel). Marcus Schiller served as the president of both these congregations, providing continuity.

....

From Exit 3, follow Taylor Street to Juan Street and turn left, park in
one of the peripheral parking lots of Old Town San Diego State
Historic Park and walk to the central plaza

....

-San Diego Jewish World, June 25, 2015

11. Exit 3

The Courthouse and the Franklins

The Colorado House
(Photo: Shor M. Masori)

SAN DIEGO — There were no televisions, radios, motion pictures, or YouTube videos back in the mid-19th Century. There were, occasionally, traveling stage productions and these were well-attended. But for day-to-day entertainment, San Diego citizens often crowded the town's small brick courthouse to attend—and later comment upon—the proceedings.

If you look at the photograph above, you can see the courthouse on the left, as it appears today in Old Town San Diego State Historic Park. To the right of it is the Colorado House, and to the right of that is an empty lot. Back in the 19th Century, that lot was occupied by the Franklin House, which was the skyscraper of Old Town, being all of three stories tall.

The Franklin House was owned by Lewis Franklin, who played a prominent role in early California Jewish history, and his younger brother Maurice Franklin, both originally from England. Lewis traveled to San Francisco almost immediately after the discovery of gold near Sacramento in 1848, and it was in his tent in 1849 that the first Jewish High Holy Day services were conducted in San Francisco. The following year, Lewis, being learned in the Jewish religion, agreed to deliver the High Holy Day sermon. By 1851, however, Lewis moved to San Diego. That year, there being insufficient Jews to make up a minyan, Franklin observed the holiday by meeting with three other Jews—the first Jewish religious meeting in San Diego's history.

Two celebrated court cases in early San Diego history involved the Franklin House and its occupants. One of these cases became known throughout the United States as the "San Diego Incident."

The first of these cases came in 1858 when the Franklin brothers started fighting with each other and things became so nasty that it resulted in the two brothers suing each other for a rightful division of the property.

In the trial, played out before a large audience of town people, it developed that the brothers' relationship had soured after Maurice had married young Victoria Jacobs, whom latter-day San Diego historians remember chiefly for the fact that prior to her marriage she had kept a diary giving the flavor of day-to-day life in San Diego. Lewis and Victoria did not like each other, witnesses testified, and matters became so bitter between them that Victoria refused to leave her room to go to the hotel dining room with her husband if she knew that Lewis would be there. Additionally, the brothers accused each other of shirking their duties at the hotel and in the ground-floor pharmacy which Maurice operated. Eventually, Circuit Court Benjamin Hayes dissolved the partnership and found that Lewis had suffered the greater financial damage. He ordered Maurice to pay his brother $1,111.64 ½ cents. Not long afterwards, Maurice and Victoria moved to San Bernardino, where Victoria died in 1861 at age 22, and was the first adult to be buried in the Home of Eternity, San Bernardino's historic Jewish cemetery. Maurice lived on to 1875.

Model of the three-story Franklin House, once San Diego's skyscraper
(Photo: Shor M. Masori)

In 1859, one year after the Franklin vs. Franklin court case, San Diego County's grand jury was meeting at the courthouse to consider a routine assault case.

Hearing that Moses Mannasse had been a witness to the assault, the Grand Jury issued a subpoena for him to testify. Anxious to finish their business that Saturday, Oct. 8, rather than have to continue it to Monday, the Grand Jurors sent Deputy Sheriff Joseph Reiner to find Mannasse. He didn't have to look too far, because Mannasse was with nine other Jewish men at Yom Kippur services being conducted two doors away at the Franklin House.

When Reiner delivered the subpoena, Mannasse declined to accompany him back to the Grand Jury proceedings. He explained that this was the holiest day of the Jewish year and that his presence was needed as the required tenth man to make a minyan.

Reiner told the Grand Jury what Mannasse said, but, unsympathetic to the Jew's request, the jurors sent Reiner back to the Franklin House with orders to bring Mannasse back, by force if necessary. This he attempted to do, but Mannasse's fellow Jews intervened, preventing Reiner from forcibly removing him. Finally, Reiner mobilized a posse to physically remove Mannasse and take him to the courthouse, where the Grand Jury awaited. While seated in the witness chair, Mannasse refused to answer any questions until after sunset when Yom Kippur had ended.

The *San Diego Herald* subsequently wrote that the Grand Jury had been "overanxious to conclude their labors before sunset, at the expense of the violation of conscience of a good citizen." Franklin, meanwhile, considering the interruption of the services at his hotel to be possibly the worst insult suffered by the Jewish nation since the sacking of the Temple in 70 A.D., wrote indignant letters to Jewish newspapers around the country describing the incident.

"I know not what feeling mostly motivates me, in recapitulating to you the occurrences which have disgraced civilization in this our remote little town of San Diego," he wrote. "Were I to say that unmitigated disgust fills my bosom, I would scarcely express myself as a wrong of the nature I shall here recount to you knows no parallel in the annals of the civilized world. An offense has been committed against all decency, and I, in common with my coreligionists, call upon you to give publicity to the matter so that the perpetrators may be marked with the rebuke of scorn by a free and independent press…"

Franklin's letters prompted a debate among Jews throughout the country, with some agreeing with him, and others suggesting that it would not have been a major problem for the minyan to have simply recessed the Yom Kippur prayer session to allow Mannasse to do his civic duty.

When I have put the question to Jewish tour groups accompanying me through Old Town, I have found a similar division of opinion.

Victoria Jacobs Franklin display
(Photo: Shor M. Masori)

***From Exit 3, follow Taylor Street to Juan Street and turn left, park in
one of the peripheral parking lots of Old Town San Diego State
Historic Park and walk to the central plaza.***

-San Diego Jewish World, July 2, 2015

12. Exit 3

Old Temple Beth Israel

Old Temple Beth Israel in Heritage Park
(Photo: Shor M. Masori)

SAN DIEGO—Many fine carriages pulled up to the new building at the corner of Second Avenue and Beech Street on a hill overlooking downtown San Diego and the Bay. Their occupants came to observe or to participate in High Holy Day services of 1889. It was the first time that the building, with windows stained with Magen David designs, and a roof line featuring the Tablets of the Law, came into official use. Up until then, Jewish religious services in San Diego were held in homes or in rented quarters. To celebrate the occasion, not only Jews, but also Christians in civic and business leadership positions, attended the Reform services.

As part of the transition from a homeless, wandering congregation to one with its own home, Congregation Adath Jeshurun, which had been the Jewish communal name since the early 1860s, changed its name to Congregation Beth Israel. It made sense because the old name roughly translated meant "The Gathering of the Faithful," whereas the new name meant "The House of Israel." And indeed, the Jews of San Diego now had a fine house of worship, which cost approximately $8,500 to build. About $1,500 of that total had been raised in March 1889 by the women of the congregation who staged a week-long Jewish Fair that featured booths, entertainment, and food. According to a congregational history celebrating Beth Israel's 150th anniversary, some of the other funds came from the sale of seats that could be reserved for family members during services.

As described in the *San Diego Union* of that period, the temple measured 56 feet by 30 feet, with two small rooms on either side of its entrance. Over the years, those rooms had such uses as an office for the clergy and a changing room for a bride. The walls of the sanctuary were painted gray, the ceiling sky blue, and 250 numbered chairs faced the Holy Ark (Aron Kodesh) carved from sugar pine with redwood panels, with an eternal light (Ner Tamid) suspended from the ceiling. The aisles were carpeted with cocoa and plain matting. A chandelier hung from the ceiling at the center of the room.

Not in evidence on the day that Temple Beth Israel celebrated its first Rosh Hashanah was a rabbi. The clergyman who previously had been employed, and who, in fact, had urged the construction of the Temple building, was no longer affiliated with the congregation. What had happened to Rabbi Samuel Freuder? The answer was that, for reasons unknown, he had converted to Christianity and was becoming a missionary for that faith.

He joined one Protestant sect after another, seemingly never satisfied with what he found. By 1915, he decided he had made a big mistake and reaffiliated as a Jew, writing a pamphlet titled: *A Missionary's Return to Judaism: The Truth About the Christian Missions to the Jews*. In the pamphlet, he decried what he considered deceptive practices on the part of his former missionary colleagues.

Mirroring San Diego's economic boom and bust cycles, the membership of Temple Beth Israel grew and shrank. The first spiritual leader to preach in the temple was Rabbi Marx Moses, whose tenure lasted three years until the Panic of 1893. In his short time as Beth Israel's rabbi, he had persuaded the City of San Diego to set aside land for the Home of Peace Cemetery adjacent to the non-denominational Mount Hope Cemetery. He also helped to establish the Mothers Club of Beth Israel which helped to support the congregation's religious school.

For the next 16 years, Beth Israel barely hung on without a rabbi, its membership at one point dwindling to 14 families. By the time the congregation felt financially secure enough to hire Rabbi Emil Ellinger in 1909, it had already undergone a split. Immigrants from Eastern Europe, who originally sought permission to worship as a separate Orthodox minyan, were unable to complete their High Holy Day worship in the one-room temple before members of the original Reform congregation asked them to hurry up and shorten their service. Incensed, they decided to form a synagogue of their own, which in 1906 they named Tifereth Israel, meaning "the Glory of Israel."

Ellinger drew the wrath of Beth Israel congregants in 1911 when he officiated at a wedding between a Jewish man and Catholic woman. Amid the anger over the intermarriage, Ellinger submitted his resignation. Over the next 15 years, until 1926, the congregation hired six rabbis in succession, none staying more than four years. But the congregation continued to grow, and in 1926, it moved to much larger quarters at 3rd Avenue and Laurel Street into a Moorish style synagogue that would last it for three quarters of a century, until 2000 when it moved to its own campus in the University City neighborhood of San Diego.

The original building at 2nd and Beech subsequently was utilized by Christian denominations and later by a Spiritualist congregation until, decaying and underutilized, it faced destruction by builders anxious to put up something more modern on that lot. Jim Milch, a congregant of Congregation Beth Israel joined forces with the Save Our Heritage Organization (SOHO) to move the old temple to county-owned Heritage Park, two blocks up Juan Street from Old Town San Diego State Historic Park. Here it was restored to its original condition and is now rented for meetings by civic and religious groups of any denomination. One of the questions I always like to ask groups that join me in Old Town tours is "whom do you think sat up there in the balcony?" Typically, people responded, "the women." But that wasn't the case. The Reform congregation permitted men and women to sit together in the main sanctuary. The balcony at one time housed an organ, as well as people who came too late to services to get a seat on the main floor.

Beth Israel at Third Avenue and Laurel Street; Tifereth Israel, which moved from 18th and Market Streets to 30th and Howard Avenue; and Beth Jacob Congregation, which was located along 30th Street, for a while were the only three congregations in San Diego. Beth Israel was Reform. Tifereth Israel switched from Orthodox to Conservative, and Beth Jacob switched from Conservative to Orthodox. The three post World War II rabbis -- Morton Cohn at Beth Israel; Monroe Levens at Tifereth Israel, and Baruch Stern at Beth Jacob -- were friendly and collegial, often guest lecturing at each other's synagogues. Later with San Diego's growth many additional synagogues were begun, and today one could say there is not one but six San Diego communities.

The first is central San Diego, where the Conservative congregation Ohr Shalom Synagogue today occupies the 3rd and Laurel building that was formerly Beth Israel's. The second area is the College-Del Cerro-San Carlos neighborhoods to which both Beth Jacob and Tifereth Israel moved in the 1970s. Here too is Temple Emanu-El, started by Beth Israel's former rabbi, Morton Cohn. The third area is the Chula Vista-Tijuana areas, with two synagogues on each side of the U.S.-Mexico border. The fourth is La Jolla and University City, where the modern Beth Israel is located today, along with such other large congregations as the Conservative Congregation Beth El and the Orthodox Congregation Adat Yeshurun, which revived the name of San Diego's first wandering congregation. The fifth and sixth Jewish communities are up the northern stretches of San Diego County along coastal Interstate 5 and inland Interstate 15.

In three of the regions there are Hillel Houses associated with local universities, and throughout San Diego there are numerous small congregations operated by Chabad.

....

From Exit 3, Follow Taylor Street to a left turn at Juan Street, pass Old Town San Diego State Park on right, and continue up Juan until arriving at Heritage Park on the left. Old Beth Israel is the first of several Victorian era buildings you will notice.

....

-*San Diego Jewish World, July 9, 2015*

13. Exit 4
Riverwalk Golf Course

Riverwalk Golf Course

SAN DIEGO — The Handlery Hotel, on the northeastern portion of Hotel Circle, adjoins the Riverwalk Golf Course, on land that the Levi and Cushman families have owned for over a century. Currently they and a developer plan to replace the golf course over a ten-year period with a 4,000-unit apartment and condominium complex, if approval can be won from the San Diego City Planning Commission and City Council. That application was pending in 2015.

Back in 1947, when the golf course was created on 200 acres of land, it was as part of the Mission Valley Country Club. It was highly rated enough to host several PGA golf tournaments prior to the San Diego Open's transfer to the Torrey Pines Golf Course in La Jolla. The list of famous golfers who played the course included Tommy Bolt, Billy Casper, Jack Nicklaus, Arnold Palmer, and Gary Player. Working as a youngster at the course, Phil Mickelson used to retrieve golf balls on the driving range, and another celebrity, boxer Muhammad Ali, once took a break from training at a nearby hotel to take a few publicity swipes at a golf ball with a borrowed 8-iron.

Originally part of a rancho, the land on which the golf course was constructed had been purchased in the early 1900s by Adolph Levi and his son Edgar, who together also purchased large tracts of land in Kearny Mesa, La Mesa, Lakeside, and Rancho de los Penasquitos. Adolph's daughter Selma married George New-bauer of San Francisco, and their daughter Helen married Elliot Cushman of San Diego. One of Helen's and Elliot's sons, former automobile magnate Steve Cushman, has served as a San Diego Port Commissioner and as a member of the San Diego Convention Center board of directors.

The Mission Valley Country Club was a center for the Levi and Cushman families' fellow Jews. Among them, Harry and Morris Wax, founders of Waxie Sanitary Supply, used to relax over card games at the club, and Jewish organizations of many types held their luncheons and dinners in the club's meeting rooms.

A perusal of the editions between mid-1956 and mid-1958 of the fortnightly and now defunct *Southwestern Jewish Press* provides the flavor of Jewish communal and social life during the period.

One of the groups that met regularly for dinner at the Mission Valley Country Club was "The Guardians," which helped to raise money for the San Diego Hebrew Home for the Aged, often through golf tournaments at the Mission Valley Country Club. Today, at various golf courses, the Guardians still sponsor tournaments for the Hebrew Homes' successor institutions, the Seacrest Village Retirement Communities which are located in suburban cities of Encinitas and Poway.

While fundraising was the announced goal of the Guardians, playful fellowship was what kept the men coming back meeting after meeting. Morrie Pomeranz, in a column, faithfully reported some of the anecdotes told during the meetings. For example, in May of 1957, he reported: "The Guardian father whose pride and joy is a first grader tells the following with a bit of understandable pride. His little boy, just starting school, was given the orientation treatment–what school meant–what was expected–what was offered in return, etc., and the teacher concluded her little talk by saying 'And when you want to go to the washroom, you should raise your hand and display two fingers like this.' The youngster mulled this over for a few minutes and then perplexed he asked: 'How will that help?'"

Later that month, Pomeranz had another story:

The scene: a downtown stationer's store–our two Guardians await for some loose-leaf inserts–said one Guardian to his little companion: 'I still say I'll be at the meeting tonight even though it's my wife's birthday–I'll get out somehow.' The listener could only add: 'Well, don't make a big *tsimmis* out of it–no sense in hurting her feelings'– but the other protested defiantly with his booming voice, 'Aw, nuts, I say I'll be at the club before 6:15' — and who do you think was at the counter directly behind the two? — the wife of course — and to those who might inwardly tend to discredit the actual wording of this little downtown vignette–and if verification be needed–just call Mildred!'

The annual luncheon of the Women's Committee of Brandeis University also was held that May, and Mayor Charles Dail installed officers of the San Diego chapter of the National Council of Jewish Women.

The roster of groups meeting at the Mission Valley Country Club over subsequent months also included the Bay City chapter of B'nai B'rith Women, the Henry Weinberger Lodge of the B'nai B'rith, which had a golf tournament there of its own, the Men's Club of Temple Beth Israel, and the Temple Beth Israel Sisterhood.

These were just the regular meetings. The Mission Valley Country Club also hosted important life cycle events, such as a bridal shower for Jane Cohn, the daughter of Rabbi Morton Cohn of Temple Beth Israel; a brunch for Evelyn Krantz, bride-to-be of Larry Solomon; and a wedding reception for Zena Feurzeig and her groom Donn Harle Kobernick, following their marriage which had been co-officiated under the chuppa by Rabbi Cohn and Rabbi Monroe Levens at Tifereth Israel Synagogue. Although he wasn't at this particular rite, the third rabbi in the San Diego trio of clergy was Rabbi Baruch Stern of Beth Jacob Congregation. They were all friends.

The pride taken in membership at the Mission Valley Country Club was illustrated by banker Fred Leeds, who upon his election as a vice president of the Cabrillo Savings and Loan Association, inserted an announcement in *Southwestern Jewish Press* stating that in addition to business, his affiliations included membership at Temple Beth Israel, the B'nai B'rith, and the Mission Valley Country Club.

In 1958, however, a Jewish Community Center, located several miles east of Hotel Circle on 54th Street between El Cajon Boulevard and University Avenue, had its grand opening and thereafter drew from the Mission Valley Country Club much of its Jewish meeting business.

This was a factor in the golf club being sold in 1962 and being renamed as the Stardust Country Club. In addition to local residents, the Stardust and its successor Handlery Hotel sought golfing guests at Hotel Circle hostelries for its revenue.

....

Hotels along the frontage roads on the north and south sides of Interstate 8 give Hotel Circle its name. Westbound traffic accesses and exits the Interstate 8 at Exit 4 on the north side of the freeway, whereas eastbound traffic utilizes freeway entrances and exits on the south side. A bridge at Taylor Street on the western end of Hotel Circle connects the north and south sides, as does an underpass at the eastern end. From the Hotel Circle exit from eastbound Interstate 8, turn left and follow the road through the underpass. Beyond the Town & Country Hotel is the intersection with Fashion Valley Road. Turn right and enter the golf course on the left.

....

-San Diego Jewish World, July 16, 2015

14. Exit 5

Westfield's Frank Lowy

Westfield Shopping Center in Mission Valley
(Photo: Shor M. Masori)

SAN DIEGO — The Westfield Mission Valley Shopping Center is one of more than 100 shopping centers in Australia, New Zealand, the United Kingdom and the United States controlled by a corporation owned by the Lowy family of Sydney, Australia, whose story of post-Holocaust success is both motivating and poignant.

Frank Lowy was a teenager when his family moved from Slovakia to Hungary in the hope of keeping safe from the Nazis' genocidal campaign against the Jews. Eventually, however, the Nazis invaded Hungary and began murdering Jews. They would have slaughtered all of them, but for the fact that the Russian Army drove the Germans back toward the Rhineland and ultimate defeat.

Frank Lowy survived, but when the Germans occupied Budapest on March 20, 1944, his father, Hugo, an Orthodox Jew, went to the train station to see if he could purchase tickets for his family to any safe destination. On that day he disappeared. Frank did not learn what happened to his father until 1991, when Myer Lowy, who had the same last name but was no relation, told of being with Hugo on that fateful day.

As told in the short documentary film *Spiritual Resistance* by Jill Margo and Laurie Critchley, they were captured by the Nazis at the train station and taken to an internment camp outside the city. Not long afterwards they were crammed into cattle cars with other Jews on the first Hungarian transport to the notorious Auschwitz death camp in Poland. With barely room to move on the cattle cars, little air and no proper sanitation, Hugo Lowy encouraged his fellow passengers to pray, thereby helping to keep up their spirits.

When the train stopped at Auschwitz, the passengers who had survived the trip were ordered to leave all of their belongings on the train platform. When a guard ordered Hugo Lowy to put his tefillin bag on the pile, he refused. The SS guard grabbed the bag and threw it onto the pile. When the guard turned his back, Hugo retrieved the bag, despite warnings from fellow Jews not to do it, to leave it there. Hugo responded: "I'm not going anywhere without my prayer shawl and my tefillin!" It's probable he knew exactly what the outcome would be.

The Nazis beat Hugo to death. His act of defiance, in the eyes of Judaism, was *kiddush Hashem*, a sanctification of God's name.

Frank Lowy

After World War II ended, Frank Lowy made his way to Palestine, but the ship on which he was traveling was caught running the British blockade. Frank and the other passengers were incarcerated on the island of Cyprus, there to stay until the British mandate over Palestine ended and the new state of Israel was born. Frank fought in the Haganah in Israel's War of Independence. He remained in Israel until 1952 when he immigrated to Australia.

The first business he opened in Sydney was a delicatessen, but later with partner John Saunders, he invested in a shopping center in the Sydney suburb of Blacktown. Successful enough to enable investment in other centers, the Westfield Development Corporation eventually grew to over 100 shopping centers. Saunders left the company in 1977, making Westfield a Lowy family enterprise.

Lowy is well known in Australia for his philanthropy and for his love of soccer. In addition to supporting research into cancer and heart disease, the billionaire is admired for a $30 million gift that established the Lowy Institute for International Policy, in which scholars focus on Australia's place in world politics. After learning how his father died, Lowy became a sponsor of an Auschwitz historical memorial, donating to the former death camp a refurbished railroad car like the one in which his father had been forced to travel. Just inside the doorway of the railroad car, Lowy placed a textile bag with a prayer shawl and tefillin inside.

The Mission Valley Shopping Center at 1640 Camino del Rio South was already 33 years old when Westfield acquired it. Built in 1961, it was the second major shopping center to be constructed in San Diego County, one year later than the College Grove Shopping Center off State Highway 94. Between the time of its construction and its acquisition by Westfield, Mission Valley Shopping Center was expanded once and remodeled once. Westfield expanded it again, adding a 20-screen multiplex and some more stores in a northeast wing, bringing the total number of stores to 131. The company had announced plans to add yet another 50,000 feet of commercial space and to develop another 450,000 square feet of land for residential use.

....

The Mission Valley Shopping Center is on the frontage road on the north side of Interstate 8, east of Exit 5.

....

-San Diego Jewish World, July 23, 2015

15. Exit 5

Morris Casuto and the ADL

Morris Casuto outside former ADL office building

SAN DIEGO — Although Jewish agencies and organizations including the Anti-Defamation League (ADL) recently have clustered their offices near those of the Jewish Federation of San Diego in the Kearny Mesa neighborhood, they used to be scattered through different parts of San Diego. The San Diego regional offices of the ADL for many years occupied a suite at 7851 Mission Center Court, and for 25 years in those offices, under the leadership of Morris Casuto, important Jewish communal work was done.

Through the years, whenever anti-Semitism was manifested with graffiti daubed onto synagogue walls, or when hateful leaflets were scattered, or the airwaves polluted with incendiary comments from neo-Nazis and other right-wing extremists, Casuto was there to speak up for the Jewish community and to denounce the haters.

As a result, Casuto often was threatened, his home telephone number and address were published by extremist websites, and he had to install monitors, locks, and other defensive devices at his home and his offices. Although he was a target for the haters, he never shied from representing the Jewish community to the media, nor in denouncing injustice.

Did he get scared? "Of course I get scared," he once told *San Diego Jewish Press-Heritage*. "Any individual who does not get scared sometimes is a fool. Does it stop me from doing what I think I have to do? Generally not."

In an interview for this series, Casuto said he placed considerable emphasis during his tenure on cultivating good relationships with local law enforcement agencies. "In the case of hate crimes," he said, "police need to understand why a person is assaulted. In most cases, the criminal and the victim don't know each other. The community the victim belongs to is being sent a message: 'You are un-important, you are unprotected, you don't belong here, we want you out.' So the degree that law enforcement organizations can join together to provide a kind of comfort, that is important.

"We realized that police are trained to look at the seriousness of a crime by injury, theft or damage, but very often with hate crimes, the injury is internal." Hate crimes are not only someone being beaten up, or property being vandalized, but "often there will be a threatening phone call in the night. Police have to know that there is a way to deal with this type of incident that the victim will be given some type of comfort, that they are not alone."

If the ADL had been only a reactive force in the San Diego community, it would not have garnered the respect and admiration that accrued to it during Casuto's tenure in San Diego prior to his retirement in 2010.

Casuto and the ADL brought the message of respect for diversity to public schools throughout San Diego County. They sponsored well-received workshops for students, faculty and administrators in a program known as the "World of Difference," which emphasized the positive aspects of pluralism and diversity in American society. As ADL director, Casuto emphasized building positive relations between the Jewish community and other minority groups, coming to their support when they were attacked, just as their leaders spoke up for the Jewish community in similar circumstances.

One of the secrets behind Casuto's success was his self-deprecatory humor. While he would emphasize the importance of fighting intolerance–a serious and potentially sensitive topic–he enjoyed making jokes about his short stature, 5'5 1/2.

After retiring, Casuto agreed to serve on important boards of directors around San Diego, including those of the Thomas Jefferson School of Law and the Joan B. Kroc Institute for Peace and Justice at the University of San Diego.

....

Mission Center Road has freeway entrances and Exit 5 on both sides of Interstate 8. To reach the building where the Anti-Defamation League kept its offices, proceed north on Mission Center Road to Mission Center Court, and turn left.

....

-San Diego Jewish World, July 30, 2015

16. Exit 6

Qualcomm Way, Qualcomm Stadium

Qualcomm Way turnoff from Interstate 8
(Photo: Shor M. Masori)

SAN DIEGO — In 1997, Qualcomm, a telecommunications industry giant co-founded by Jewish electrical engineers Irwin Jacobs, Andrew Viterbi and others, paid the City of San Diego $18 million for San Diego Jack Murphy Stadium to be renamed for 20 years as Qualcomm Stadium and for Stadium Way, which runs from Interstate 8 north to Friars Road, to be renamed as Qualcomm Way.

By taking Qualcomm Way to Friars Road and turning right, travelers can, within a short distance, access the parking lot of the stadium where the San Diego Chargers play in the National Football League and the San Diego State Aztecs play college football. The stadium once housed the San Diego Padres of baseball's National League, but that team moved to its own stadium in Petco Park in downtown San Diego in 2004. In 2015, the Chargers were considering moving to a new stadium in Los Angeles County.

Qualcomm, an abbreviation for "Quality Communications," was created in 1985 after Jacobs and Viterbi left Linkabit, a company they previously had founded, to serve as consultants in the telecommunications industry.

During their reign, Linkabit consulted to the National Aeronautics and Space Administration (NASA) on methods of sending data and photographs from space probes; with the U.S. military to relay information to aircraft anywhere in the world; and with such commercial entities as Holiday Inns, 7-Eleven, and Walmart to enable their headquarters to transmit videos to their companies across the nation. They sold the company in 1979 to M/A-Com, and decided to leave that company's employ in 1985.

Initially, Qualcomm sold Omnitracs software to trucking companies to enable them to stay in touch with their fleets, wherever in the country their trucks might travel. They also acquired Eudora, a company whose email program was compatible with Omnitracs. For a while, Qualcomm also manufactured cellphones, but sold that business to Kyocera. The reason: Far more profit could be made in developing communications software that could be sold to multiple cellphone manufacturers. In this, Qualcomm had a distinct advantage, in that Viterbi had patented the Viterbi Algorithm for separating telecommunication signals from noise in the atmosphere. Building on this knowledge, Qualcomm developed Code Division Multiple Access (CDMA), a proprietary technology for use in cellular communications.

The company thereafter grew by leaps and bounds, becoming one of San Diego County's largest employers.

The street name "Qualcomm Way" corresponds to the ethics statement of Qualcomm employees, which they call "The Qualcomm Way." In it the employees make four pledges. 1) "We act with integrity in everything we do." 2) "We lead by example with transparency, and by encouraging each other to raise concerns and ask questions." 3) "We trust each other and are responsible and accountable for our actions, while interacting in a collaborative, respectful and professional manner." 4) "We have a collective drive for success and are constantly thinking of new and innovative ways to do things."

Qualcomm Stadium in Mission Valley (Photo: Shor M. Masori)

(Following adapted from *Schlepping Through the American West: There Is a Jewish Story Eveywhere* by author Donald H. Harrison.)

Qualcomm Stadium, as it is called in its third incarnation since opening in 1967, is a massive concrete structure described as "modernist" by some architects, "brutalist" by others. Either way it is a celebration of structural forms and building materials. Its massive slabs of unadorned concrete give the impression of overwhelming power, not unlike that of a 320-pound tackle advancing on a 180-pound quarterback. Modernism is an architectural style that was made popular in San Diego four years earlier when polio vaccine discoverer Dr. Jonas Salk and architect Lous I. Kahn, two admired Jewish leaders in their fields, unveiled the Salk Institute for Biological Studies, an eye-arresting complex of buildings in La Jolla, starkly beautiful and overlooking the Pacific Ocean.

When the stadium opened for business, it was called simply San Diego Stadium. On Sept. 9, 1967, the San Diego Chargers, then of the American Football League, played the first official game of the season here. They had a Jewish coach by the name of Sid Gillman, who previously had led them through their paces at the now demolished Balboa Stadium. In 1963, under his guidance, the Chargers won the league championship with a commanding 51-10 defeat of the Boston Patriots. Perhaps because of all the excitement engendered by a new stadium, it looked like the Chargers would dominate the league again in 1967. In their first ten games, they ran up a record of 8-1-1, but then disaster, in the form of the Oakland Raiders, struck. Having handed the Chargers their only loss earlier in the season, the Raiders did it again 42-21. The dispirited Chargers then lost the next three games to end up in third place with an 8-5-1 record. When Gillman and his all-American lineman Ron Mix, also Jewish, looked at each other, there was really only one thing to say: "Gevalt!"

If Gillman had something to cheer about, it was that NFL Commissioner Pete Rozelle took him up on his idea of having a game played between the champions of the National Football League and the American Football League. Today the Super Bowl is an American institution.

Another Jewish sportsman, Gene Klein, had purchased the Chargers in 1966 and held onto the team until 1984. He also owned the Seattle Supersonics of the National Basketball Association and raced thoroughbred horses. A friend and fan, Lou Harris, recalls that when Klein was asked to compare football and horse racing, he responded that when his horses win, they never ask for an increase in salary.

In 1968, the Chargers got some professional sports company at the stadium. A new tenant was the minor league Pacific Coast League team known as the San Diego Padres. In 1969, the Padres were accepted as an expansion team in the major leagues and were assigned to the National League.

In the first game of its major League season, the Padres won 2-1 against the Houston Astros, but after that things just got worse and worse. The Padres wound up their season dead last with a record of 52-110.

Although there have been distinguished moments in the history of the two professional franchises, the sad fact of the matter is that since the Chargers' establishment, the team has thus far played in only one Super Bowl. The Padres have a slightly better record, having fought their way to two World Series. However, the two San Diego teams lost all three of these championship contests.

In 1980 *San Diego Union* sportswriter Jack Murphy died, and in appreciation for the key role he had played in getting professional teams to move to San Diego, and persuading voters to approve the bond issue to build the 50,000-seat stadium (it has since been expanded to over 70,000 seats), the stadium was renamed in his honor as San Diego Jack Murphy Stadium, or "the Murph" for short.

Later on, in 1997, naming rights for the stadium were sold for $18 million to Qualcomm, but Murphy is still remembered because Qualcomm Stadium surrounds what is called Jack Murphy Field.

There is a statue of Murphy and his black Labrador hunting dog, Abe of Spoon River, standing between one of the entrances of the stadium and the platform of the San Diego Trolley station serving Qualcomm Stadium. True, Murphy was Irish but in his Labrador, there was a Jewish story. Abe was short for Abraham. One of the puppies that dog sired was named Isaac. Alas, he wouldn't hunt, so Murphy gave him away. The name of his third dog? You guessed it, Jacob.

As the Chargers early in their franchise had a Jewish player in Ron Mix, so too did the Padres have theirs in Brad Ausmus, who made his major league debut as a catcher in the 1993 season and stayed with the team until 1996 when he was traded to the Detroit Tigers, the team for which he became the manager in 2013.

Gillman, Mix, and Ausmus all have been inducted into the National Jewish Sports Hall of Fame in Suffolk County, New York.

Not all the Jewish stars who performed at Qualcomm Stadium are so kindly remembered. In 1990, Roseanne Barr decided to make a comedy act out of singing the National Anthem before a Padres game against the Cincinnati Reds. She screeched out the words, and then in imitation of a baseball player, scratched her crotch and spat. The crowd didn't care for the satire and the booing, in the form of controversy, continued for many weeks thereafter.

Although the Chargers got to play in only one Super Bowl, the stadium has hosted three such contests featuring other teams. In 1988 the Washington Redskins defeated the Denver Broncos 42-10. Ten years later, in 1988, the Denver Broncos defeated the Green Bay Packers 31-24. And in 2003 Tampa Bay Buccaneers beat the Oakland Raiders 48-21. Many Jewish San Diegans have been privileged to attend all three games, among them Charles Wax, chairman and chief executive officer of Waxie Sanitary Supply.

There also have been two All-Star Games played here. The National League won 7-3 in 1978, in a game in which a fellow who was often thought to be a Jew—but wasn't–played. That was Rod Carew, then a first baseman for the Minnesota Twins. When *Saturday Night Live's* Adam Sandler wrote his Chanukah song, one of the lyrics said that "Rod Carew is a Jew—converted"–but in fact he wasn't and hadn't. His wife was Jewish and their child was being raised Jewish, but Carew himself remained Christian. The other All-Star Game at "The Murph," in 1992, saw the American League prevailing, 13-6. Another All-Star game will be played in 2016 in San Diego, but it will be at Petco Park, the Padres new home.

Jews have moved in and out of the Padres front office as a succession of management teams came and went, but one well-known Jew who has been more or less a fixture for the Padres has been radio announcer Ted Leitner, who used to be the TV sportscaster on KFMB-TV, Channel 8. Leitner has the knack of giving running play-by-play descriptions while filling in those moments between the action with anecdotes about almost every professional player in every sport ever played in San Diego.

The Padres moved from Qualcomm Stadium in 2004 to Petco Park in downtown San Diego, and the San Diego Chargers have been campaigning for a new stadium as well, more than broadly hinting if one to their liking is not forthcoming the franchise will be moved to another city.

Meanwhile, Qualcomm Stadium remains the home field for the San Diego State Aztecs as well as the host to two College Bowl games played in the winter -- the Holiday Bowl and the Poinsettia Bowl -- each of which has enthusiastic fans. It also has been the venue for numerous concerts, religious revivals, games of the short-lived San Diego Soccers, and has served as an evacuation center when major wildfires forced thousands of San Diegans to flee their homes.

A point of personal pride: When the late Tony Gwynn retired at the end of 2002 from baseball after playing all 20 seasons of his major league career for the Padres, there was a ceremony at Qualcomm Stadium that involved various VIPs followed by Tony and Alicia Gwynn walking through a 9-foot diameter baseball that had been crafted from balloons. The Jewish angle was that my daughter, Sandi Harrison Masori, and her husband, Shahar Masori, owners of Balloon Utopia, made that giant baseball portal!

....

From Interstate 8, take Qualcomm Road north to Friars Road, turn right, and follow to stadium entrance.

....

-San Diego Jewish World, August 6, 2015

17. Exit 6

Susan Davis's Congressional Office

District office of Congresswoman Susan Davis

SAN DIEGO — The distance between this city and Washington D.C. is approximately 2,690 miles, or a five-hour jet plane ride. Impractical to go back and forth every day between work in Washington and constituents in their districts, as, say, a member of Congress from Maryland or from Virginia might be able to do, California's congressional representatives depend on multi-tasking staff members at home to keep them informed about their constituents' concerns.

A visit to the offices at 2700 Adams Avenue of Congresswoman Susan Davis (D-San Diego) provides an enlightening look into the mechanics of a well-run constituent service operation in which the English-language equivalent of *tikkun olam* – making the world better – is a watch phrase for her staff.

I recently had the opportunity to meet with Jessica Poole, district director, and Daniel Hazard, field director, for the congresswoman whose 53rd Congressional District picks up much of its population along portions of the Interstate 8 in urban San Diego, La Mesa, and El Cajon. Other parts of the district include Lemon Grove, Spring Valley, and the eastern portions of Chula Vista.

Poole explained to me that each of the six staff members in the district office, herself included, is given a mixture of geographic areas and issue areas in which to specialize, so that each staff member can give a briefing by memo or in person to the congresswoman on a range of subjects.

At the same time, staff members in the congresswoman's office in Washington, D.C., similarly have been assigned responsibility for various issues, so that on any given problem at least two staff members -- one in Washington, D.C., close to the legislative process, and one in San Diego, close to the constituents -- can consult while formulating an issues-briefing for the congresswoman.

In her own case, said Poole, she is not only the district director, or administrator of the San Diego office, but she also has the responsibility of keeping Congresswoman Davis informed on the goings-on in Lemon Grove, Spring Valley, and the North Park neighborhood of San Diego near the office on Adams Avenue, where used book stores and antique shops abound.

Additionally, she is responsible for keeping the congresswoman informed about constituents' concerns in the areas of health care, social security, and women's issues.

Hazard, as field director, is responsible for creating events for Davis during congressional breaks, and serves as liaison between the congresswoman and San Diego's large military community and its biotech community. He also serves as the liaison between Davis and the Jewish community, of which they are both a part.

Other members of Davis's district staff in 2015 were Lee Steuer, the senior community representative who, like Hazard, had previous Washington D.C. experience; Jessica Mier, community representative; Margaret Hernandez, district scheduler; and Armita Pedramrazi, staff assistant and coordinator of Davis's intern program. As many as six interns at times will come into the office to help answer phones, conduct research, draft letters, and learn the ways of government, according to Poole.

Davis, elected to the Congress in 2000 after service on the San Diego Unified School District Board and in the California State Assembly, serves on two committees in Congress: the Armed Services Committee, reflecting the large military presence in San Diego, and the Education and the Workforce Committee, reflecting her service on the San Diego Unified School District's board as well as her experiences as director of the Aaron Price Fellows Program, which as stated on its website, came about as follows:

The Aaron Price Fellows Program was created in 1991 by the Price Family to honor the life of their son, grandson, and brother, Aaron. Every spring, a class of 9th grade students from four public high schools is selected for a three-year journey that includes an "up close and personal," behind-the-scenes look at government, business, non-profit and cultural institutions.

The goals of the program are to: foster friendships between Fellows from diverse ethnic, religious, and economic backgrounds; teach Fellows about government, cultural, business and non-profit institutions to illustrate their significance and relevance in their lives; and expose Fellows to exciting career opportunities.

One of the graduates of that program was Todd Gloria, who went on to serve on Davis's staff, eventually becoming her district director, before setting out upon his own political career. He won a seat on the San Diego City Council, and in the wake of a sexual harassment scandal that drove Mayor Bob Filner out of office, Gloria also served as the city's interim mayor until Filner's replacement, Kevin Faulconer, could be elected. As of this writing in 2015, Gloria was a candidate for a seat in the California State Assembly.

Davis has long been active in San Diego's Jewish community, worshiping at Congregation Beth Tefilah, which subsequently merged with Adat Ami Synagogue to become Ohr Shalom Synagogue (Conservative). She later joined Temple Emanu-El (Reform) and she often attends community events. I remember seeing her and her husband, Dr. Steve Davis, in the audience at one speech given at the Melvin Garb Hillel Center at San Diego State University, and they were unsuccessfully coaxed to leave seats in the middle of the room to take places of honor in the front of the audience. She tends to shy away from such perks of office, preferring to introduce herself as "Susan" rather than as "Congresswoman Davis," and, so Poole told me, preferring to sit along the side of a conference table rather than at its head, when she holds meetings whether with staff or visiting groups.

Hazard told me that Davis "engages with the wide diversity of groups and opinions" in the Jewish community. "Not everyone has the same views, obviously, so she talks to AIPAC, she talks to J Street; she will go to Hillel and talk to people on a regular basis, and people come to see her from the Jewish Federation and Middle East advocacy groups," Hazard added. "People see her as a leader, not just for the local delegation from here, but she is also a senior member of Congress."

Given the polarization in the Jewish community over Middle Eastern issues, including the nuclear pact with Iran, I asked how Davis manages to stay friendly both with AIPAC and J Street — with AIPAC generally more supportive of the policies of Israel's government under Prime Minister Binyamin Netanyahu and J Street generally more opposed.

"She understands the positions of both sides, and she starts from a position of respect from both sides, so I don't think that she has to prove one thing or another," Hazard said. "I think they know where she stands in terms of supporting Israel, supporting U.S. diplomacy, and supporting the President, as appropriate. When you start from that position, it is easier to stay in favor with both sides. People see her as trusted and someone who has the best interests of American security, Israeli security and human rights at heart."

Poole said that Davis, whatever the issue, "has a reputation of listening and she listens to all sides. She is very deliberate before she takes a position. Even at the end of the day, if a group doesn't agree with her, if she has given them time and consideration, it can help."

The physical configuration of Davis's offices offers some insight into how business is conducted. In the reception area, where C-SPAN coverage of meetings of the House of Representatives plays on a monitor, there are small desks where visitors needing help dealing with one federal agency or another can fill out papers under the helpful guidance of Pedramrazi. Off the reception area is a short hallway in which there is a private office for Davis to use when she is in the district — although, according to Poole, she prefers to work in the staff room.

Davis utilizes her modest private office or the conference room only when meetings with constituents so dictate; otherwise, she likes to work at one of the desks in the open-floor-plan staff room, in which staff members face each other in a circle and throw out questions to one another as necessary.

Poole, having previously worked for U.S. Senator Barbara Boxer, joined Davis's staff as soon as she took office in January 2001. As a Davis staffer, she worked under other district directors until she, herself, became one in 2008. Hazard, after graduating UCSD, moved to Washington, D.C., obtaining a staff job with Davis in which he first "shadowed" senior staff, and later was assigned responsibility for liaising with the Department of Defense (DOD) — an important assignment given Davis's position on the Armed Services Committee. He obtained a master's degree at the National Defense University, which is sponsored by the Department of Defense.

Defense issues with which Hazard dealt included strategy concerning such Middle East players as Iraq, Hezbollah, and Iran, so foreign policy in the Middle East became a natural extension of his responsibilities. But after seven years in Washington, Hazard elected to return to San Diego to raise his young family. Having him and Steuer on the district staff, with their previous Washington experience, makes communication between the two offices even more efficient, said Poole.

An important portion of the district office's work is helping constituents deal with federal agencies, ranging from the Social Security Administration, to the Veterans Administration, to the various Cabinet-level secretariats of the Executive Branch. "The case work we do is like the social work function of the office," said Poole. "We receive a lot of requests from people who need assistance with a federal agency, or sometimes with local matters as well. If it is a federal agency, we contact that agency and try to get the matter resolved for them."

Asked what makes for a smoothly functioning district office, Hazard answered: "I think it starts with the member, the elected official, they set the tone for their offices. In my experience, it's true in Washington and it is true here. When you start with someone of Susan's caliber and dedication to constituents, it is easy to follow in her path. We know what we are supposed to be doing. Everyone is passionate about public service; you don't have to prod anyone to go out and help people." Noting that the staff refers to itself as "Team Davis," Poole recalled that the first time she met her boss, she was being interviewed by the congresswoman and others. "I felt like I was the only person in the room, the way she acts with individuals. Her focus is on people. She is listening. That carries over and sets the tone, how she works with people, how we try to work with people."

Working with people was one of the important criteria for where the district office is located. "We wanted something that was accessible for the community, so being in a neighborhood was a great option for that," Poole explained. "It is very central to the district as well. And if you spend any time here, it is very well traveled both in terms of traffic and pedestrians. It is very open, like a storefront, and we wanted people to feel free to stop by and access our services."

From Texas Avenue Exit, proceed south on Texas to a left turn on Madison Avenue, followed by a left turn on Oregon Street. Office is on northeast corner of the intersection of Adams Avenue and Oregon Street.

-San Diego Jewish World, August 13, 2015

18. Exit 6

Synagogues on the Move

Former home of Tifereth Israel Synagogue
(Photo: Shor M. Masori)

SAN DIEGO — Although San Diego's Jewish community started in Old Town San Diego in the 1850s, moving to downtown and environs in the late 1800s and early 1900s, it was on the move again after World War II, with 30th Street in the North Park neighborhood becoming a focus of activity.

Here's a quick chronological overview:

San Diego's first Jewish house of worship, Temple Beth Israel, had been constructed in 1889 at Second and Beech Streets as a Reform institution with men and women sitting together and facing a raised stage on which both the Holy Ark and the reader's table were located.

Not recognizing Reform liturgy, which was an amalgam of liberal German Judaism and some of the mannerisms of American Protestantism, Orthodox Jews who arrived in San Diego from Eastern Europe formed a separate *minyan* to conduct their services.

But in 1905, when Yom Kippur came, there was a conflict over who could use Beth Israel's one-room Temple building. The Orthodox *minyan* had started prayers early in the day and were still engaged in prayer when the main Reform group arrived, and asked them to vacate.

The Orthodox angrily adjourned to the nearby home of Elias Jacobson to complete the service, and thereafter decided to form their own congregation, which they named Tifereth Israel Synagogue. The congregation found a location sixteen blocks east and about ten blocks south of Beth Israel near 18th and Market Streets, a venue which since has been obliterated by the construction of Interstate 5.

The congregation remained on 18th Street until 1948, when it moved to a larger space 12 blocks farther east and considerably to the north at 30th Street and Howard Avenue on land the congregation had purchased during World War II. The new location was not the only change for the synagogue. A new rabbi, Monroe Levens, persuaded the congregation that in order to grow it should switch from the Orthodox movement to the Conservative movement. One salient difference was that whereas for Orthodox Jews driving a car is forbidden on the Sabbath, for Conservatives, it is permissible if it is being done for a religious purpose such as traveling to synagogue. That meant Tifereth Israel could draw its membership from a larger area than what was within walking distance.

Baruch Stern, a survivor of Adolf Hitler's concentration camps, had served as a Hebrew teacher at Tifereth Israel Synagogue. Moss Addleson, a synagogue member, introduced Stern to his brother, Rabbi Nathan Addleson of Los Angeles, with whom Stern studied for ordination as an Orthodox rabbi.

Beth Jacob Congregation's first home
(Photo: Shor M. Masori)

Second home of Beth Jacob Congegation
(Photo: Shor M. Masori)

About the same time, in response to Tifereth Israel's switchover, Beth Jacob Congregation, which had established itself in the late 1930s as a Conservative congregation, decided to switch and become an Orthodox congregation. The newly minted Orthodox congregation hired Stern as its rabbi. From a home on Myrtle Avenue, it moved to a building at 4473 30th Street between Monroe and Meade Avenues.

Meanwhile, in the mid-1920s, Temple Beth Israel moved from Second and Beech to a Moorish-style synagogue at 3rd Avenue and Laurel Street. (In 2000, the congregation moved again to a campus east of La Jolla in the University City area of San Diego. Its historic second home at 3rd and Laurel subsequently was occupied by the Conservative Ohr Shalom Synagogue.)

Rabbis Stern and Levens were close colleagues, who also had cordial relations with Rabbi Morton Cohn of Temple Beth Israel. Jerry Levens, son of Monroe Levens, recalled that the Orthodox and Reform rabbis would often come to their house for dinner. Rabbi Stern could eat there because the food was kosher and Rabbi Cohn "would eat anything anywhere, as long as it was good."

This was a golden age for San Diego's Jewish community, with the three rabbis being close friends, who often would deliver lectures at each other's congregations and frequently co-officiate at life cycle events.

The North Park era of the Jewish community lasted approximately 30 years. In the late 1970s, the congregations sold their buildings along 30th Street and followed their members farther east to the College and San Carlos communities of

San Diego. Today Tifereth Israel is located at 6660 Cowles Mountain Boulevard and Beth Jacob Congregation is at 4855 College Avenue.

···

To see the former homes of Tifereth Israel and Beth Jacob, take the Texas Street off ramp to Madison Avenue and turn left (east) to 30th Street. Turn right (south). The former site of Beth Jacob Congregation is at 4437 30th Street, between Madison and Meade Avenues. Proceed farther south beyond major intersection at El Cajon Boulevard to Howard Street. Tifereth Israel Synagogue occupied the large building at the corner.

···

-San Diego Jewish World, August 20, 2015

19. Exit 8

San Diego Family History Center

San Diego Family History Center, operated by Mormon Church

SAN DIEGO — It may seem strange that a book focusing on "Jewish stories" along the Interstate 8 would direct you to a facility operated by the Church of Jesus Christ of Latter-day Saints, but if it is genealogical research that you are interested in, there is no place better for tracing your family's roots than the San Diego Family History Center, regardless of your religion.

I have used this facility at 4195 Camino del Rio South on many occasions for historical research and have always found the people there to be courteous and helpful. And if you are concerned that someone at the library may engage in proselytizing, I can say that has never been my experience the many times I have been there.

For members of the Mormon Church, family research is not only fun, it is what we Jews would call a mitzvah. Mormons believe that once a person has died, his or her soul continues to have a will, and that soul may be willing to accept posthumous conversion to the Mormon faith. So for Mormons, finding out who one's ancestors were is a step toward potentially uniting the generations of one's family.

You don't have to be Mormon to utilize the research facility, nor do you have to turn any of the information you access over to the LDS Church. Very simply, as a gesture of good will towards people of other religions (or even no religion), the Latter-day Saints make their voluminous microfilm records available.

If you haven't done family research, guides will teach you how to begin, and direct you to the appropriate microfilm records. If you don't know how to operate a microfilm reader, they will show you. If you become discouraged in your search, they will help you. The guides here and at Family History Centers across the country really go out of their way to be accommodating, with no fee or donation asked.

So what can you find at a Family History Center? One of the basics is Federal Census records, which are compiled every 10 years. If you know where a member of your family lived in 1940, 1930, 1920, or any decade before, you may be able to find without too much difficulty the information about that relative and other family members living at the same address.

You also can access birth and death records, marriage records, trans-Atlantic passenger manifests for immigrants, and naturalization papers. Because on such records as these, people are asked to provide information about themselves and their families, it sometimes is possible for one record to lead to another, to another, and so forth, further and further back through the generations.

In addition to these kinds of genealogical records, the Family History Center also maintains a well-stocked library about different places around the world, including the cities or shtetls from which your ancestors may have emigrated.

Eastbound traffic should remain on the right side of the Mission Gorge/Fairmount Exit ramp so that you can make a right turn. Almost immediately turn right again on the frontage road, Camino del Rio South. The San Diego Center for Family History is part of the Church of Latter Day Saints complex on the left at 4195 Camino del Rio South.

-San Diego Jewish World, August 27, 2015

20. Exit 8

Mission San Diego

Mission San Diego, first in the chain of California missions

SAN DIEGO — Under any circumstances a trip to Mission San Diego is worthwhile because it is the oldest mission in the chain that runs more than 600 miles along the coast of California and served as an instrument of this state's European settlement. One really cannot encounter California history without knowing about Father Junipero Serra and the other Franciscan friars who taught Christianity to the indigenous people, known in this part of San Diego County as the Kumeyaay.

Mission San Diego is the inspiration for much of the nomenclature of San Diego, including the name of the neighborhood known as Mission Valley; the names of many important streets such as Friars Road, Mission Center Road, and Mission Gorge Road, and even to the moniker of the baseball team — the San Diego Padres.

San Diego is referred to as St. Didacus in Latin and, according to some experts, is a name that is derived from Santiago, which is equivalent to "Saint James" in English. He was a lay friar whose medical healing during the 16th century was thought by the King of Spain to be nothing short of miraculous, even to the point that touching a part of Diego's body after his death was believed to bring about cures. It was on San Diego's feast day in 1602 that the explorer Sebastian Vizcaino renamed the bay and its surroundings for him. The area first had been spotted and claimed by explorer Juan Rodriguez Cabrillo in 1542.

Cabrillo had named this area San Miguel, but San Diego was the official name by the time Father Serra and his party celebrated a mass atop Presidio Hill in 1769, where the mission was located for five years before being moved up-river to its present location. It should be noted that in 2015, Pope Francis canonized Father Serra, thereby elevating him to the status of a Catholic saint.

One finds at Mission San Diego numerous statues and busts of many important figures in Catholic belief, but none captured my Jewish attention more firmly than that of St. Joseph, as the husband of Mary is called by Christians. He stands in a garden with his left hand held to his heart and his right hand, holding a lily, at his side. In Christian iconography, a lily represents purity.

Many Jews are familiar with the Catholic concept that Mary was a virgin impregnated by God, and that Joseph was at first suspicious of her, but was a kindly enough man that he did not intend to make a public issue of her pregnancy.

Somewhat later, according to Christian Scriptures, God's action and plan were made known to Joseph, who thereupon performed the *mitzvah* of serving as Mary's protector.

So, what would have happened if Joseph had made a public issue of Mary's pregnancy?

According to *Deuteronomy* (or *Devarim* as the fifth book in Torah is known in Hebrew), if a man learns that his wife had deceived him about her virginity, then the city elders "shall take the girl to the entrance of her father's house and the people of her city shall pelt her with stones and she shall die, for she had committed an outrage in Israel, to commit adultery in her father's house, and you shall remove the evil from your midst."

As Mary's protector, and husband by law, Joseph fulfilled another important function in the interplay of Hebrew and Christian scriptures. According to Christian belief, Jesus was a direct descendant of King David. In Hebrew Scriptures, the prophet Jeremiah (23:5) predicts that "days are coming–the words of Hashem– when I will establish a righteous sprout from David; a king will reign and prosper and he will administer justice and righteousness in the land. In his days, Judah will be saved, and Israel will dwell securely."

Christians refer to the person so described as the messiah, so it was important that Joseph, as the legal father of Jesus, was a direct descendant of King David. However, there is an apparent conflict in Christian Scriptures. *The Gospel According to St. Matthew* (1:1-17) reports that Joseph was descended from David via his son King Solomon, whereas the *Gospel According to Saint Luke* (3:23-31) says he was a descendant of David's son Nathan. Matthew gives the name of Joseph's father as Jacob (thus paralleling the genealogy in Genesis), whereas Luke says Joseph was the son of Heli.

It should also be noted that in the genealogy as given by Luke, there are many more generations separating Jesus from King David than in the genealogy reported by Matthew. There is a tradition in Christianity that the genealogy recited by Luke really charts the ancestry of Mary, not Joseph, but substitutes the name Joseph because he is her husband. The importance of this interpretation is that it would mean that Jesus was descended from David biologically through his mother, and for legal purposes through his human father.

Another issue affecting Joseph -- who, as bumper stickers often proclaim, was a "Jewish carpenter"-- is the Catholic idea that Mary remained a virgin throughout her life. How can this be reconciled with the idea that Joseph and Mary were man and wife? According to Catholic theologians, Joseph was quite old and a widower when he married Mary, and apparently was beyond the age of sexual function. Accordingly, Joseph often is represented in Catholic iconography as an older man.

Catholics consider Joseph to be both a protector of travelers and of pregnant women. A year after San Diego's 1769 founding, a ship bringing supplies to the mission was overdue. The military commander with whom Serra had traveled — Gaspar de Portola — feared the ship was lost and food was only sufficient for a return expedition to Baja California. To stay any longer without additional provisions risked starvation. He reportedly urged Serra to return with the soldiers to Baja California, but Serra was resolute about staying.

St. Joseph

Instead, Serra said he would pray for nine days -- an act known as a noven -- to St. Joseph for the safety of the ships, and, if no ship was spotted, those in his party could leave if they wanted. On the ninth day, which happened to be St. Joseph's Feast Day, March 19, a supply ship heading for Monterey Bay lost its anchor at sea and was forced to enter San Diego Bay thus saving, by chance or miracle, the expedition.

Traditionally, St. Joseph's Day also is the day when swallows return each year to the mission at San Juan Capistrano.

This explains why the statue of St Joseph, along with those of St. Francis of Assisi -- for whom the Franciscan order is named -- and San Diego occupy special places of honor at Mission San Diego.

From the Mission Gorge Exit, proceed east to a left turn on Twain Avenue, which will eventually become San Diego Mission Road. The mission will be on the right.

-San Diego Jewish World, September 3, 2015

21. Exit 8

Dr. Garfield and the Kaiser Hospitals

Kaiser Hospital on Zion Avenue

SAN DIEGO — Two of my grandsons were born at the Kaiser Permanente Hospital that towers over the intersection of Mission Gorge Road and Zion Avenue. Given that the hospital's address is 4647 Zion Avenue, I sometimes joke that these descendants were natural born "Zionists."

But no such flights of fancy are needed to tell the "Jewish story" of this hospital. This hospital, as well as all the Kaiser-Permanente facilities, were an outgrowth of the innovative spirit and farsightedness of a young Jewish physician from Los Angeles -- Dr. Sidney Garfield -- who in 1933 established a 12-bed hospital in Desert Center, in the far reaches of the Mojave Desert, to tend to the health of 5,000 Metropolitan Water District workers who were building an aqueduct to bring water to Los Angeles from the Colorado River.

Dr. Paul Bernstein, San Diego regional medical director for Kaiser Permanente, is quite knowledgeable about Garfield, having told his story in the novel *Courage to Heal*. While some of the conversations and the love story in that book were products of Bernstein's fertile imagination, he said he hewed strictly to the facts in describing Garfield's progress as a doctor and Health Maintenance Organization (HMO) administrator.

Bernstein told me that as a boy Garfield wanted to be an architect. But his mother thought him becoming a doctor was more fitting. He trained as a surgeon at Los Angeles County Hospital, which today is known as USC Medical Center, "where they were bringing injured workers from the aqueduct on a six-hour ride to treat them for trauma, and a lot of them died on the way," Bernstein said. Workers called the ambulance "the oven on wheels."

So Garfield went out to Desert Center because "it was the Depression and there weren't a lot of other jobs, and second because there were thousands of workers who needed health care. With a $2,500 loan from his father and by getting a lot of incentives from some companies — surgical companies, air conditioning companies, General Electric — he was able to create a small hospital in the desert. By the way, this was the first hospital in America to have air conditioning where the patients were and not where the doctors were. It was unique, caring about how the patients were feeling."

For the next part of the story, Bernstein depended on "Kaiser lore" rather than on documented facts. According to the oft told story, industrialist Henry Kaiser, who had been a prime contractor on the Boulder Dam (now called the Hoover Dam), literally jumped off a train near Desert Center to get in a successful bid for the Six Companies consortium to build the Parker Dam. He suffered minor injuries and, accompanied by his insurance executive Harold Hatch, encountered Garfield at the desert hospital.

Kaiser and Hatch learned that rather than wait for patients to be hospitalized, Garfield was an advocate of pre-payment for health care. Workers were asked to contribute 5 cents per day to insure themselves against huge medical bills in the event of an accident. Well over 90 percent of the workers did so, enabling Garfield to further capitalize his small hospital.

For an additional nickel a day, workers were able to pre-pay the costs for treatment for non-work-related illnesses that might befall them. This plan also proved to be a success, not only financially, but more importantly, in how it gradually changed the outlook of the hospital world. With income already assured via prepayment, hospital personnel needn't hope that enough sick patients would be wheeled through the doors to defray expenses and salaries, nor were they tempted to order unnecessary tests just to jack up the fees. Instead the doctors and nurses could emphasize preventative medicine, helping enrollees to stay healthy, and – as is said in KP's advertising slogan voiced in TV commercials by actress Allison Janney (*The West Wing, Mom*) —to "thrive."

After the aqueduct construction was completed, Garfield was invited by Kaiser to set up a similar plan at the construction site of the Grand Coulee Dam, enrolling 6,500 workers and family members. Not long after the dam was completed, the Japanese attacked the U.S. Naval Fleet at Pearl Harbor in Honolulu, Hawaii, precipitating American entry into World War II. There was tremendous urgency to rebuild America's naval fleet and to win back control of the Pacific Ocean from the Japanese. Some 30,000 workers were hired by Henry J. Kaiser, under a U.S. military contract, to build ships at six facilities in the San Francisco Bay Area.

Once again Kaiser wanted Garfield on his team. Together they set up first aid stations at the shipyards, as well as a field hospital in Richmond, and a major hospital in Oakland for the most serious cases. This was the beginning of Kaiser-Permanente, into which members of the public were permitted to enroll as World War II wound down. The era of the health maintenance organization (HMO) had begun, and Kaiser-Permanente Hospitals branched out from the San Francisco Bay Area to other parts of the nation, including San Diego.

In the Summer 2006 issue of *Permanente Journal*, a peer-reviewed quarterly journal of medicine, doctors pondered the contributions to the medical profession made by Garfield, who, since and before his death in 1984 had attained legendary status.

Dr. Jay Crosson recalled that Garfield "was a fount of ideas—virtual intellectual fireworks—admittedly igniting a few duds among the brilliant rockets. The ideas ranged across the entire spectrum of health care, from delivery models to financing to hospital design."

Crosson suggested that four ideas, in particular, resulted in innovations for which Garfield will be remembered. In addition to pre-payment, these included: group practices with multiple medical specialties; an emphasis on keeping people healthy; and utilization of technology for accurate medical record keeping.

Crosson quoted Garfield as saying, "The computer cannot replace the physician, but it can keep essential data moving smoothly from laboratory to nurse's station, from x-ray department to the patient's chart and from all areas of the medical center to the physician himself."

In a personal remembrance, Dr. Robert Feldman wrote: "Over the 15 years of our collaboration, I spent a great deal of time with Dr. Garfield working on research regarding health care delivery. I saw him almost daily under many different circumstances. He was a remarkable man – patient, tolerant, always considerate, soft-spoken, almost shy, but strong – a complete gentleman. He treated construction workers as he would important administrators or physicians. He was generous and unpretentious. I never heard him gossip or criticize his medical colleagues. He said he sought out and tried to employ the strengths of the people he worked with. He readily acknowledged a good job, and if he didn't have anything positive to say he didn't say anything. He was dapper and dressed well in custom-made clothes. He didn't carry a wallet, just a credit card and a few large bills—he had class."

Bernstein never met Garfield personally but he was a resident at the Zion Avenue Kaiser Hospital in 1978, the same year that Garfield popped into the Emergency Room at 2 a.m., identified himself, and asked to be shown around so he could see "how things work in San Diego." Dr. Jeffrey Selevan, a fellow Jew, was serving as chief of the emergency room at the time, and he showed him around. "He was obviously excited to meet him," said Bernstein. Seleven incidentally went on to become the chief financial officer for the Kaiser Medical Group for a number of years.

After World War II, Kaiser-Permanente became more and more successful as a result of labor unions and businesses enrolling their members in the pre-payment plan. While Kaiser and Garfield agreed on many things, "like brothers, they had their differences too, which resulted in 1955 in our famous civil war between Sidney Garfield and Henry Kaiser, that was between the medical group and the business arm, which we call the 'health plan.' They had a disagreement that almost disintegrated the Kaiser-Permanente plan back in the 1950s," Bernstein related. "Henry Kaiser felt strongly that he could do a better job of controlling outcomes and costs than physicians could, so he started to want to control it just like his businesses of steel, aluminum, shipbuilding and cars, to name a few, because he was very controlling. He wanted to make medical decisions and the doctors pushed back. The doctors believed they should make all decisions about patient care, whereas Kaiser felt that businessmen could make those decisions as well, and more cost effectively than the doctors."

"They came to impasse," Bernstein continued. "Henry Kaiser said, 'Great I will sell you the whole program. Give me $3 million and I will give you the hospital and everything.' Doctors at that time were making $600 per month, so they couldn't afford anything near that. The doctors, Henry Kaiser, and his business group got together at Henry Kaiser's famous mansion at Lake Tahoe, called *Fleur du Lac* (Flower of the Lake) where years later they filmed a segment of *The Godfather* movie — the part where the Godfather's brother is taken out to the lake and is done away with. That meeting in 1955 resulted in our current medical services agreement on structure.... The doctors make all the medical decisions, and they work with the health plan to make business decisions, a fully integrated system of care. Sidney Garfield had been head of the medical group at the time, but he stepped down as part of the agreement and went over to work with Kaiser on the health plan side."

The basic agreement, still in effect today, has generated the Kaiser concept of "the right care based on medical guidelines and outcomes and what is going to help that patient get well, and not just order tests randomly to generate fees," Bernstein said. "It is health care based on wellness and prevention and not the traditional sick care based on treating patients only when they are ill. We want to do everything we can to keep the patient healthy, so that if you look at our testing rates for colonoscopies and mammograms, we lead the nation in preventive care, and this is in contrast to ordering inappropriate tests, such as MRI's, for anyone with a headache, where it is not always indicated." Such decisions, he said, are based on national studies and guidelines.

In Bernstein's office is a large photographic mural of Sidney Garfield, together with his saying: "Keep your arms on each other's shoulders and keep your eyes on the stars for innovation and change for the future." Outside Bernstein's office is a full size stand-up poster of Garfield, his hero.

"Almost everything we do in American medicine today was really developed by him," Bernstein said admiringly. "Think about it, prevention and wellness, he came up with in the 1930's. Focusing on a patient from everything from air conditioning in the patients' rooms to providing care that keeps them healthy, to getting them in sooner for care rather than later. ... Back then our morbidity and mortality from pneumonia were significantly less than any hospital in California because patients came in before their colds and upper respiratory infections turned into pneumonia. At the same time patients with appendicitis did well because they came in before their appendix ruptured because they didn't have that barrier in terms of fees. They came in sooner so we had the best care and outcomes. The same thing applies today in terms of prevention."

A new Kaiser Central Hospital near the intersection of Interstate 15 and Clairemont Mesa Boulevard is scheduled to open in 2017, at which point some of the specialties will be housed there and others will continue to be housed at the Zion facility, according to Bernstein. "Our Central Hospital in Kearny Mesa will be more advanced and innovative than any hospital in San Diego. It will include a neurosurgery center of excellence, cardiac center of excellence, and, a maternal and child center of excellence. Zion will become a center for orthopedics, hematology and oncology, and other centers still under development. We will have emergency rooms at both."

Dr. Paul Bernstein with mural of Dr. Sidney Garfield

From eastbound Interstate 8, take Mission Gorge Exit, turn left onto Mission Gorge and follow to Zion Avenue. Turn right and the hospital will be on the right.

-San Diego Jewish World, September 10, 2015

22. Exit 9

A World Champion's Tennis Club

Lake Murray Tennis Club

SAN DIEGO — Soft-spoken, easy-going Saul Snyder is easy to underestimate. An opponent once told him, "you look like my accountant," but that was before he faced Snyder across the tennis net, and lost. He learned, as many others had before and since, that Snyder, who is an octogenarian, is one of the finest tennis players in the world.

No, that's not hyperbole; Snyder has rooms filled with plaques, awards and "golden balls" attesting to his prowess on the tennis court—whether the surface be hard, clay, or grass. In 2008, he was the United States Tennis Association's (USTA) singles champion for men 75 and over in both hard court and clay court play. In 2012 he was the Southern California Tennis Association's Senior Player of the Year, as well as USTA's 2012 doubles winner in clay court competition in Virginia Beach.

He won the gold medal at Israel's 14th Maccabiah Games in 1993, and 20 years later in Croatia, he and Joyce Jones won the gold medal for mixed doubles play for people over 80 — a world championship!

Although he hasn't won a grass court championship—there are few such courts in Southern California on which to practice—Snyder says that he really likes the feel of them, and how "you can expect everything to be below your knees when it is coming at you." He reached the quarter finals in one grass court tournament, along the way beating a fellow who was seeded No. 1.

Snyder is based at the 10-hard-court Lake Murray Tennis Club at 7003 Murray Park Drive near the junction of the San Carlos and Del Cerro neighborhoods of San Diego. The city-owned facility overlooks a San Diego reservoir that is part of the sprawling Mission Trails Regional Park. Snyder lives approximately three blocks from the courts, and he likes to joke that now that he's "retired," his biggest decision is whether to walk or drive to a match.

He's not exactly "retired" because as a former real estate broker, he listened to his own sales pitches about how valuable apartment house properties are, and now he and his wife Sonia own apartment complexes in San Diego; Riverside, California; and Houston, Texas. Although a management company looks after the properties, he says he likes to do a little work around them now and then—mainly pulling up weeds and picking up papers. Playing tennis prepares him well for such tasks, he acknowledges; he often has to pick up balls from the surface of the courts.

Danielle Bryan, one of the tennis teachers at the club which has been managed since 2000 by her parents Dan and Kathy Emmerson, says that the strength of Snyder's game is that he is fast – he can reach most balls that other people would let go – and that he excels at shot placement.

Asked if he agreed with that assessment, Snyder said he was fortunate to have developed good speed and stamina, as well as a drop shot that has opponents rushing to the net to return, and which he follows with a lob shot over their heads. His serves don't smoke by any means, but they go where he wants them to – often in the opposite direction from where his opponent think he's looking.

I asked if as one whose 83rd birthday was in September 2015 he has a special diet or physical regimen to keep himself fit. He responded that he makes certain to eat light meals more than two hours before a match, so that he has time to digest them, and that he always, but always, engages in stretching exercises before he plays. Opponents whose meals are too heavy, he noted, tend to feel sluggish and by the time the match gets around to the third set, they can be too tired for vigorous competition. Generally speaking, he likes to follow a "Mediterranean diet: salads, fruit, fish, chicken, very little beef, no pork. I also stay away from trans fats, watch my cholesterol, and I stretch, exercise."

He also said that he tries to remain relaxed and jovial up until he gets on the court, but as soon as it's time for the first serve of the match, he concentrates fully on his game. In fact, he gives full attention to his opponent in the warm-up period prior to the match, in an effort to determine whether that person has a weak forehand or backhand, or is out of shape. "I will play against those weaknesses," he readily concedes. "They do the same thing to me."

En route to any match, Sonia reminds him to "focus, focus, focus!"

Is that because he gets distracted? I asked.

Snyder responded that most of the time, he has no difficulty concentrating, except when members of his family are in the stands watching, or there has been distressing family news such as someone's sickness or marital problems.

What's the problem with members of his family being in the stands? Sometimes, instead of watching, he said, "they're reading books."

That will knock down any tennis player's ego.

Snyder began playing tennis shortly after World War II while a student at Beverly Hills High School. At that point, he was far from the phenomenon he is today. In fact he was tenth on the school's tennis ladder, meaning he sat on the bench when the Normans played other high school teams. The top five players were the ones that usually got to compete.

Later at UCLA, he continued to play, but more for fun rather than for school competitions. However, one contest against a fellow Beverly Hills High School alumnus he considered to be a grudge match. The fellow had won an award for sportsmanship even though "on the court he was not a good sport, and I resented it. Even though at the time, I was overweight, I struggled through three sets and I beat him."

Until he was about 60, he played recreational tennis, just having fun, and never thought about entering tournaments until some friends told him, "you are really better than you think you are" and "you should get better equipment." He traded in his wooden racket for an aluminum one and joined the San Carlos Tennis Club, which closed after a year so that the landowners could develop condominiums.

At that point, San Diego City Councilwoman Judy McCarty, sensitized to the needs of the tennis community by a daughter who was taking tennis lessons, came to the rescue, winning funding for construction of the Lake Murray Tennis Club, where membership is open to all. Initially eight courts were built, but the citizen board that runs the club decided to raise the money to construct two more.

Snyder served one year as president of the Lake Murray Tennis Club's Board of Directors, drawing perhaps on his experience as a vice president for membership for Congregation Beth Tefilah, a Conservative synagogue that since merged with Adat Ami Synagogue to form Ohr Shalom Synagogue.

Meetings of the relatively few board members of the Lake Murray Tennis Club were held in the clubhouse with a few chairs being drawn up near the sofas. Some of the issues Snyder remembers from his term were whether women's teams could import players from other clubs (no!) and whether to build those new courts. Other issues were relatively minor, he recalled.

A plaque inside the clubhouse tells of the United States Tennis Association rating it as an "outstanding facility" in 2001. What makes the place so special? I asked.

"I think it's the friendliness of the players, that we have a clubhouse that doubles as a meeting place," he responded. "It has two bathrooms (with a shower), a pro shop, where you can get stringing, and purchase rackets and shoes. Kathy and Dan Emmerson are outstanding managers of the club."

Occasionally some young elementary school-age relatives will ask Snyder for some pointers about tennis, and he likes to quote from a book by Ed Collins, who is an instructor at the Peninsula Tennis Club in Ocean Beach. "Watch the ball, bend your knees. That will be $20 please."

Of all the trophies, medals, and gold balls he has received, Snyder seems to hold one in which he was named "Sportsman of the Year" by the San Diego district tennis association in highest esteem.

"Most of the matches we are in, we call our own lines," Snyder related. "If you are not a sportsman and you are looking only to win and you are willing to cheat, there are opportunities to do that, but you would become quickly known for that quality. I think sportsmanship is quite important."

Unfortunately not everyone in tennis acts so honorably. "I have played against cheaters," Snyder said. "One time in Rancho Mirage I was beaten in a close match, and about an hour later a stranger came up to me, and said he had watched the match and that "several of the balls you hit were called out but weren't."

In a doubles match, he recalled, he and his partner were in a tie breaker game against a twosome whom they had never beaten. "They hit some balls that were pretty close. When it is near your feet and deep, it is hard to call, and I called their balls 'fair!' and we lost." When the game was over, one of the opponents told him, "Saul there is one more thing that you need in your armament – line calls," meaning that I should have called some out that were out."

In another match, he was playing a fellow "who hits the ball as hard as you will ever see, and following that game I was to play a mixed doubles game with Roz King. Roz was watching the singles match against this fellow, which he won. She came storming on the court and said 'don't you ever do that when you are playing with me! You gave him 4-5 points.' He hit the ball so hard, I had to turn my head to see where it landed, and if it is close, I can't call it out."

Given the choice between winning a championship, and being an honest and sportsman-like competitor, Snyder said there is no question that he would choose the latter.

"When this game stops being fun," he declared, "that's when I'm going to hang my racket up!"

In the meantime, he says, tennis provides him plenty of exercise and the chance to socialize, while keeping the mind active—an important ingredient for warding off dementia. "Tennis is played worldwide and affords a person an opportunity to meet people from all over the world and all walks of life," Snyder said.

Saul Snyder, tennis champion

From Interstate 8 take the Waring Road Exit (it only goes in one direction) to a left turn on Navajo Road. Turn right on Park Ridge Boulevard and follow it to the end. Entrance is just beyond the intersection with Murray Park Drive.

-San Diego Jewish World, September 17, 2015

23. Exit 9

Benjamin Branch Library

Benjamin Branch Library entrance

SAN DIEGO — At this point I still can't tell whether the tale of the reclusive bibliophile who only came to the public's attention after he died, very much alone, is a "Jewish story" or not. As the man in question, Edwin Arthur Benjamin, is the namesake of the city's Benjamin branch library, I suppose if it turns out he was not Jewish, we could always fall back upon the fact that the library is located at the corner of Waring Road and *Zion* Avenue to claim our Jewish story.

There's divided opinion about whether Benjamin was Jewish, or perhaps the son of a Jewish father, or perhaps simply someone bearing the surname of one of the 12 Jewish tribes. The records that I've searched don't tell his religion, and he certainly didn't make that fact about himself generally known, since recluses in any event don't talk much about themselves. Census records report that his father was born in England, and his mother, Martha Phelps, in New York.

Calvin Metz, a Christian friend of Benjamin's, might have been able to tell us all about the bibliophile, but Metz is also dead. One of Metz's daughters, Kathryn, who used to call Benjamin "Uncle Ed," told me in a telephone interview from Loma Linda, California, that Benjamin didn't practice any religion, but rather had been an atheist. However, she added, it's possible that his father, H.R.

Benjamin, who served as a doctor in an Iowa regiment in the Civil War, had been Jewish. Kathryn simply was unable to say one way or the other.

Edwin Arthur Benjamin, born in 1875, was discovered dead in his North Park home near 30th Street in August 1963 while the Metzes were away from the city on vacation. Kathryn, who grew up to be a school teacher, doesn't recall if she ever was told where he was buried, or if his body was disposed of by some other means. One of the items she received from his estate was his family Bible—which included both the "Old" and "New" Testaments—but the fact that he was in possession of Christian Scriptures doesn't really answer the question of his religious/ethnic background. On my own reference shelf is a King James version of the Bible in addition to the Stone version of the Tanakh and the Plaut Torah commentary.

How the Metzes came to be friends with Benjamin, who socialized with practically no one else, was a matter of serendipity. While a pupil in public school, Kathryn went door to door to collect for the neighborhood Bookmobile. Benjamin, for whom books was a passion, contributed a few from his collection, which Kathryn later learned was quite extensive, perhaps as many as 10,000 volumes, all carefully bound.

"His whole house was lined with custom-made book shelves," she recalled. "I remember some of them were signed first editions of Mark Twain's. He also had an extensive collection about Lincoln."

It wasn't the book collection—which she said was donated to the public library—that resulted in the distribution across the country of a UPI news story about his demise. It was the fact that this urban hermit left an unsolicited $500,000 gift to the City of San Diego to be used for library purposes. Today, $500,000 may not sound like that much, but it was an astounding amount of money back in 1963, especially to have been accumulated by someone who lived so far beneath the general public's radar.

Benjamin's chance encounter with Kathryn led to a friendship with her father Calvin, a fellow lover of books, who was the principal of Pepper Drive Elementary School in El Cajon. Metz was a highly regarded educator, even being among a group to receive awards at the White House, his daughter reported.

The Metzes moved from their home in North Park to another home in Allied Gardens, which is the neighborhood in San Diego where the Benjamin branch library is located. Even so, they kept in close touch with Benjamin—which wasn't always easy—because he refused to have a telephone that might disturb his solitude. Nor did he have a refrigerator—another one of them newfangled devices.

Kathryn said that for companionship Benjamin had his beloved cat, Rusty, and additionally engaged in fairly frequent business discussions with his stockbroker, who helped him invest in the Melville Corporation which eventually morphed into the CVS drugstores.

When it came to socializing, the Metzes were just about his only friends. "He would come over on holidays, and on Sundays for dinner," Kathryn remembered. He helped to develop Kathryn's love of literature. She recalled fondly that he gave her the Lady of the Lake poem from Alfred Lord Tennyson's *Idylls of the King*.

Calvin Metz was among those who called for the Allied Gardens branch library to be named after Benjamin. The city did so, utilizing some of his bequest to build the Benjamin Branch Library, which opened March 22, 1965. The Benjamin branch marked 2015 as its golden anniversary. Meanwhile, the city had outside consultants invest the corpus of Benjamin's bequest, so that in 2015, even after various withdrawals to build or improve other branch libraries, the fund still amounted to more than $1.2 million.

Two withdrawals from the fund came in 1986. These were $55,000 for design and construction of a Point Loma branch library expansion, and $130,000 for land acquisition and expansion of the North Park library. In 1994, another $200,000 was taken from the fund to be put toward construction of the Rancho Bernardo branch library.

Metz, who became an unofficial watchdog of the fund, considered these appropriate uses of the money left to the city by his old friend. But he balked at an effort in 1985 to use money from the fund to pay for a computer system to help the library in its fundraising.

After Metz testified on the matter, the San Diego City Council directed the City Manager to find money for the computer system from some other place.

Computers—the very idea would have been abhorrent to an old bibliophile who didn't even like such devices as telephones or refrigerators!

THIS BUILDING IS DEDICATED
TO THE MEMORY OF
EDWIN ARTHUR BENJAMIN
1875 - 1963
SCHOLAR · HUMANITARIAN · INVESTOR
WHO GAVE HIS FORTUNE
TO THE SAN DIEGO PUBLIC LIBRARY
SO THAT OTHERS MIGHT SHARE
HIS LOVE OF BOOKS

From Interstate 8, take Waring Road Exit, and continue to Zion Avenue. Library is at the coern of Waring and Zion.

-San Diego Jewish World, September 24, 2015

24. Exit 9

Young Israel of San Diego

Young Israel of San Diego entrance

SAN DIEGO — "Rabbi" means "teacher" and Rabbi Chaim Hollander teaches Judaic Studies at Soille San Diego Hebrew Day School in the Kearny Mesa neighborhood and at Young Israel of San Diego in the San Carlos neighborhood, where he is the pulpit rabbi.

Born in post-war Germany to Holocaust survivors Leah and Karl Hollander, he was a year and a half old when the family immigrated to Youngstown, Ohio, where he attended secular schools and played pitcher, short stop, and first base in Little League, Pony League, Babe Ruth League, and for a semi-pro team called McCauley Awnings.

He grew up at the Conservative Temple Emanuel in Youngstown, a congregation that had several Orthodox teachers and an Orthodox cantor. Hollander's mother came from a Chassidic background, kept a kosher home, and "was really determined that I should have a more religious life." A possibility arose when he was 13 to study at a yeshiva in Skokie, Illinois, "but I wasn't sure that was the direction I wanted to go in life" so Hollander declined the offer, preferring to stay at home.

Fate intervened when at age 15 ½ Hollander slipped and fell, breaking his instep. He couldn't put any pressure on his foot, which meant he could not go to his school where one had to walk up three flights of stairs because there was no elevator. So, for eight weeks, recalled Hollander, "they used to send me homework, but I didn't need seven hours a day to finish homework. So, I had a lot of time, and I was reading and I was thinking. I was growing up in the '60's, a time of real idealism. I put my idealism toward religion rather than anti-war protests and all that stuff, although when I got to college I did protest against the conditions of Soviet Jews."

Within a year of that religious exploration, Holocaust survivors Joseph and Edith Mann, who were Sabbath observant, moved into the neighborhood and took Hollander under their religious wings. They invited him to celebrate Shabbat with them, and under their influence, he became increasingly observant. Around this time also a Rothschild family moved to Youngstown, where Mr. Rothschild became the administrator of the Jewish Community Center. Rothschild was a graduate of Yeshiva University in New York City, and recommended that Hollander consider going there. Applying and winning acceptance, Hollander learned that YU offered three tracks of study. "One track was for those who had very little Jewish background, such as myself." Another track was for students who were interested in doing their learning in Hebrew. The third track was a "strict yeshiva, a theological seminary, where every day they studied six hours of Talmud and so forth."

Hollander enrolled in the first track "and I really enjoyed it. It began to click, and I decided that I would work hard to graduate from that program and get to the yeshiva part." Reflecting on that period of his life, Hollander said he had realized that if he had decided when he was 13 to go to the Skokie yeshiva, he'd have been much further ahead in his studies, "and I wanted to make it up as much as I could, so I began to study more intensely to the point that not only did I study during regular classes but in the last couple of years, I had a good friend tutor us. We used to study three hours in the evening after our secular classes and after we finished our homework."

"I worked very hard," Hollander continued. "In fact, one summer I went to a Yeshiva University camp in the Poconos, where there was a Kollel in which a small group of fellows, perhaps 12 to 14 guys, sat together and learned all day. There was a three-hour break in the middle of the day. It was a wonderful opportunity. It really advanced my learning to the point that in my senior year when I was going to graduate from Yeshiva University, I decided that I wanted to continue to rabbinical school."

About this time, Hollander was introduced at a mutual friend's Shabbos dinner to Tema Reisman who, like Hollander, was active in protests in front of the Soviet Embassy to the United Nations over the treatment of "refuseniks" — Jews who were denied permission to emigrate to Israel or to the United States, and who were held in suspicion and sometimes thrown in jail for wanting to do so.

A woman who knew both families played the role of *shadchan*, asking Hollander if he would like to start dating Reisman with an eye toward marriage. He was willing, but first, he decided, there was something he wanted to make clear to her. After graduation from Yeshiva University, he planned to live at least a year in Jerusalem so he could study at the Chofetz Chaim Yeshiva. When he told that to Tema, known as "Temi" to her friends, she said she thought it was a wonderful idea. Soon they were married and on their way to Israel together. Three months later, Temi became pregnant with the first of eight children, six of them boys and two of them girls. Most of them are either rabbis or married to a rabbi.

By mid-2015, the Hollanders' children had blessed them with 30 grandchildren. This is a matter of great sentimentality to Hollander, who explained "my father had five siblings. Of those six, only he and my uncle survived the war. My uncle never married, and my father was the only one who had children. We have to replenish the world!"

After returning to the United States from Jerusalem, Hollander began his teaching career. Too kind to mention names of schools where he was unhappy, he said it was sufficient to say that they were in the Northeast. At the first school, he spent a year teaching with no senior personnel observing his classroom until near the end of the year. When the principal told Hollander that if he came back the following year, he'd make a better teacher of him, Hollander responded that there had been a whole year to do that, but now he planned to move on. He "wasn't thrilled" with the next school either, and this caused a career crisis. Maybe, thought Hollander, he was intended to do something else; maybe he should pick up a few more units in accounting.

At this point Tema intervened. Before he did anything else, she suggested, he should attend the annual memorial lecture for the father of Rabbi Hanoch Leibowitz, the Rosh Yeshiva of the Chofetz Chaim Yeshiva in New York City. Hollander wasn't at all certain about the idea; it was a two-hour drive to New York City, and a two-hour drive back, and he had to teach the next day. "You can do it," Tema told Hollander. "Just go."

Following the lecture, Hollander stood in line to greet the Rosh Yeshiva, who bade him to sit down and tell him what had been going down in his life. "It impressed me that there were maybe 100 guys behind me and the Rosh Yeshiva treated me as if I was the only guy in the world, and everyone else could wait. I told him all my frustrations, and he said, 'You know, if something comes up, I will give you a call.' I felt good that someone had listened to me, but I didn't think anything would come of it. But sure enough, it couldn't have been more than five or six weeks later when I got a call from the Rosh Yeshiva. Actually, his rebbetzin called me and when I came to the phone she said, 'I will pass the phone to the Rosh Yeshiva' and Rosh Yeshiva said, 'There is something developing in New Orleans.'"

To attract good quality teachers, a yeshiva in New Orleans had decided to create a mini-Kollel, at which adult students could learn intensively for half a day, and teach younger students the other half day. "A lot of fellows at that point had several children, so it was hard to continue learning but this was an opportunity to learn and still make money, and also their wives could get jobs teaching in the school as well."

Accordingly, the Hollanders moved to New Orleans, where they greatly enjoyed the learning and the camaraderie with other mini-Kollel students and their wives. During this time, Hollander received his *smicha*—he was now an ordained rabbi.

In July 1981, a former classmate from the Chofetz Chaim yeshiva, Rabbi Simcha Weiser, invited Hollander to join him in San Diego, where Weiser was becoming the headmaster at San Diego Hebrew Day School (which later was renamed Soille San Diego Hebrew Day School after Rabbi Henri Soille, a benefactor). Hesitating to leave the Kollel, Hollander needed a couple of days to think about the offer, but eventually accepted.

"I came here as a teacher with the idea that I would be in charge of the Judaic Department which I was for many years." However, he grew restless with administrative duties and consulted with the Rosh Yeshiva who asked if he was well enough paid as a teacher. "Yes," said Hollander, "thank God, Rabbi Weiser pays me very well." So, asked the Rosh Yeshiva, "why do you want to be an administrator; what do you need the headache for? I realized the Rosh Yeshiva was right."

Meanwhile, Young Israel of San Diego had been created in 1989 in the San Carlos area, attracting a small group of Orthodox families. Like many start-up congregations, the membership of Young Israel initially met at each other's homes, and eventually had grown sufficiently to warrant renting a succession of small spaces.

Its founding Rabbi, Daniel Korobkin, served four years before moving on to Allentown, Pennsylvania, and then to Canada, where at this writing in 2015 he heads a very large congregation, Beth Avraham Yoseph of Toronto.

The second rabbi of Young Israel of San Diego, Rabbi Elchanon Snyder, was retained in 1993, the same year that Richard Goodwin was chosen to become the congregation's president. Goodwin served from 1994 to 2003. Snyder departed in 1998 to take a position in New York City.

For a booklet that saluted Rich and Julie Goodwin while celebrating the congregation's 20th anniversary in 2009, Rabbi Snyder wrote from New York about the origins of the Young Israel movement with which the congregation had affiliated.

The Young Israel movement began in the early years of the 20th Century. The Orthodox shuls at the time were modeled on the European pattern, no singing and only married men leading the prayers and receiving aliyot. The youth began a movement to fight the religious apathy of the day. They wanted shuls that appealed to the youth, for the youth to run the prayers, to have singing and for the sermons and lectures to be in English. The Young Israel movement was the first movement to prove that orthodoxy was compatible with human life.

In the wake of Rabbi Snyder's planned departure, Rabbi Hollander heard that a part-time position for a pulpit rabbi would be opening. After consulting with headmaster Rabbi Weiser at Soille San Diego Hebrew Day School, he applied for the position, certain that it would not interfere with his duties at the school. Morning prayers are held early in the morning at Young Israel, before school starts. And this, it turns out, is to the benefit of the school because one is not supposed to talk until one's prayers are said. In that Rabbi Hollander already has completed his prayers by the time the students gather, he is free to offer commentary during the service.

In addition to its morning services, said Hollander, Young Israel of San Diego meets at nights and on the weekends, neither time conflicting with the school's schedule. About the only time that Rabbi Hollander experiences a conflict is when he has to officiate at a congregant's mid-week funeral, which, thankfully, has not occurred very often and about which Rabbi Weiser has always been compassionate.

Getting the Young Israel job required the Hollanders to move from their home in the College area, near Beth Jacob Congregation, where he *davened,* to a home in San Carlos, which is about seven-tenths of a mile from Young Israel. Normally this is not a demanding walk, but after the rabbi had knee replacement surgery in 2015, it was more than he could negotiate on foot. A non-Jewish colleague from Soille San Diego Hebrew Day School kindly agreed to push him in a wheelchair to Shabbos services until such time as he could complete the walk on his own volition.

Young Israel's schedule of early morning services and evening services and classes, also makes the congregation a good neighbor for the several businesses that are fellow tenants in the small shopping center at the southwest corner of Navajo Road and Golfcrest Drive. In the morning, the only shop that is open is a donut shop—which probably would get a lot of business from shul-members if only it had kosher certification. Evenings, the only place open is a Cotijas Taco Shop, which with *carnitas* (a pork product) featured on its menu, definitely is not kosher.

But a friendship has arisen, nevertheless, between the Mexican restaurant and the Orthodox synagogue, Hollander said. If there is a problem with the air conditioning, or other electrical equipment on Shabbos, when observant Jews may not turn electricity on or off, the non-Jewish personnel of the taco shop cheerfully come over and help fix it.

✶   ✶   ✶

I asked Rabbi Hollander what, in his opinion, makes a good teacher, and although his answer applied to his role as an instructor with nearly 35 years tenure at the Hebrew School, it could be extrapolated to also pertain to his experience as a pulpit rabbi since 1999 at Young Israel. As I listened, I thought of the teachers he had told me about who had been important in his life, starting with the religious neighbors who influenced him as a teenager, and continuing even to the late Rosh Yeshiva.

"The most important thing -- I really believe this -- is to develop a one-to-one relationship with every single student," Hollander told me. "I really try to do that.

Every day at lunchtime, rather than staying in my room to eat lunch, or being in the teachers' lounge, I go out there every day. I will sit down with the kids or they will sit down with me, and it is a time when everyone has a chance to just 'let it down.' It's not a classroom, and so especially in the sixth, seventh, and eighth grades, they really get to know me well. A lot of kids have had issues and they have felt comfortable enough to talk to me about them. I don't know if I have helped them or not, but I have tried to. That is really important because that is an age when you are going through some tough physiological changes and it is hard to talk to your parents at that age because you are not quite sure what your relationship is with them. But I am not their parent.

"There have been a few kids who have felt that I have challenged them -- I represented religion to them and they were rebelling against religion -- but most kids are not like that," Hollander continued. "Most kids view me as a person they can be comfortable to talk to. I think that I have kept the confidence of every child that I have spoken to, and I think that is important."

The friendships he forms with his students, both boys and girls, have mutual benefits.

"In the classroom itself, I am there to teach; I have a curriculum and I have to cover the curriculum," he stated. "Every school has to have some kind of discipline system, so we have one too," he said. "If a child misbehaves, you give him a warning, then another warning, and then you send him down (to the principal) with a note. I have never had to do that. There have been times when I have told a child, 'I'm sorry, you are going to have to sit outside the class for a couple of minutes and think about what you have done,' and then I go and talk to them for about 30 seconds, and they realize whatever it was, and then they come back. When I talk to the kids, I tell them 'I really expect a lot more from you than that; I really have a great regard for you, and I have a great deal of respect for you, and you are disappointing me.'"

He noted: "That was the attitude of the Rosh Yeshiva. I remember our yeshiva had a concept *gdulat ha'adam,* the greatness of man, and we as human beings have to live up to our greatness and that is how I view the kids too. I'm not saying I never have discipline problems; I am not perfect, but that is my attitude in teaching."

His own children attended Soille Hebrew Day School, and he instructed all of them, in turn, except Pnina, who attended classes for children with special needs. He told his other daughter and six sons that they were not allowed to call him "Tati," which means 'Daddy' in Yiddish, but rather when in the classroom they should call him "*Rabbi* Hollander—that is what I am," he related. "I suppose there were times that I was stricter with them than I was with the others because I didn't want any of the students to feel, 'look, he is favoring his own kids.' I remember there were some other kids in the school who had their parents teaching and in the class room they called the teacher 'mommy' or 'daddy.' How would another child feel? In fact, several of my children were so careful, that when they invited other children over to the house—for Shabbos or whatever—that in front of their friends they would always call me 'Rabbi Hollander' not 'Tati.' They got so used to it with their friends."

I asked what lessons as an educator carried over to being a pulpit rabbi. "What is a rabbi, but a teacher?" he responded. "I teach the children; I teach adults, I teach teenagers. I think I have a certain ability that God gave me to be able to teach and I use it in the shul as well."

Having taught for nearly 35 years at the day school, some of his students are now well into their 40's with children of their own. Several of his students have become members of Young Israel of San Diego, Hollander noted.

"We have seen growth in the shul," he said. "I am not just talking about numbers. Thank God, it has grown in numbers, it has perhaps tripled or quadrupled in size (to about 55 families). But you see the spiritual growth of people, which is what I am interested in. You see people growing as human beings and in their consideration and in their love of God and their love of Judaism – that is a very warm feeling."

It has gotten to the point that Young Israel, which has occupied its space at 7291 Navajo Road since 2002 is not always able to accommodate the crowds at regular Shabbat services, let alone those held for the High Holy Days.

"We need to strike it rich and find somebody or some people who will give the wherewithal to buy a building, number one, and number two, decide where to put the building. You can't move too far away because people have made commitments in buying homes within walking distance, so it has to be somewhere very near where we are now."

Continued growth will occur, he said, especially if congregants buy into the concept of reaching out to people, and inviting visitors to their homes," Hollander said. "When a person walks into the shul and someone comes over, saying 'Here's a *siddur,* here's a *chumash.* Can I help you with something else?' then right away they are made to feel welcome."

Knowing that first-timers to the Orthodox shul might be somewhat intimidated by a Torah service, the congregation is making an effort to introduce its members to the general public. Hollander would like people to know how interesting and accomplished some of Young Israel's congregants are. Recently, the shul hosted a talk by a member who had served in the Israeli army, and other talks in the "get to know us" type series included a member who had been a first responder in New York City on 9-11, and a younger member who had participated in the March of the Living, which takes teens on visits to the Nazi concentration camps in Poland and continues on to visit the State of Israel.

Many Jews have a fear of Orthodoxy, Rabbi Hollander told me. "One of the biggest accusations against Orthodox is that we are closed-minded, and I just feel that people who are not Orthodox tend to be close-minded themselves. They are not willing to hear. I am not expecting them to become Orthodox, but at least they should hear it, and respect us for what we believe."

The rabbi wound up our interview with a story, which he said was not a parable, but an actual occurrence. A bearded man, wearing a black coat, while riding on a train, was hissed at by an assimilated Jew. "You know, it is really disgusting the way you look," said the other man. "Why do you have to look like that? What's the matter with you? Why don't you look American?"

The bearded man looked up, and said, "I bet you think that I am a Jew. But I am not. I am Amish."

"Oh," said the man, now terribly embarrassed. "I am so sorry. It's so wonderful that you practice your beliefs."

The bearded man smiled, certain the man would understand the lesson. "Actually," he said. "I am a Jew."

Rabbi Chaim and Tema Hollander

From Waring Road Exit 9, proceed south to a left turn on Navajo Road. The synagogue is located in a small shopping center just before the corner of Navajo Road and Golfcrest Drive.

-San Diego Jewish World, October 1, 2015

25. Exit 9

Tifereth Israel Synagogue

Tifereth Israel Synagogue entrance

SAN DIEGO — Tifereth Israel Synagogue's third home at 6660 Cowles Mountain Boulevard is a spiritual home filled with Judaic art and music.

Formed initially as an Orthodox congregation in 1905, the congregation's first synagogue at 18th and Market Streets no longer exists. That building was torn down to make way for a portion of the Interstate 5 freeway. Before that time, however, the congregation had sold its property and had moved to the corner of 30th Street and Howard Avenue in the North Park section of San Diego, at the same time choosing to affiliate with the Conservative movement of Judaism.

Rabbi Monroe Levens was the congregation's first and only senior rabbi during the three decades prior to the second building's sale to the Covenant Evangelical Presbyterian Church.

Charting the demographic shifts of San Diego's Jewish population, Tifereth Israel next moved to the hilly San Carlos neighborhood in the eastern portion of San Diego. The congregation chose a plot of land somewhat larger than four acres at the northwestern corner of Cowles Mountain Boulevard and Tommy Drive. The synagogue was built close to the eastern foot of Cowles Mountain, which at 1,593 feet reaches the highest summit within San Diego's city limits.

Cornerstones from the first two synagogue buildings were placed in the third synagogue's western wall during a ceremony on July 16, 1978. The building's dedication came nearly a year later on June 2, 1979, following a short uphill march by congregants and their new senior rabbi, Rabbi Aaron S. Gold, from the East San Diego Masonic Temple located at 7849 Tommy Drive. The Masons had graciously permitted Tifereth Israel to use its spacious facility as a temporary home during the interim period.

With congregants taking turns cradling the Torahs as they marched to their new permanent home, they were joined by Rabbi Emeritus Levens, and, in a bipartisan show of support, by San Diego Mayor Pete Wilson and San Diego City Councilwoman Lucy Killea. Wilson, a Republican, would go on to become a U.S. senator from California, and later would serve as the state's 36th governor. Killea, a Democrat, would go on to win a seat in the California State Assembly and later advance to the state Senate. Near the end of her public service, she pointedly changed her voting registration from Democrat to Independent in a call for greater bipartisanship in the state's politics.

The Silverman Sanctuary into which the Torahs were marched on that June day features an imposing Aron Kodesh (Holy Ark) set against four large stained glass windows depicting the Burning Bush where God first spoke to Moses. Local art historian Karen Hjalmarson, writing in a bound volume celebrating Tifereth Israel Synagogue's centennial in 2005, noted that each of the windows designed by glass artist Leslie Perlis measure 3 feet wide by 10 feet high and that "vivid hues of red, orange and yellow comprise the dancing and swirling flames." The bottom segment of the composition, depicting 'the Burning Bush that is not consumed' "has a decidedly cooler palette, ranging in color from blue to black." Within the flames, a careful observer can read various names of God. Light from outside, said Hjalmarson, bathes "the entire composition in an ethereal illumination."

The Ark itself is protected by two 16-inch high welded bronze doors created by sculptor Shirley H. Lichtman, whose works had been shown nationally. Hjalmarson remarked that the abstracted and beautifully textured doors "seem to form a golden interlocking vine that climbs majestically to the top of the ark," leading the eyes of views to the Ner Tamid, or Eternal flame, which also was sculpted by Lichtman.

One side of the sanctuary is dominated by a 10-by-14 foot stained glass window, consisting of 20 panes of glass. Depicted are a colorful menorah juxtaposed against white Hebrew letters spelling out "Kadosh, Kadosh, Kadosh" meaning "Holy, Holy, Holy." Leslie Perlis was the artist for this window as well as for another window on the opposite side of the sanctuary depicting the cycle of Jewish holidays. If one studies the stained-glass windows' design curling around a large Cabinet bearing the Holocaust Torah, one can detect a shofar for Rosh Hashanah, the lulav and etrog of Sukkot, and the Kiddush cup of Shabbat. Thus, the joy of the holidays and the sadness of the Holocaust are juxtaposed.

Such juxtaposition is not unusual to Jewish ritual; often sad times are remembered amidst the happy ones—as for example when a groom breaks a glass under his foot during a wedding—the shattering said to be a remembrance of the destruction of the ancient temple in Jerusalem. This sanctuary has seen *aufrufs* (engagement announcements), weddings, and baby namings, but it also has been the venue for funerals. One of the saddest of these was that for Marla Ann Bennett, a San Diegan studying in Israel, who was killed in 2002 by a terrorist bomb at the Hebrew University in Jerusalem. Her family were members of the Reform congregation Temple Emanu-El, but because it then had a much smaller space, arrangements were made for the funeral to be held at Tifereth Israel. The rear walls of the sanctuary were folded back so that the social hall became part of the sanctuary and still there were not enough seats for some 2,000 mourners. For many San Diegans, Bennett's death personified the terrible human cost of political terrorism.

Inside the Holocaust Cabinet is a Torah that had been removed from the central synagogue of Prague by the Nazis for a museum in which they had planned to document their destruction of the Jewish people. Among many returned to the use of the Jewish people, the Holocaust Torah is read on Yom HaShoah by members of San Diego's New Life Club of Holocaust Survivors, as well as on other occasions of remembrance. A Torah cover, also known as a mantle, designed by Chilean-born artist Jacqueline Jacobs shows some butterflies trapped by barbed wire in the darker lower portion of the mantle but other brightly colored butterflies rising above the barbed wire into the sunlight and freedom. The top of the mantle bears the Hebrew words, "Ani Ma'amin" – "I believe." Jacobs thus conflated several Holocaust memories: the barbed wire of the concentration camp; the song Ani Ma'amin, which expresses the belief in the coming of the Messiah, and became an anthem for some inmates in the Nazi concentration camps; and the butterfly symbolizing freedom. The butterfly was central to the poem "I Never Saw Another Butterfly," written by a young Pavel Friedmann in which he told of being penned up with fellow Jews in the Terezin ghetto. "The dandelions call to me/ And the white chestnut candles in the court./ Only I never saw another butterfly."

There are other art works in the sanctuary as well, among them a 72 by 84 inch Jerusalem tapestry by Susan Hart Henegar; a cast bronze David's Harp by sculptor David Gluck accompanied with words from the Prophet Isaiah: "For my house shall be called a house of prayer for all people;" a Chanukiah by Sylvia and Samuel Chernov featuring nine brass urns placed in an abstract design; and a Chuppah by Marjorie Gosz and Helen Levine, bearing legends from the Song of Songs: "I am my beloved's and by beloved is mine" and from the Prophet Hosea: "And I will betroth thee unto me forever."

In the main foyer leading to the sanctuary, there are other significant art pieces. Occupying the most striking position is Leslie Perlis's stained-glass evocation of the 12 tribes of Israel. The grid has three vertical and four horizontal rows of 18-inch square panels. A black granite bench is placed in front of the art work to allow easy viewing. Many are the parents who delight young children by sitting with them in front of the stained-glass creation and asking them what they see. "Do you see any animals?" a parent might ask. "Can you point them out to me?" "Good, do you also see a boat?" "How about a spiral?" "Can you tell me which of the pictures have the color orange in them?" "How about blue?"

On a wall near the entrance to the sanctuary is a 12-foot wide, 8-foot-high plaque featuring a Tifereth Israel tree of life by Josef Pelzig. Plaques honoring people or remembering their simchas are mounted near the tree of life.

The foyer leads directly into the Cohen Social Hall in which numerous simchas are celebrated and congregational dinners are held. For example, the annual Purim Shpiel -- which often will use a popular musical or play as a vehicle to retell the story of how Queen Esther saved the Jews -- is performed on the stage at one end of the hall.

A pass-through counter to the kosher kitchen is at the other end of the hall, which is partially illuminated by a large chandelier in a six-pointed Star-of David configuration. This social hall is the home of the Tifereth Israel Community Orchestra (TICO) which offers several concerts a year under the baton of maestro David Amos, who has conducted professional orchestras all over the world. The orchestra brings together retired professional musicians and skilled amateurs of all religions. Amos programs many varieties of music, often with well-known guest artists. He particularly enjoys programming symphonic music built on Jewish themes in addition to more well-known secular orchestral pieces.

From the main foyer, one may follow another corridor to the office of Rabbi Leonard Rosenthal, who succeeded Rabbi Gold as rabbi in 1992. He and his wife Judy raised their son, Rabbi Adam Rosenthal, at this congregation. Two daughters, Adina and Margalit, also are deeply involved in the Jewish community. Near the rabbi's office and study are the office and work spaces of the synagogue's administrator and staff. Beyond their area, the small Goodman chapel, suitable for intimate services, is located. "Crown of Glory," another work by glass sculptor Leslie Perlis, helps to establish a mood for prayer and study. The abstract design includes the crowns of three Torahs, and smaller representations of a Torah scroll, a tallit, and tefillin.

The sanctuary, social hall, offices, and chapel comprise the main building on the Tifereth Israel campus. There is also a two-story stretch of classrooms which formerly housed the San Diego Jewish Academy, located today on its own multi-building campus in the Carmel Valley area of San Diego. The classrooms continue to be used by Tifereth Israel Synagogue's own Silverman Pre-School and the Abraham and Anne Ratner Torah School as well as by a well-stocked library, named for a former elected member of the San Diego Unified School Board and her husband, Sue and Richard Braun.

The campus also includes a playground, as well as room for a large congregational sukkah within which the holiday of Sukkot is annually celebrated.

The Twelve Tribes

From Waring Road Exit, proceed south to left turn on Navajo Road. Follow to Cowles Mountain Boulevard, turn left, and left again on Tommy Drive. Entrance to synagogue is off Tommy Drive.

-San Diego Jewish World, October 8, 2015

26. Exit 10
Temple Emanu-El

Temple Emanu-El courtyard

SAN DIEGO — Temple Emanu-El, swathed in Jerusalem stone, houses a Reform congregation that has occupied this property in the Del Cerro neighborhood since 1978. Initially, there was a former Baptist church where the courtyard and sanctuary stand today. After some remodeling that original building served Temple Emanu-El's membership until 2007, when it was razed to make way for this edifice designed by the late La Jolla architect David Raphael Singer with input from Rabbi Martin S. Lawson and a temple committee.

The interior designer was Laurie Gross Schaefer of Santa Barbara, who has helped to beautify and delineate Jewish sacred spaces throughout the United States. Besides at Temple Emanu-El, her work in San Diego County may be seen at Congregation Beth Israel and at Temple Adat Shalom. Temple Emanu-El's architectural theme is expressed by a quotation from the Prophet Amos (5:24) that hangs in the vestibule: "Let Justice Roll Down as Waters; Righteousness as a Mighty Stream."

On a courtyard wall, there is a waterfall of recycled water; the blue carpeting in the sanctuary and in the social hall undulate in wave-like pattern; and the doors of the Aron Kodesh, backed by blue curtains, resemble a water surface or waterfall glistening in the sunlight. Amos' words are repeated above the door of the Aron Kodesh, but in Hebrew. The element of water is contrasted with that of fire by the Ner Tamid, which is solar powered descending from a skylight.

Rabbi Morton J. Cohn parted in 1964 from Congregation Beth Israel, which he had served as Senior Rabbi since the end of World War II. Along with his wife Sally, who became the first Sisterhood president, he and some devoted followers from Beth Israel started Temple Emanu-El that year in quarters rented from the Rolando Methodist Church at 4876 Seminole Drive. In 1976, Rabbi Martin S. Lawson joined Rabbi Cohn, serving as the assistant rabbi and educator for two years.

In 1978 when the congregation moved to Del Cerro, Rabbi Cohn retired as senior rabbi and was succeeded by his associate, Rabbi Lawson, who remained as the senior rabbi until his own retirement in June 2012. Cohn, as founding rabbi, remained an important part of the congregation and it was for him that in 1990 the Torah School was named in an educational complex shared with the Price Family Pre-School. Today, Rabbi Lawson, as rabbi emeritus, continues in the tradition of being an asset to his successor. She is Rabbi Devorah Marcus, who was selected by the congregation following a year of interim service rendered by Rabbi Richard Shapiro.

The rebuilt sanctuary building was dedicated in September 2008, after congregants spent 17 months worshiping at temporary facilities at First United Methodist Church in Mission Valley. The dedication festivities drew San Diego Mayor Jerry Sanders; Congresswoman Susan Davis, who is a member of the Jewish community and Temple Emanu-El; Councilman Jim Madaffer, and two Jewish candidates for elective office, who were successful that November: Marty Block and Marti Emerald. Block, then president of the San Diego Community College Board, subsequently was elected to the state Assembly, and some years later to the state Senate. Emerald, a former "troubleshooter" newscaster for KGTV-Channel 10, was elected to the San Diego City Council, succeeding the termed-out Madaffer.

Also present was architect Singer who once was asked by *the La Jolla Light* who or what inspires him. He responded: "Irving Gill and Luis Barragon for the timeless quality of their buildings; Simon Rodia, the builder of Watts Tower, which expresses the idiosyncratic and poetic vision that an individual can achieve; Studs Terkel, the interviewer of ordinary people with extraordinary stories; Abraham Heschel, the 20th century Jewish philosopher and civil rights activist; the archeological remains of the Southwest Indians, the Mayans, the Incas, the Nabateans (Petra); the courtyard houses of Mexico and the Middle and Far East; and the variety and splendor of nature (i.e. the Galapagos, Anza-Borrego Desert and the seals at Children's Cove.)"

Describing the dedication ceremony for *San Diego Jewish World*, Sheila Orysiek, a congregant, wrote: "The mild evening, typical of San Diego, added to the beauty of the Temple courtyard which was filled with the happy people, groaning tables of catered food, laughter and chatter. The Jerusalem stone with which the building is faced was lit with mellow landscaped lighting to echo the golden glow of the Western Wall as it is lit at night in Israel's ancient capital. Enclosing the courtyard is more Jerusalem stone interspersed with vines, leaves and pomegranates in wrought iron with water streaming down one wall in a soft murmur. The wrought iron gates into the courtyard are a sculpted menorah but though the courtyard is thus 'enclosed' it is not enclosing."

In September 2015, Jewish Family Service's College Avenue Center moved from Beth Jacob Congregation to Temple Emanu-El. As a result, the social hall, lobby, board room, and sanctuary are in use throughout the week.

Rabbis Morton Cohn and Martin Lawson

....

From the College Avenue, Exit 10, proceed north on College Avenue to left turn on Del Cerro Boulevard. As you start up the hill, the buildings on the left are the Temple Emanu-El synagogue and school complex at 6299 Capri Drive.

....

-San Diego Jewish World, October 15, 2015

27. Exit 10

College Avenue Center

JFS Older Adult Center director Elissa Landsman with Harry Rosen

SAN DIEGO — Older adults who seek a low-cost meal plus intellectual and physical stimulation often drop by the College Avenue Center operated by Jewish Family Service in space rented from Temple Emanu-El at 6299 Capri Drive.

The center relocated to Temple Emanu-El in September 2015 from Beth Jacob Congregation, transitioning to the social hall of a Reform congregation from that of an Orthodox one.

The College Avenue Center is a San Diego County nutrition site, and to people over the age of 60, it serves healthy and hearty meals such as I sampled recently. On my plate were pepper steak, vegetables, mashed potato, fruit, and a slice of bread, all to be washed down with decaffeinated coffee.

The cost: only $4, and that was not the best part. I sat with Gloria Rimland, whom I recognized as the pioneering first female president of Tifereth Israel Synagogue, and was introduced to two of her tablemates, both PhD professors emeritus at San Diego State University: Dr. Harold Wald, chemistry, and Dr. Kurt Eisenmann, mathematics.

I found attendees at the College Avenue Center to be quite friendly and open. Before lunch, in fact, two gentlemen had told me a little bit about their lives. Harry Rosen, born in Germany, had "a taste of the Nazis but thank God, my father was a very realistic person. He was from Poland and he remembered the pogroms. We were smuggled out to Belgium after they threatened to arrest him and send him to Dachau because he was against the fuehrer."

That was in 1934, when Rosen was 11 years old. Belgium proved inhospitable. "We couldn't get permanent residence, we were refugees without papers." So next they moved to Haifa, in what was then Mandatory Palestine, and Rosen fought in Israel's 1948 War of Independence. He was married the following year (1949) to the wife who only recently died after 63 years of marriage.

"I don't want anybody else," Rosen told me. Not that he hasn't been getting offers, but he is wary that the women are more interested in what he can offer than in him. "They know I am still driving so everyone is coming close to me, and I have an apartment with two rooms. I've been approached already, by a woman, who wanted to know why I don't rent one room out. Sure, driving, having my own apartment, and being in good shape!"

He had made his way from Israel to New York in 1960, and then pushed on to San Diego. "I didn't speak any English at the time—and it was a hardship I didn't want my family to go through. Besides when you come with family, you can't stay with friends."

The New York winter almost did Rosen in. He came down with bronchitis and doctors advised him to either return to Israel or go somewhere else in the United States where it is warm. A friend, who also had escaped Germany, invited him to settle in San Diego in 1961, a time, he remembered, when Mission Valley was nothing but dairy land. Liking it here, he sent for his family.

Rosen had worked in San Diego at the aircraft plants, mostly at Rohr Aircraft, sometimes at Convair. "We accepted subcontracts from the big companies, and I used to build parts for the airplanes," he told me.

Another man came up to me, introducing himself as Abraham Yarhi, formerly from Alexandria, Egypt.

"Since I've come here to Jewish Family Service, I don't need any more medication," he told me. "I am so lucky with the exercise and the food, it is a blessing. It keeps you alive and healthy. It's a blessing for people who live close."

About Alexandria, he said that it was a far more modern, cosmopolitan city than Cairo because "it is right on the Mediterranean Sea. Many boats came, and the people who lived there saw what people from other places wore, what they did, and the city became more modern than Cairo. The summer there is very nice to go to the beach. Many people from Cairo go to Alexandria in the summer to go to the beach."

Earlier still, Elissa Landsman, program manager at the College Avenue Center, told me a little bit about the operation. It had started as a senior center at the old Jewish Community Center on 54th Street. When that facility closed in 1998, following the JCC's move to La Jolla, the older adult program was moved to the social hall of Beth Jacob Congregation. It stayed there 17 years until relocating in September 2015 to Temple Emanu-El.

Landsman, who has a degree in recreation and leisure studies from Cal State Long Beach as well as a certificate in gerontology from San Diego State University, began volunteering in 1985 for Jewish Family Service and in 2000 was presented with an opportunity to become program director for the College Avenue Center.

"I know my purpose and I know my calling when I see the clients here; they are very friendly and loving," she said. "I am a cheerleader and a shepherd and a planner, but I know that they feel very strongly about me and I feel very strongly about them."

Particularly satisfying for her, in addition to keeping the seniors happy and busy with plenty of activities, is "when they have a pressing issue that they need help with, I can give them that help through our agency. I can refer them on to get some extra assistance...The nice thing about this population is that most of them are very happy, healthy and engaged, and it is very rewarding. We have a great program!"

In addition to the hot lunch, "we have things ranging from lectures, movies, dances, classes, exercise programs like aerobics, tai chi, and yoga. We have painting classes, a bingo group, line dancing, ballroom dancing, drawing classes, and current events classes. Sometimes we have Sunday lunches, and one Sunday it was salmon, and afterwards Yale Strom (a klezmer violinist) and his wife (Elizabeth Schwartz, a vocalist) were here to entertain us. We have entertainment on Fridays as well. We also have ancillary programs where people can meet with health insurance counselors. We have an attorney who comes here monthly. We have an AARP driving program (a refresher course on the rules of the road)."

Landsman said the center doesn't count the people it serves as they come through the door, but rather monitors how many people attend activities. Thus, if someone attends a morning exercise class, and an afternoon current events discussion, that person might be counted twice as a visitor.

On the average, she said, there are about 200 visitors per day, 70 of them exclusively for the lunch, and the rest attending the various activities. "I would say that the average age is between 68 and 72," Landsman said. "When I started here 15 years ago I would say that 75 to 80 percent of the clients were Jewish. Today, I would say that the clientele is perhaps 50 percent Jewish. Mostly we serve people from the College area, Del Cerro, San Carlos, and Allied Gardens (neighborhoods of San Diego), and La Mesa."

The group is multicultural, with various religions and backgrounds represented. "I do have Hispanic, African-American and Middle-Eastern clients, so you do have some diversity," she said. Various classes such as aerobics, feeling fit, and arthritis exercise are taught without fee by San Diego Continuing Education, a division of the San Diego Community Colleges, she said.

Even a short visit to the College Avenue Center will confirm that the place buzzes with energy.

....

From the College Avenue, Exit 10, proceed north on College Avenue to left turn on Del Cerro Boulevard. As you start up the hill, the buildings on the left are the Temple Emanu-El synagogue and school complex at 6299 Capri Drive.

....

-San Diego Jewish World, October 22, 2015

28. Exit 10

San Diego State University

San Diego State University campus
(Photo: Shor M. Masori)

SAN DIEGO — Before I even get started on this chapter, I want to acknowledge a debt to Lawrence "Laurie" Baron, a professor emeritus of history at San Diego State University, who also is my colleague at *San Diego Jewish World*. Laurie wrote a paper on the Jewish history of SDSU and has given me permission to borrow from it liberally.

While serving as the longtime director of the Lipinsky Institute for Judaic Studies, Baron was the organizer of the Western Jewish Studies Association, which brings together scholars from throughout the western states. One of the problems facing researchers in American Jewish history and other disciplines has been a tendency to focus on the Jewish communities of the East Coast, treating Jewish communities out west, at best, as an afterthought. Thanks to Baron, Jews from the western states are getting far more academic attention. Since 1995, WJSA meetings have been held in a variety of western cities, including Vancouver, British Columbia, during the organization's 20th anniversary in 2015.

The Lipinsky Institute for Judaic Studies was so named because of an endowment given by Bernard and Dorris Lipinsky whose names also grace the Lipinsky Hospitality Center. Above it rises the Lipinsky Tower, to which students without watches or cellphones refer regularly whenever they want to know the time.

Besides being a philanthropist, Bernard Lipinsky had a long history with San Diego State, so his story is a good place to start our Jewish exploration of SDSU. He attended SDSU in the 1931-32 academic year, and among his favorite history professors was Abraham P. Nasatir, an Orthodox Jew who was so popular with his students and colleagues that since 1986–a dozen years after his retirement–the eastern wing of the former Humanities-Social Science Building has been officially named Nasatir Hall.

Nasatir Hall

Nasatir came to San Diego State in 1928, three years before the college moved from its original home in the Normal Heights area, to what was then known as Montezuma Mesa. With no Orthodox shul close to the new campus, Nasatir "opened his home for a daily *minyan* for male students who wanted to daven before they went to classes," according to Baron.

Lipinsky recalled that Nasatir "sometimes asked his students to purchase him a movie ticket for Saturday matinees because he observed the tradition of not carrying money on Shabbat." Specializing in the history of South America as well as Spanish colonialism in North America, Nasatir authored 18 books. When he died in 1991, he indirectly provided for even more scholarly endeavor. Until the grant ran out, an annual Nasatir Lecture on American Jewish History was a feature of the SDSU calendar.

While Nasatir was apparently well-liked by Jew and Gentile alike, discrimination at the off-campus fraternities and sororities was commonplace at San Diego State and other colleges and universities through the 1960s, when it was outlawed. Reportedly, because he was Jewish, sports enthusiast Bob Breitbard (see previous story on Valley View Casino Arena for his biography) was blackballed by one member of a fraternity he had sought to pledge. In the 1930s, such anti-Semitism led to the creation on the rim of the campus of the Aleph Phi Pi fraternity, in which Lipinsky served as chancellor, Bob Breitbard as vice chancellor, and another member was Sol Price, the future founder of the Price Club warehouse stores. Female students in 1933 formed a local chapter of the B'nai B'rith Junior Girls Auxiliary.

The 1940s brought World War II, with many students volunteering to fight. Among local Jewish students who volunteered was Herman Addleson, who first had to have an operation on a cleft lip in order to medically qualify. Unable to afford such an expense, he feared he would have to sit the war out, but Boston Red Sox batting champion Ted Williams–who had grown up in San Diego–came to Addleson's rescue. He helped pay for the operation that qualified Addleson to apply for the paratroopers. Sadly, Addleson was killed while parachuting behind Nazi lines in France on D-Day, June 6, 1944. His name is listed with other KIA on a monument on the San Diego State campus.

Following the war, with many members of the military coming home with their GI benefits, San Diego State hired new faculty members, among them three who became active in the Jewish community: Ernest Wolf, Harry Ruja, and Oscar Kaplan. Along with Abraham Nasatir, they successfully campaigned for the establishment of a Hillel chapter on the San Diego State campus. The chapter was inaugurated in a ceremony attended by 650 people at Congregation Beth Israel at which the president of Brandeis University, Abraham Sachar, was the keynote speaker.

In 1948, San Diego State students elected their first student president who was Jewish: Duane Kantor, who had remained neutral in a campus battle over whether fraternities and sororities should be required to abandon their discriminatory practices. Students Larry Solomon and Bob Levy subsequently led the campaign to create Beta Tau as a local Jewish fraternity. In 1951, it became part of the national Zeta Beta Tau (ZBT) Jewish fraternal organization. Two other Jewish fraternities, Alpha Epsilon Pi and Sigma Alpha Mu, were chartered on the SDSU campus, respectively in 1970 and 1983.

Jewish women meanwhile created Alpha Epsilon Phi sorority, with Harry Ruja an advisor. One of its members, Judy Gumbiner, said she pledged the sorority to meet other Jews and to remain Jewishly active. She was also active in campus-wide activities, and was honored three times as Woman of the Year by the Associated Student Council.

In 1962, a campus group advocating free speech invited the neo-Nazi George Lincoln Rockwell to address the campus, and his speech–or perhaps the controversy surrounding it–attracted 2,000 persons. Rockwell denigrated Blacks and Jews, prompting Jewish student Ed Cherry to jump up on the stage to argue with him, and when Rockwell wouldn't let him speak, Cherry punched the Nazi. Other students pelted Rockwell with eggs and rocks, and also vandalized his car. Cherry and two other students were disciplined.

Even as study programs were being established on campus regarding African Americans, Native Americans, Chicanos, and Women, so too did a Jewish Studies minor come into being. The Jewish faculty group Yavne was formed in 1969 and nine of its members agreed to teach courses on Jewish subjects. The Jewish student population at that time was estimated at 1,000.

In the 1969-70 school year, Rabbi Robert Weisfeld, then director of the San Diego Bureau of Jewish Education, taught courses in Hebrew and Judaism on a voluntary basis. The following year Irving Gefter was given a tenure position to teach Hebrew and Jewish Heritage, and the year after that Ida Sheres taught Bible and modern Jewish literature.

In Brage Golding, San Diego State University had its first Jewish president. He also was the father of San Diego's first Jewish Mayor, Susan Golding. Brage Golding served SDSU from 1972 to 1977 and reported never encountering anti-Semitism on the campus, not even in late 1973 when the so-called Yom Kippur War pitting Israel against its Arab neighbors broke out, nor two years later when the United Nations passed a resolution equating Zionism with racism — a resolution that it rescinded some years later.

In 1970, the Lubavitcher movement opened a Chabad House near the campus. Subsequently, with Rabbi Yonah Fradkin at its head, the campus Chabad fostered a network of Chabad Houses throughout San Diego County. A 1972 SDSU graduate, Lorie Geddis, recalled "traditional Shabbat dinners with lots of kosher wine and stories of the Baal Shem Tov late into the night." Geddis also attended "Pathways Through the Bible" classes taught by Rabbi Samuel Penner, spiritual leader of nearby Congregation Beth Tefilah, a Conservative congregation.

The United Jewish Federation of San Diego helped Hillel purchase a new building adjacent to the campus, and Rabbi Jay Miller became its director. For a time, Hillel was called the Jewish Campus Center, but it subsequently reverted to the Hillel name. Jackie Tolley succeeded Miller and became the longtime director of the SDSU Hillel House.

In the 1980s, the number of Jewish students enrolled at SDSU climbed to an estimated 3,000. Yet, impending budget cuts imperiled most Jewish studies courses. Students and faculty lobbied the University's Development Office to approach potential donors in the community, and Jewish faculty members issued an appeal for support from the community.

Prof. Jacob Goldberg of Tel Aviv University was retained to speak at a fundraising event to enlarge the formal Jewish Studies program–a proposal that garnered considerable support in the local Jewish community after Nation of Islam firebrand Louis Farrakhan had been scheduled to deliver an anti-Semitic speech on campus. SDSU refused a demand from Farrakhan that his own armed body guards come on campus to protect him, and the speech was cancelled. Meanwhile, at the urging of SDSU's then-President Thomas Day, Bernard Lipinsky decided at this point to endow a permanent chair in modern Jewish history and to underwrite an annual visiting Israel professor.

Before Baron took over as director of the Lipinsky Institute for Judaic Studies, there was a temporary director chosen from the faculty. He was history professor Bob Filner, who later would serve as a school board member, San Diego city councilman, and a member of Congress before being elected in 2012 as mayor of San Diego. In a plea bargain, Filner resigned as mayor a year later after a scandal erupted in which he was accused of sexually harassing many women.

Another Jewish development on the campus took place in secret. The Fred J. Hansen Institute for World Peace was created from the estate of a local avocado grower, whose executors asked for proposals for advancing the cause of international peace either in the field of marine biology or agriculture. In the wake of the Camp David agreement of 1979, bringing peace between Israel and Egypt, San Diego State University proposed to administer a program in which agricultural experts from the two former enemy nations could meet quietly, out of the public limelight, to discuss ways to cooperate in ways to grow foods in their deserts. The Jewish director of the Hansen Institute, Robert Ontell, was able to organize such meetings on the campus. Gradually and without publicity other Middle Eastern countries–including some that had no diplomatic relations with Israel–allowed their agricultural experts to participate.

This program led SDSU President Steven Weber to invite Israel's former prime minister and future president, Shimon Peres, to receive an honorary doctoral degree from the university in 1997, one of only a few that had been granted up to then. The others had been conferred upon U.S. President John F. Kennedy and Bernard Lipinsky. Weber and a delegation from SDSU also attended the inaugural international board meeting in Israel of the Peres Center for Peace, and ten years later returned to Israel for the dedication of the Peres Peace House in Jaffa.

Following Weber's retirement as SDSU's president, Elliot Hirshman became the second Jewish president in the university's history. Previously he had served as provost and senior vice president for academic affairs at the University of Maryland.

During Baron's tenure at the Lipinsky Institute, the Jewish Historical Society of San Diego, under the leadership of Stan and Laurel Schwartz, decided to locate its archives at SDSU's Love Library in collaboration with the Special Collections Department.

Baron, now professor emeritus, was succeeded as director of the Jewish Studies program by Risa Levitt Kohn, who also served as a curator of a Dead Sea Scrolls exhibition at San Diego's Natural History Museum in Balboa Park.

Today names of some additional Jewish philanthropists grace the SDSU campus. There is a Viterbi Digital Plaza outside the KPBS Building, the plaza having been named for the family of Andrew Viterbi, the co-founder of telecommunications giant Qualcomm. Among well-known personalities on the KPBS television and radio news broadcasts was Gloria Penner, a member of the Jewish community who died in 2012 after nearly a half-century long career with the public broadcasting station.

Other Jewish contributors to the campus are Lee and Frank Goldberg, for whom is named the plaza that serves as a central courtyard for the Aztec Student Union, opened in 2013. Frank Goldberg founded a furniture store in suburban Chula Vista that grew into a chain of 11 stores in California and Nevada.

Following in her father Bernard's philanthropic footsteps, Elaine Lipinsky endowed a program for an Artist in Residence associated with the Jewish Studies Program. Ethnomusicologist Yale Strom, a documentary film maker, composer, and klezmer musician, has taught and performed at SDSU under the auspices of that program since 2006.

Like many campuses across the United States and Canada, SDSU saw an upsurge of pro-Palestinian, anti-Israel activity in 2014 in the form of the Boycott, Divestment and Sanctions movement against Israel. Some Jewish students complained of being intimidated by increasingly vocal and hostile demonstrations against the Israeli government, while others rallied to Israel's defense, nurtured by such pro-Israel organizations as StandWithUs.

*   *   *

Professor Baron's article "From Minyan to Matriculation: San Diego Jewry and Jewish Studies at San Diego State University," was published in 2003 as a chapter in *California Jews*, edited by Marc Dollinger and Ava Kahn, and published by Brandeis University.

From College Avenue, Exit 10, turn south (right from eastbound I-8), and you will be at the SDSU College Campus. Parking structures are on the periphery of the campus.

-San Diego Jewish World, October 29, 2015

29. Exit 10

SDSU President Elliot Hirshman

Elliot Hirshman

SAN DIEGO — Elliot Hirshman already had obtained a degree in economics when he decided that instead of going to Harvard Business School he would apply instead for a PhD program in cognitive psychology at UCLA. His mother, Edna May Hirshman, had this to say about his decision:

"I don't think you should be one, I think you should see one!"

Hirshman's mother was used to speaking her mind. Long active in the Jewish community, she was the first woman to be elected as president of Temple Ansche Emeth in New Brunswick, New Jersey, her son reported proudly.

Hirshman's father, Harold, was no stranger to leadership either. He worked his way up the ladder to become associate vice president for student services at Rutgers University.

"I often say that I went into the family business," confided Hirshman, who was born in 1961 to a family "who rooted for the underdog. Whatever it was, they were always concerned whether it was fair and just. That was the kind of environment I was raised in and it is, I think, very congenial with the university environment with many students, faculty and staff who are really focused on trying to make the world a better place."

Today Hirshman is president of San Diego State University, the second Jew to hold the office. The first was Brage Golding. "I have an economics degree and a psychology degree and I use them both in equal measure," Hirshman confided during an in-office interview.

"Obviously," he explained, "a university is a very large enterprise and while you wouldn't want to call it a business, there are budgets to be managed and there are personnel issues, organizational and structural problems." At the same time, he said, there are human and cultural elements that must be considered, and that's where psychology comes in handy.

Occasional debates break out among students about whether SDSU should participate in the BDS (Boycott, Divestment and Sanctions) movement against Israel, and that debate offers some insight into how Hirshman conceptualizes his role as a mentor.

"One of the things that I try to emphasize to people is that my role is to facilitate a healthy discussion, a safe discussion, a discussion that will be a model for students and prepare them for the real world," the SDSU president said. "Whatever the issue—whether it is BDS or fossil fuels—if I get in the middle of the discussion and say, 'No, the right answer is this!' that actually is going to impede student development. It is going to give them the message that some other authority resolves those issues as opposed to the concept that part of being a democracy is that democracy as a whole resolves them.

"I am very careful to not engage and say, 'This is the right or wrong way' early in the day," the SDSU president said. "Now, ultimately, if it is a recommendation that comes to me, I will act on it one way or the other and I'm obviously glad to do that in a way I believe will be in the university's best interests. But the more important part is that the students have learned how to have a discussion and that they have been able to practice articulating their views and thinking through. I think you would be surprised how many students through these discussions actually come to different views than they had initially."

Hirshman shared that "I often get members of the Jewish community who will say, 'You need to shut this discussion down' and I don't think that is the right approach. I think supporting the discussion and letting the issues come through is more true both to academic principles and Jewish tradition."

I asked how one balances the need for such discussion with the right of Jewish students to go to college without feeling intimidated by anti-Israel demonstrators.

"One of the things that you want to do for all groups -- racial, ethnic, religious -- is to have outreach programs that are supportive -- finding smaller communities within the larger campus," he responded. "If you look next to the campus, you will see a brand new fantastic Hillel building—I have been there a number of occasions—and that is a great opportunity for a university to have a welcoming community. Rather than playing defense about what is bad and how you want to fix it, is really to have that outreach.

"In terms of challenges, we always want to be advocating for free speech and expression but there is a line—usually not involved with speech—but there is a line where people might intimidate physically or harass somebody and then it is the university's responsibility to protect the students and to keep them safe. We have not had anything even remotely like that on our campus, but if we did, whatever group it was, we would work very strongly to protect the group. So, for example, there are many concerns about student safety because of sexual assault and I think if you look at both our policies and our practices in that area you will see that we are working very aggressively to support student safety and we continue to improve our practices.

"I think this is true of most universities—students should be excited about engaging in a discussion even if it makes them a little uncomfortable sometimes, and then if there are cases where there is any physical or safety threat that is where everyone needs to come together as a community to keep people safe. We are committed to that."

Hirshman noted that San Diego State University has "an international focus—we have literally hundreds of exchange programs, and study abroad opportunities. I think we were ranked 22nd in students abroad, and we had eight Fulbright scholarships last year." Israel is among the mix of nations with which SDSU collaborates, "for example our Entrepreneurship Center which has trips to Israel and outreach to Israeli entrepreneurs which I think is an area where a lot of universities are interested, given the success that Israeli entrepreneurs have. We are certainly open to a range of relationships. We visit with the consuls-general of Israel and many other nations in terms of building relationships and will continue to do so."

Hirshman came to SDSU in 2011 after serving as vice president for academic affairs and provost as the University of Maryland, Baltimore County. Soon thereafter he established a goal for SDSU to become ranked within the top 50 research universities within the country. In 2015, SDSU was in a seven-way tie for the 149th ranking by *U.S. News and World Report.*

"The importance is that the research university, as a public entity, provides so much more to students and to the community than a more generic institution. The students have the opportunity to interact with state-of-the-art, or state-of-the-field knowledge of cutting-edge technology. It really enriches the experience whether it is through direct research or through engagement with the faculty members and all the knowledge they bring to bear in their instructional role."

He said two areas of research, in particular, hold out exciting possibilities for SDSU. One is viromics, "which is the study of the DNA of viruses and how that then affects human hosts and environmental hosts. That is an area where we have multiple leading figures in computer science, where we do analysis, and in biology, where we do the actual DNA restructuring."

A second area, he said, "is clinical and cognitive neuroscience where we have people in language, people in autism; there is a whole range of people who have interests, and I think it is growing on the campus. When we build our new Engineering-Interdisciplinary Science Complex (approved in May by the State University and College Board of Trustees), it will have functional Magnetic Resonance Imaging so that our researchers can image the brain of people who have neuro-degenerative diseases or image the brain as they are performing tasks so that we can understand in a greater way what is going on in the brain, both the diseased and the healthy brain."

Remembering that his own field was cognitive psychology, I suggested he may one day want to get out of the president's office and head over there.

"Perhaps!" he laughed.

I asked how the emphasis on research would fit with California Governor Jerry Brown's goal to produce one million college graduates to fill California jobs by 2025.

"Nationally the average graduation rate is about 59 percent, and so it really is not a question of a dichotomy between educating students and pushing them through, so to speak," said Hirshman. "Rather, think of the potential loss if 59 out of 100 are making it but the remainder aren't. Our graduation rate is in the low 70's now, quite a bit above the national average, but still we would really want it to be 100 percent. So, our focus in insuring student success. We want to see whoever comes here being successful and graduate. And, of course, if they can do it faster that will be better for everyone because it will cost them less, it will cost their family less, it will reduce debt loads. ... What he (Brown) is saying is 'let's be sure we are successful with more students and when possible let us try to do it faster.' I think those are reasonable things to talk about."

At SDSU, Hirshman added, "one of the things that we have seen historically is that commuter students have struggled relative to students who live on campus. So we have taken a number of steps to make sure that our commuter students are more likely to succeed, all the way from more tutoring, supplementary instruction, to having a commuter center where people get together and get involved in activities."

Living on or near campus, he suggested, results in students being "more immersed in what the work of the student is. The farther you get away from campus, the more possibilities there are for diversion. Just as a practical matter if you think about students who commute an hour each day, they are losing two hours a day that they could be more fully engaged. I think there are practical reasons where the more you are engaged with the campus, the better you are going to do. We see that repeatedly. The time loss in driving can have a big impact on a student."

....

From College Avenue, Exit 10, turn south (right from eastbound I-8), and you will be at the SDSU College Campus. Parking structures are on the periphery of the campus.

....

-San Diego Jewish World, November 5, 2016

30. Exit 10

Jewish Historical Society

Dome of SDSU's Love Library

SAN DIEGO — Room 363 of the Love Library at San Diego State University is the home of the Jewish Historical Society of San Diego, which lovingly preserves the written records and photographs of this county's Jewish community. The room is also known as the Irving and Sylvia Snyder Reading Room, co-memorializing a wife and a businessman who donated $50,000 to honor her.

The reading room includes a lifetime collection of Judaic books that was donated to SDSU's Lipinsky Institute for Judaic Studies by the family of Seymour Camp. The family advertised in the *New York Times* that they were looking for a suitable home for the books, and the then-director of the Institute, History Prof. Lawrence Baron, answered the advertisement.

Between its founding in 1980 and the approach of the year 2000, SDSU and the Jewish Historical Society of San Diego led separate existences.

The society had been founded in 1980 at the suggestion of Nathan and Sophie Gass, parents of member Arnold Gass, who were visiting from Lynn, Massachusetts, where they had founded their own local Jewish historical society. A small cadre of Jewish history enthusiasts—including Henry Schwartz, Mollie Harris, Audrey Karsh, and Prof. Abraham Nasatir of SDSU – promptly embraced the idea. Meeting at the Jewish Community Center, which then was located on 54th Street between El Cajon Boulevard and University Avenue, the Jewish Historical Society conducted business in a low-key fashion.

Henry Schwartz popularized the society by writing regularly about episodes in San Diego Jewish history for the fortnightly newspaper *Israel Today*, which later changed its name to *San Diego Jewish Times*.

Stan and Laurel Schwartz were not related to Henry Schwartz, and it was by coincidence that after Henry died, people of the same surname were elevated to the leadership.

The couple had moved to San Diego from New York State where, at colleges located miles apart, she had majored in art and minored in Judaic Studies, and he had majored in business. Laurel and Stan met in Israel while taking a two-week bus tour sponsored by the American Jewish Congress. Laurel had accompanied an aunt, while Stan had traveled on his own. There were three busloads on the tour, and Stan and Laurel were the only passengers then in their 20s.

As might be imagined, they gravitated toward each other, and eventually, encouraged by busloads of would-be *shadchans*, decided to sit with each other for the balance of the tour. Thereafter the progress of their relationship was a regular topic of conversation for the other travelers. Months after returning to New York, they announced their engagement, to the accolades of their former traveling companions. The American Jewish Congress was so excited by the successful match that the organization began to advertise singles tours to Israel.

History was among the young couple's common interests, and they attended annual meetings held in cities around the country of the American Jewish Historical Society, at which researchers presented papers on local topics.

When the Schwartzes decided in 1978 to move to San Diego for its weather, their parents Anne and Martin Press and Mildred and Harry Schwartz, as well as Stan's grandmother, Ida Steinberg, soon decided to follow them. Although they initially worked at other jobs, Laurel and Stan found a new passion in 1989 – buying and selling Judaic books.

"When we moved out here we were interested in antique furniture and we visited a lot of antique shops," Stan recalled. "I noticed Jewish books lying on the shelves. I thought, 'What good are the books doing in this place?' So we would buy the books and I had a small collection and I was working in computer sciences at the time, on a military contract. I got laid off and Laurel said, 'Why don't you start selling some of the books, and I did.'" Thus, the business known as Schwartz Judaica was born.

After Henry Schwartz died, Stan and Laurel rose to top leadership roles. At their behest, the organization began to collect dues, more extensively publicize its activities, and expand its membership. They invited both scholars and long-time San Diegans to address their society.

Among the speakers were Harriet Rochlin, author of *Pioneer Jews*; Elana Saad, who made a study of the Jews of Tijuana; and Vernon Kahn, whose memoir told of creating Vernon's Delicatessen and the North Park Bakery.

But times, they were changing. Jews were moving from East San Diego to La Jolla and to northern San Diego County communities located along the Interstate 5 and the Interstate 15. The center of Jewish population was moving farther and farther away from the old JCC at 4079 54th Street, which had been dedicated back in 1958. The new Lawrence Family JCC was built in the 1980s, and although the East San Diego community tried hard to hold on and keep the 54th Street JCC open, eventually expenses outran their ambitions. The property was sold in the 1990s to a church, which itself was later torn down to make way for a housing development.

Meanwhile, in 1991, Rabbi Morton J. Cohn, who had been the senior rabbi of Congregation Beth Israel, and later in his career the founding rabbi of Temple Emanu-El, died in 1991, followed five years later by his wife, Sally. Their children, closing up his home, invited the Jewish Historical Society to take custody of his papers. "Pick them up today?" the rabbi's son, Mort Cohn Jr., asked.

Rabbi Cohn "had five 4-drawer filing cabinets filled with his papers," Laurel recalled. "We went out to his house on Barbarossa Drive, realized that this was a very large collection, and called Congregation Beth Israel, and asked if they could help us with this."

Stan picked up the story: "I was friends with Stuart Simmons (then executive director of Beth Israel) and he sent over several men who worked there with a truck."

It meant first taking all the papers out of the filing cabinets and putting them into boxes, then moving the empty cabinets and filled boxes to Congregation Beth Israel (then located at 3rd Avenue and Laurel Street, the present home of Ohr Shalom Synagogue), where the contents of the boxes were put back into the filing cabinets and stored in a garage area.

The collected papers of Rabbi Morton J. Cohn thus became the first collection of the Jewish Historical Society.

As the year 2000 approached, marking the 150th year of Jewish settlement in San Diego, the Jewish Historical Society of San Diego and the Lipinsky Institute for Judaic Studies at SDSU came to a symbiotic understanding. The Jewish Historical Society could keep its archives in the Snyder Reading Room, where its staff and volunteers could curate the collections, placing documents and photographs into acid-free folders and cataloging the collections. When these are ready, the Jewish Historical Society formally donates each collection, with archival notes, to the Special Collections and University Archives at SDSU's Love Library.

With such transfer of ownership, the collections are assured a permanent home, and will be available to scholars.

At this writing in 2015, there are 85 collections that have either been donated to SDSU's Special Collections or are in the process of being curated by the Jewish Historical Society, which is always on the look out for more.

Among other contributors who followed the lead of the Cohn family was Seymour Okmin, who gave the Historical Society records and photographs from the Weinberger Lodge of the B'nai B'rith. Lenore Fefferman of B'nai B'rith Women donated her collection. Longtime Cantor Sheldon Merel of Beth Israel, when he moved to Seacrest Village Retirement Community in Encinitas, operated by the Hebrew Homes, couldn't take all his material with him, so he donated "pictures, notices, programs, and CDs," said Laurel. "He wanted access to the collection, so we photographed every page of his scrapbooks and we gave him a digital file."

In the instance of Ruth Doris Jacobson, who was the commander of Post 185 of the Jewish War Veterans, the family allowed the Historical Society to digitally photograph her papers and scrapbooks, but kept the originals in their possession.

The Jewish Federation of San Diego County turned over to the Jewish Historical Society 20 boxes of records including over 30,000 photographs dating back to the 1940s. And, the most recent collection obtained by the society included some of the papers of former San Diego City Councilwoman Abbe Wolfsheimer Stutz and her father, Col. Irving Salomon. The colonel was an internationalist who was appointed by President Dwight D. Eisenhower to the U.S. delegation to the United Nations, and who hosted Eleanor Roosevelt at his Rancho Lilac in Valley Center, and who was the first Jewish layman to become a papal knight. Other of Salomon's papers were donated to the Valley Center History Museum, near Escondido.

Today, Laurel Schwartz serves as the Jewish Historical Society's archivist and her husband, Stan, as its president. The Lipinsky Insitute for Judaic Studies has been replaced by the Jewish Studies Program of SDSU, headed by Prof. Risa Levitt Kohn.

When I visited the reading room recently, Stan and Laurel were both there along with the society's treasurer Gerri Brech. Together the society's three officers were sorting through thousands of photographs from the Jewish Federation of San Diego, captioning those that they could, and putting all of them into acid-free sleeves.

Brech, I learned, is the former Gerri Goldstein, whose public school education was at a trio of San Diego schools named for U.S. Presidents — Andrew Jackson Elementary School, Woodrow Wilson Junior High, and Herbert Hoover High School. From there she went to San Diego City College, becoming a medical assistant, and after raising her family, continued her education at Grossmont College and San Diego State University. She eventually became a preschool teacher at the 54th Street JCC and after that worked at the JCC Building Fund Campaign Office.

Her family were members of Tifereth Israel Synagogue when it was located on 30th Street, but by the time she was raising a family of her own, she was a member of Temple Emanu-El, now located in the Del Cerro area. After her family grew up, she moved to Rancho Bernardo, becoming a member of nearby Temple Adat Shalom in Poway.

She recalled that teens in the 1950s liked to go to drive-in restaurants at which car hops would bring food orders to your car, some of them racing to and fro on roller skates. Girls, she recalled, went to the drive-in restaurants with other girls, and boys with boys, and they would check each other out, not unlike the characters in the movie *American Graffiti*. Brech also was a member of B'nai B'rith Girls, which met at Temple Beth Israel, and on a few occassions was persuaded to be a hostess at dances sponsored by the Jewish Welfare Board for military personnel.

Brech said she volunteers for the Jewish Historical Society because "I like everything Jewish" and because she greatly admires Stan and Laurel Schwartz for their dedication to the cause of historic preservation. "They tell me what to do and I do it," she laughed.

Other regulars: Al Kohn and his late wife Fern; and native San Diegan Marilyn Smith Tom.

The society welcomes volunteers and researchers and material donations. Call or email for an appointment via laurelschwartz@cox.net or phoning (619) 232-5888. Its collections can be accessed via two websites: www.jewishstudies.sdsu.edu/archives.htm and www.jhssandiego.pastperfect-online.com

Home of Jewish Historical Society of San Diego archives

From College Avenue, Exit 10, turn south (right from eastbound I-8), and you will be at the SDSU College Campus. Parking structures are on the periphery of the campus.

-San Diego Jewish World, November 12, 2015

31. Exit 10
Hillel at SDSU

Exterior of Hillel Center at San Diego State University

SAN DIEGO — The Melvin Garb Hillel Center, dedicated in October 2014, is a place for Jewish students to hang out, socialize, and make Jewish connections.

Here, says Hillel's SDSU's campus director, Jackie Tolley, the students "engage in programs that help to fulfill Hillel's mission to be 'a vibrant Jewish campus presence and to involve the maximum number of university-age Jews in ways that foster a lasting commitment to Jewish life.'"

The environmentally conscious, LEED-Gold certified, 10,500-square-foot building at 5717 Lindo Paseo, adjacent to the San Diego State University campus, is so attractive that other campus organizations occasionally rent its large second-story meeting room.

However, Tolley notes, there are provisos. Outside groups are not allowed to use the kitchen, unless they have a recognized kosher caterer, and they can't bring products like pork or shellfish onto the premises.

Lounge area at Hillel of San Diego
(Photo: Shor M. Masori)

Having such a facility, with a lounge, kosher kitchen, coffee bar, pool table, smaller meeting rooms, free wi-fi, and a patio for outdoor barbecues, is a far cry from a small, leaky house on Montezuma Road where the local Hillel got its start in the late 1970s as the Jewish Campus Center, or a later interim building not far from the present facility. The fundraising drive for the $9 million project was led by SDSU alumnus and former United Jewish Federation President Herb Solomon. The Melvin Garb Foundation made a lead gift of $2.5 million.

Tolley came to San Diego in 1977 with her husband Mark Berger, who had been hired to serve as the planning and budgeting director of the United Jewish Federation of San Diego. Having taught 5th grade in Maryland, and 8th grade in Pennsylvania, Tolley figured she probably would teach one grade or another here in California.

Rabbi Jay Miller, local director for the Jewish Campus Centers, "had moved to town the same month we did, so Jay and my husband were the two young Jewish professionals in the community, and so we knew him and his family socially," Tolley recalled.

While Tolley was waiting for news of a teaching job, Miller suggested that because he was often elsewhere, she should keep the Montezuma house at SDSU open and meet students who should come inquiring. She recalled thinking that the job would be a nice stop gap until a teaching job came through. Her responsibilities grew exponentially in the ensuing 37 years, during which the Jewish Campus Centers morphed into Hillel of San Diego. Today, Tolley concedes happily, she is at Hillel to stay.

In a way, the arcs of her career and that of her husband crossed. Tolley got into the world of Jewish communal work and Berger got out of it. Today he serves as executive director of Partnerships With Industry, a program that finds jobs and work projects for adults with developmental disabilities.

For some students, Hillel is a touchstone—a place to come, perhaps, for a Friday night dinner, or to listen to a lecture, or to gather for a *tikkun olam* project somewhere out in the community. For others, Hillel is a home away from home— the place to go when there are hours rather than minutes between classes, the home where they can laugh with friends and staff in good times, or draw comfort from them in bad times.

Hillel is the community agency responsible for working with the campuses in San Diego. The on-campus Jewish Student Union is affiliated with the Associated Students of SDSU. Jews at SDSU, similar to those at other universities across North America, must contend with efforts by the Students for Justice in Palestine to vilify and isolate Israel with resolutions and demonstrations calling for boycotts, divestment and sanctions against the Jewish state.

Tolley said as important as it is for Jewish students to stand with Israel, which the Hillel group takes quite seriously, members of the outside community may get the wrong idea about the reality of Jewish life at SDSU. "They don't understand that all campuses are not undergoing the same kind of tension," she said.

"They think because the divestment hearings get very heated that there are tensions every day, all year long. That is not the case—maybe on some campuses, but certainly not in San Diego," she added.

Hillel, the Jewish Student Union, and another group called Students Supporting Israel (formerly Aztecs for Israel) all vigorously defend the Jewish state, she said. However, "Being Jewish can't be just about fighting," she said. Hillel seeks to imbue in students appreciation for "all the wonderful, positive, life-enhancing things the Jewish community and Judaism have to offer."

Indeed, there are many offerings for Jewish students both on and near campus in addition to Hillel. A few blocks north of the campus is Temple Emanu-El, which not only houses a Reform congregation but also hosts the senior citizen-oriented College Avenue Center, operated by Jewish Family Service with a kosher kitchen and plenty of opportunities for student volunteers. Within a shorter walk of the campus is the Chabad House, with many programs geared to students. South of the campus is Beth Jacob Congregation, an Orthodox synagogue.

On campus, there is a Jewish Studies Program, whose director, Prof. Risa Levitt Kohn, is also the faculty advisor to the Jewish Student Union. Hillel and Chabad alternate Friday night Shabbat dinners to which students are invited and Hillel offers student-led Shabbat services before dinner. On the afternoon of Chabad nights, Hillel has started a lunch 'n' learn program, inviting local rabbis and Jewish educators to teach over lunch. On Rosh Hashanah afternoon, Hillel joins members of Temple Emanu-El and the Conservative Tifereth Israel Synagogue in Tashlich services at Lake Murray.

Among community members who have come to Friday night Shabbat dinners is Elliot Hirshman, the president of San Diego State University and member of the Jewish community. He and his wife Jeri also attended Hillel's High Holy Day services and he was a speaker at the Melvin Garb Hillel Center's dedication.

Hillel offers community service projects throughout the year, many in cooperation with Jewish Family Service. Some occur during vacation periods. For example, over a recent Spring break, Hillel House sponsored a trip to Arizona to build houses under the auspices of Habitat for Humanity. The chance of catching a Spring Training baseball game in Arizona was for some students an additional incentive.

"Especially in the west, Jewish students are not coming to campus looking to Hillel to meet their needs for kosher food, or a daily minyan," Tolley said. "They may at some places back East, but you don't find that on the West Coast. We are not just a synagogue on campus; we are conscious of the fact that it takes more than saying, 'Hey come to Friday night dinner,' to get students involved. They are looking for all kinds of things on campus and we have to provide a real broad cross section of activities to engage them."

What students are looking for, "although they don't use the language, is 'community.' If you ask Jewish students who walk in the door why are you here, they are not going to say, 'Oh, I am looking for a Jewish community,' but that is exactly what they are looking for. They will articulate that 'I want to meet people. I want to make friends,' but the drive to find a place where you belong, that is as strong as ever. This is one place they know they can have that experience on campus."

Tolley tallies at less than 10 percent the Jewish population of SDSU's 30,000 student body. Of these, about 400-500 students stay in regular touch with Hillel by attending a meal or some other function, she estimated. "When we have a big barbecue at the beginning of the semester we get maybe 200 people. When we have a Shabbat dinner and services we get anywhere from 60 to 130. When we had a Mitzvah Day program it attracted about 100 students, although they were not all Jewish because with a lot of our programs we reach out to other organizations."

Tolley's warmest memories of her Hillel years often come from alumni who formed strong Jewish connections through Hillel at SDSU. She told of a former student who died at age 48, and a large contingent of people who attended his *shiva* were people he had met at Hillel 25 years before, "and they continue to support his family."

"Could they have made friends with each other without Hillel?" she asked rhetorically. "Maybe but to know that Hillel brought them together and their connection was so strengthened that they continue to be a source of strength and companionship for others, it is enormously gratifying."

Hillel staff members play multiple roles in students' lives, Tolley reflected. "There is a programmatic role. We work with student leaders to develop their leadership skills, to plan programs, to involve other students. We are their confidantes, role models, connectors—we are their life coaches as well."

To avoid campus construction, from Exit 10, go south on College Avenue to a right on Montezuma Road, to another right on 55th Street and a final right on Lindo Paseo.

-San Diego Jewish World, November 19, 2015

32. Exit 10

Chabad at SDSU

Chabad at San Diego State University

SAN DIEGO — The large menorah standing two stories tall on the front lawn immediately differentiates this house at 6115 Montezuma Road from the fraternity houses nearby. And if you go inside to the large, comfortable sitting room, one look at the bar will confirm that the parties thrown here definitely are not booze fests.

Instead of liquor bottles behind the bar, there are shelves of leather-bound Jewish books. "I'll have a Tanya, please," one can imagine a visitor saying.

This house is the Chabad House that serves San Diego State University. Rabbi Chalom Boudjnah has been building the congregation since arriving in San Diego in 1999 at the invitation of Rabbi Yonah Fradkin, whom he succeeded following a two-year apprenticeship.

Fradkin today serves as the senior Chabad rabbi in San Diego County, which from an organizational standpoint makes him the "boss" of the other Chabad rabbis in the county. He is based at the Chabad Hebrew Academy in San Diego's Scripps Ranch neighborhood.

The Boudjnahs' connection to this particular Chabad House predated the arrival of the French-born Rabbi, although this wasn't immediately apparent to Rabbi Chalom and Mairav Boudjnah. Early in Rabbi Fradkin's tenure at San Diego State University, BatSheva Zalkind, a Jewish student from Cape Cod, Massachusetts, was on a spiritual quest. After enrolling at San Diego State, she had flirted with Eastern religions, and one day, noticing the Rabbi putting on tefillin, she asked him the meaning of this ritual.

This led to a discussion of Jewish spirituality, Kaballah and reincarnation, and before long, the student became a regular visitor to Chabad House, ultimately deciding she had found in her own religion exactly what she was looking for. After about a year of study with Rabbi Fradkin, she eventually went to Minnesota to study under Rabbi Manis Friedman at the Bais Chana Institute of Jewish Studies, which specializes in teaching Judaism to women with very little background in their religion. From Minnesota, she went to Israel to complete her studies and there married Rabbi Reuven Drori.

Many years later, after her daughter Mairav became of marriageable age, Mrs. Drori met in New York City with Rabbi Fradkin's sister-in-law who serves as a *shadchan*, or matchmaker. About the same time, the *shadchan* also met Rabbi Boudjnah. She decided to put one and one together, without any of the parties realizing that Boudjnah was serving as assistant to the very same Rabbi who had helped Mrs. Drori find her way back to Judaism. It was only after Mrs. Drori started asking many questions about Boudjnah's background and prospects that her family's life was to turn a full circle. Rabbi Chalom and Mairav Boudjnah eventually would play the same mentoring roles in the life of SDSU students that Rabbi Fradkin had played in that of Mrs. Drori.

Being there for students in times of trouble, or loneliness, or crisis is an important aspect of the Boudjnahs' lives.

Rabbi Boudjnah told me of one young man. "He recently lost his mother and we had to take care of everything for him. He is a single boy, with no father, so he was alone."

On other occasions, the Rabbi said, he and the Rebbetzin help students facing different levels of hardship or adversity, for example, "a girl who broke up with her boyfriend and she just wanted to talk to someone besides her friends or her mother. So Mairav does that, and I do the same with the boys."

There was also a boy "whose father went to prison and he had a very hard time with that morally," Rabbi Boudjnah recalled. "There are all kinds of different issues and these kids are just 18 or 19 years old. They think they are adults, and they are young adults, but they just left home, and so it is nice that they have someone to come to. We have a family, and so they have a family. For us, they are just like family, and we're not just a Rabbi and Rebbetzin It's not a one-man show. We love each of them. We care about them, and the advice I would give them, I would give to my own kids."

At the time I visited Chabad House, the Boudjnahs had six children, four girls and two boys. The eldest, Sara Batya, was 13 in 2015. She was named after a great-great grandmother. Next came Chana Rachel, 12, also named for a great-great grandmother. When Chaya Luba finally came along, the couple gave her a name meaning "life and love" or "love of life" in celebration. "Luba is also after Lubavitch, where Chabad started," the Rabbi said.

Next came the first son, Menachem Saadya, Boudjnah said. The name "Menachem" honors the late Lubavitcher Rebbe, Menachem Mendel Schneerson, especially when linked with Rabbi Boudjnah's own middle name which is "Mendel." The boy's middle name, Saadya, was after Mairav's grandfather, "who was born in Yemen, a holy man, whom even the Arabs used to go to see him to pray for rain. He was an amazing person."

The next child born to the Boudjnahs was Shoshana Nadra, the middle name being Yemenite in origin, and meaning light. That was the name of Mairav's grandmother, who had passed away two years before the baby's birth.

Finally, there was a second boy, Dovber, who was a large baby, in the 95th percentile of weight. Dov and Ber both mean "bear," one in the physical sense, the other in the spiritual sense. Putting the two names together "the spiritual is supposed to overcome the physical," Boudjnah explained.

There are 15 bedrooms upstairs in the Chabad House. The Boudjnahs have a separate home within walking distance of Chabad House. The upstairs bedrooms at Chabad House are rented to college students and other single men living in the neighborhood. These tenants, in addition to Jewish students from San Diego State University and Grossmont College in El Cajon, as well as other community members, are invited on alternating Friday nights to Shabbat dinners. On these occasions, the *mechitzah* is rolled away, and tables and chairs are laid out in the pattern of the Hebrew letter "shin" so that as many as 140 people can be accommodated in the sanctuary for kosher dinner.

The free dinners are times when students are exposed to the joy of Jewish life and much singing accompanies the meal, Boudjnah said, his eyes sparkling.

The idea is not to turn Jewish students into Chabadniks, but instead to familiarize them with Judaism and the mitzvoth, the Rabbi said.

Boudjnah told of one very strict Orthodox man, who was not a member of the Chabad movement, who watched disapprovingly as students danced on Simcha Torah with the Torahs. Taking Rabbi Boudjnah aside, he commented that the students didn't look religious, that they probably didn't keep kosher, or keep the Shabbat or go to synagogue. So why, he asked, would they be permitted to dance with the Torah? Commenting that Chabad believes that "one mitzvah leads to another," Boudjnah said the fact that the students were not religious, and still wanted to dance with the Torah, meant wonderful Jewish things may continue to be in prospect for them.

The reason that Chabad serves kosher meals every other Friday night, rather than every week, is because, by agreement, the Hillel organization of San Diego welcomes students on the alternate Friday nights. Boudjnah said rather than being in competition, Hillel and Chabad expose students to different faces of Judaism – Hillel typically is non-Orthodox. There were some unexpected benefits in working so closely with Hillel, he added. Whereas some students were reluctant to visit Chabad on their own, fearing that Orthodoxy is too strict for them, they were willing to come with friends from Hillel on the alternate weeks. Once at Chabad, they enjoyed the warm and cordial atmosphere, Boudjnah said, and then were willing to attend other events.

Besides students, the Chabad House serves a small community of Bukharin Jews, who immigrated to the United States from some of the Asian Republics of the former Soviet Union. The Bukharin Jews follow a Sephardic rite, with which Boudjnah, a French Jew of Algerian ancestry, feels very comfortable. He has become the life-cycle rabbi for this small community, officiating at their weddings, *brit milah* ceremonies, and funerals.

In appreciation, members of the Bukharin community built for the Chabad House a finely decorated Aron Kodesh as well as a ceremonial Elijah's chair for brit milah.

Such donations are the mainstay of a Chabad House. The rabbi, known as a *shaliach*, or emissary, and his wife are expected to support themselves through fundraising. They neither receive funds from nor are expected to donate funds to Chabad's headquarters in Brooklyn. Boudjnah said there never is any money left over, and if there were, he would not be doing his job right. Whenever there is money, Chabad expects it to be spent wisely on Jewish programming.

Besides the Shabbat meals, Boudjnah offers on the other four weekdays at the Chabad House a kosher meal plan in which so far 20 students are enrolled.

"My mission is to reach out to as many Jews as possible and to give them a positive experience about Judaism," he says. "Mainly we focus on college students because we are right next to campus. I am honorary brother for AEPi, the Jewish fraternity at this campus, and we do a lot of events."

A class is offered at Chabad House about the "moral values that the Ten Commandments brought to the world," and Chabad House sponsors social events such as a "welcome back" beach barbecue. "We jet ski and play volleyball at the beach so we reach out to them in many different ways. We have minyan on Shabbos on Friday night and Saturday, but also on Sunday morning and Sunday night, which we combine with a class."

Boudjnah said Chabad House is "not a full-on community; there are perhaps 30-40 people who come for services on Shabbos, not a huge number, but it is a close group of people from different backgrounds. There are a couple of people who are Chabad and there is a family who are Israelis. Some are single guys or single women who come here. And we have the Bukharin community."

The rabbi said that except in rare instances, Chabad emissaries make a career-long commitment to the community that they have built up, rather than jumping from post to post. He and Mairav plan to stay at San Diego State and to continue to build up the College Area community of San Diego and nearby cities. Were they to leave, he said, the people who have been attracted to Chabad because of its family atmosphere might feel bereft.

....

From Interstate 8, Exit 10: Take College Avenue south to Montezuma Road and turn left. Chabad House is on the right.

....

-San Diego Jewish World, November 26, 2015

33. Exit 10
Mikvah Israel San Diego

A mikvah, with waterproof instructions on the wall.

SAN DIEGO — Susan Shapiro estimates that 200 women in San Diego County regularly go to a mikvah (ritual bath) every month to infuse their marriages with spirituality and passion. Of these, the mikvah attendant estimates, between 60 and 80 visit Mikvah Israel in a quiet neighborhood near San Diego State University. The others utilize mikvahs in La Jolla and in Poway.

Mikvah Israel occupies the back portion of a duplex at 5170 La Dorna Street. The front portion of the home, sealed off from the back, is rented to an unrelated tenant. Entering the back portion of the house, one encounters a reception area where one may wait until a preparation area becomes free.

In the preparation area, which is a well-supplied shower and bath room, a woman after seven days following the cessation of her menstruation, is commanded by Torah (Leviticus 15, 18) to cleanse her body thoroughly from "top to bottom." For example, she will remove all nail polish, make-up, hair-dye, anything that would come between her natural self and the waters of the mikvah pool. Mikvah Israel has two such preparation rooms and two mikvah pools, both attached to a source pool which initially had been filled with ritually-required rainwater.

When a woman has completed her preparations (which she may also do at home), she will call for the mikvah lady to escort her to the mikvah pool. There she will immerse herself completely, dunking under water three times. She will recite a blessing (conveniently transliterated on a waterproof card affixed to the wall of the mikvah pool) and when she leaves the mikvah, the attendant will hold a robe for the woman as she emerges, preserving modesty. An observant Jewish woman will resume sexual relations with her husband only after she has participated in this monthly rite.

Shapiro has been a mikvah attendant for 28 years. Not long after she and her husband moved to San Diego from Cape Town, South Africa, they wanted to send their children to the Chabad Hebrew Academy but tuition was a problem on the salary of her husband, Aharon Shapiro, a mashgiach (one who supervises kashrut.)

So, Senior Chabad Rabbi Yonah Fradkin suggested that she take a job as a mikvah lady (there are five at this facility) to defray the expense. In that she, herself, was a regular user of the mikvah, Shapiro was quite familiar with its rules and procedures. Her children have long since graduated from the Chabad Hebrew Academy, but Shapiro, who lives within walking distance of the mikvah, continues at her post. It is clear that she feels fulfillment in helping others to observe the mitzvah (commandment) of mikvah.

Mikvah Israel is available only to married Jewish women whose husbands also are Jewish, Shapiro said.

"Any mitzvah you do gives you an extra spiritual connection," she says. "There is a concept that when you are in the water, and you are literally not touching anything – when you pull your feet up from the floor—you literally feel like a baby in the womb. You are spiritually and physically getting reborn."

Furthermore, said Shapiro, "the whole idea of the water in the mikvah whether it was snow or rain—natural water—is that it was connected to all the waters of the Earth, including those that flowed through the Garden of Eden. In this way, we are connected to all the women through all the years and all the generations."

It is particularly emotional, she said, when a bride-to-be is brought to the mikvah by her mother, and sometimes by aunts and grandmothers as well, in celebration of the fact that the mitzvah is being passed on, generation to generation, Shapiro added.

In addition to saying the prescribed Hebrew prayers, a woman, while in the mikvah, may linger in the waters for more personal prayers or meditations.

Shapiro has observed some transcendent moments. While names of mikvah users are kept private, Shapiro felt free to relate one of her most memorable experiences. She recounted that one woman came to the mikvah wearing "a tanktop and slacks—obviously not an Orthodox woman (who would have covered her body from foreign eyes)—and she got herself ready, knocked on the door to call me to escort her, and in the pool she started making the *baracha* (blessing) and then she started sobbing, so much it was like she was making tidal waves in the pool.

"One of the things we don't do is talk when they are in there; it is just not the place for chitter chatter," said Shapiro. "She came out, and I said, 'I don't know your story but you clearly need a hug.' I gave her a hug and she started sobbing on my shoulder, telling me the doctors told her that there was no way she could have children, and that her rabbi said, 'You need to go to the mikvah.'

"I asked her if she had been to the mikvah before, and she said she went when she first got married but then when she didn't have children, she became upset about it and stopped coming. So I said to her if she made a commitment to this mitzvah, I was sure that Hashem would give her a blessing. It was one of those strange things, I had no right to promise anyone anything, but the words came out....

"Three or four months later she called for an appointment. You know you never ask any woman if she is pregnant, that is etiquette, but when she walked in, I said, 'I don't normally ask this question but (pointing to the bump in her tummy) what is this?' And she said to me, 'I got pregnant that night!' – after the doctors had told her there was no chance she could get pregnant. So we sobbed and we hugged..."

A postscript to the story: Two of Shapiro's daughters had babies only two days apart. And the woman from the mikvah had a baby boy, on the day exactly between the births of the mikvah lady's two grandchildren.

Shapiro notes that observing Jewish laws of family purity—that is, waiting for seven days after menstruation before resuming sexual relations—generally means that married couples will engage in sexual intercourse at approximately the same time as the woman ovulates. Coupled with the fact that both partners have abstained from sexual relations for approximately two weeks' time, this practice also tends to build both anticipation and passion in the love-making.

During the period between the onset of menstruation and the completion of the mikvah ritual, explained Shapiro, "we don't just not have relations; there is no touching, no physical contact–even less contact that you would have with your brother and sister, which is why just handing your husband a piece of paper can be very exciting; it makes the little things that you do very exciting."

The mikvah lady is not at all shy discussing such matters, believing in the Jewish teaching that sexual intercourse between husband and wife is itself a mitzvah – Be fruitful and multiply, God has commanded us.

Whereas pregnancy is considered a particularly wonderful blessing arising from family purity practices, Shapiro said that women will continue to go to the mikvah even if they have no intention or ability to become pregnant, as for example, after menopause.

"I have one woman who comes here in her pajamas. She has showered at home and she comes in her pajamas." That woman doesn't want to have to dress to go to the mikvah, then undress to go into it, then redress after leaving it, only to undress again when she meets with her husband.

"Not everyone who uses the mikvah here is Orthodox observant," says Shapiro. "This is one of those mitzvahs that you can do and nobody knows that you are doing it — it is totally between the woman and her husband" and the ever-so-discreet mikvah ladies.

"If you were doing kosher, you can't eat out with your friends. If you are doing Shabbos, you are not available for many social occasions. But this mitzvah is so private, we have some women who do this and don't necessarily keep anything else." Shapiro told me.

"This one is important to them. It happens that there are benefits in the marriage. There is the anticipation of getting together because it has been about two weeks that you've been apart so the anticipation builds even long after many years of marriage when you would imagine that it would have faded in the relationship. There is still that so-called excitement" – honeymoon night all over again.

Mikvah membership is $250 yearly, or $25 per visit.

Susan Shapiro

From Exit 10, take College Avenue south to Montezuma Road, turn left, and then make another left turn at La Dorna Street. Those wishing an appointment are urged to telephone at least 48 hours in advance to (619) 287-6411. A mikvah attendant will call back to confirm an appointment.

-*San Diego Jewish World, December 3, 2015*

34. Exit 10

Beth Jacob Congregation

Beth Jacob's pomegranate roof

SAN DIEGO — Approaching Beth Jacob Congregation, the first thing most people notice is the unusual protrusion from the red roof. No matter what might have been intended by the architect, Synagogue Administrator Rand Levin says the story is told at the Orthodox synagogue that it represents the stem of a pomegranate, which is a fruit rich in symbolism in the Jewish religion.

Traditionally, a pomegranate is eaten on Rosh Hashanah—its seeds representing the fruitfulness with which one hopes the New Year is imbued. According to tradition, there are 613 seeds inside the pomegranate, exactly the same as the number of commandments, or *mitzvoth*, contained in the Torah.

In Levin's view, the seeds of a pomegranate represent "all the various people inside. Not one, but many, bringing a sweetness to the congregation."

Both on the inside and the outside, the walls of the synagogue are heavily textured, representing those times when Jews "wail and cry when we pray," he said.

Triangular patches of ground provide areas for contemplation, recreation, and in the case of the Israel garden, more symbolism. Here are grown a real pomegranate tree, as well as a fig tree, olive tree, palm tree, and grapes – five of the seven species of Israel. "The only things we are missing are wheat and barley," said Levin. "It has become a real serenity garden, if you will. People can sit here and schmooze."

On another patch of ground is a small playground, providing a place of recreation for young and old throughout the week.

At the helm of Beth Jacob Congregation is Rabbi Avram Bogopulsky, only the third rabbi to serve there since it became an Orthodox institution after World War II. Beth Jacob Congregation and Center had been founded as a Conservative congregation in the late 1930s, but switched affiliations at the same time that the older Tifereth Israel Synagogue moved from the Orthodox to the Conservative movement.

Rabbi Baruch Stern, a survivor of the Holocaust who had trained as a Sunday school teacher at Tifereth Israel Synagogue during its Orthodox period, in 1947 became the first Orthodox rabbi of Beth Jacob. Up to his retirement in 1977, he permitted some of the congregation's previous customs to continue, such as mixed seating. Rabbi Stern's retirement coincided with the congregation's move from a building on 30th Street in the North Park neighborhood of San Diego to its present location at 4855 College Avenue.

The next to lead the congregation was Rabbi Eliezer Langer, who had *mechitzahs* installed in the new building to conform Beth Jacob with contemporary Orthodox practice. After he accepted an assignment in Israel, he was succeeded in 1996 by Rabbi Bogopulsky.

En route to ordination, Rabbi Bogopulsky studied under Rabbi Berel Wein and Rabbi Laibel Reznick at the Yeshiva Shaarei Torah in Monsey, New York. According to the congregation's website, "it was the inspirational words and messages of Rabbi Wein that instilled with Rabbi Bogopulsky a desire to be of service to Klal Yisrael."

Today, Rabbi Bogopulsky is aided by rabbinical assistant Pinchas ("Pinny") Roth, who coordinates the educational component of the synagogue, specifically the Monday night "Partners in Torah" program in which a teacher and student are paired.

Other staff members include Yisroel and Malka Weiser, who lead the youth programs. Both also teach at Soille San Diego Hebrew Day School, Yisroel in fact being the son of the Jewish day school's headmaster, Rabbi Simcha Weiser.

The Steiman Sanctuary, named posthumously for philanthropists Morrie and Barbara Steiman, seats 300 people with men in the middle and women on the two sides. As one might expect, the sanctuary is also rich in symbolism.

Upon the Aron Kodesh (Holy Ark) are engraved representations of the Ten Commandments, and when the doors are folded open to reveal the Torahs inside, the Ten Commandments appear on the fold-out sides of the doors as well, so that these words of God are always before the congregation.

Concerning the Ner Tamid, or Eternal Flame, "There is a legend that the glass ball at the top, which is visible, is attached to a motor that turns it to give the effect of a flame when light hits it," Levin said. "I'm not sure if it true, we've never taken it apart to find the motor, but it was put here in 1977."

On the walls on either side of the Holy Ark are large, matching, seven-branched menorahs. They were fashioned for the congregation after an electrical fire in a back room destroyed a wall of the sanctuary but not before Rabbi Langer and congregants were able to whisk the Torahs to safety.

Across from the Holy Ark is the Shulchan (or reader's table) at which prayer leaders stand to recite prayers and read the Torah. The prayer leaders, like the congregation, face East during prayers. Reading stands, known as shtenders, enable congregants located at the front of the sanctuary to keep their siddurim (prayer books) and Chumashim (Bibles) within easy reach.

In the back of the room, paneled walls can open to enlarge the sanctuary for High Holy Day services and other occasions attended by larger-than-normal crowds. Otherwise these overflow spaces can be used for a variety of purposes, such as for study and rehearsals.

Both inside and outside, there are small memorials. One inside a wall niche is a photograph of the entrance to a concentration camp, with barbed wire in front of the photograph conveying some of the terror. In a garden, there is also a memorial erected by Russian-speaking members of the congregation to those who were lost in World War II.

Another important room in the Beth Jacob complex is the *beit midrash*, a study hall that also is used by daily minyans for prayer services. Along the back wall are four stained glass windows which, according to a description on the synagogue's website, "depict highlights from the Garden of Eden, Exodus from Egypt, building the Holy Temple, its destruction, the return and rebuilding of Israel."

History and modernity, spirituality and pragmatism, exist side by side at Beth Jacob Congregation and Center, at which secular enterprises help to support a flourishing observant community that Levin estimates at 125 family units, with at least another 25 non-member families. "We don't just service members, we service the entire Jewish community," said Levin. "We hope those whom we serve who are not yet members someday will be."

On the other side of the entrance foyer from the sanctuary is a large social hall, which is served by Beth Jacob's own kosher kitchen. Approved kosher caterers are permitted to rent the kitchen, providing the synagogue another revenue stream. Rabbi Bogopulsky serves as the mashgiach for these uses.

Having greater impact as a revenue source are a block of 50 apartments on the grounds of the Beth Jacob campus, which are rented not only to congregants wanting to be within an easy walk of services, but also to college students studying at nearby San Diego State University, and other occupants.

Levin said the apartments are "open to the public. We don't discriminate, so there are many from the general population. It happens that about half the tenants have some connection to the synagogue, but we have Jews and non-Jews alike. It is a very diverse community."

I asked if tenants can prepare non-kosher food.

"Absolutely," he responded. "In the privacy of their own homes they can do what they want."

For 14 years, Levin was a video journalist for KNSD, covering various news assignments in addition to serving as a co-producer for Ken Kramer's popular "About San Diego" series, which also aired on the Public Broadcasting station, KPBS. After layoffs hit KNSD, Levin worked 4 ½ years for himself as a freelance video journalist, during which time he also served as the lay president of Beth Jacob Congregation.

"While I was president, I didn't realize that I was training for my new career" as the synagogue's administrator, he said.

As a boy, Levin had attended an Orthodox Day School and a Yeshiva in Los Angeles for one year, then completed his education at a public high school and at San Diego State University. His mother's family was Orthodox, while his father was secular, he said.

"I moved to this community in 1998 and every day has been a day of spiritual growth for me," said Levin.

Rand Levin in Beth Jacob's aron kodesh

From College Avenue, Exit 10, head south on College Avenue past San Diego State University. Beth Jacob Congregation will be on the left at the corner of College Avenue and Mesita Drive.

-*San Diego Jewish World, December 10, 2015*

35. Exit 11

Lake Murray

Lake Murray in shadow of Cowles Mountain

SAN DIEGO — In 1916, engineer James Murray came to San Diego from Montana to build a bigger reservoir than the one that had been created in 1895 when a small earthen dam had been constructed on a creek running through Alvarado Canyon. Hired by Colonel Ed Fletcher (for whom the Fletcher Hills community of El Cajon is named), Murray built a dam 117-feet-tall and 870 feet wide, inundating the old earthen dam.

Murray's efforts resulted in the creation of a 198-acre reservoir, capable of storing 4,818 acre feet of water. Today, the source of the water no longer is the rainfall that makes its way to Alvarado Canyon. Waters from the Colorado River and from the California Water Project are transported hundreds of miles to Los Angeles, where they are mixed by the Metropolitan Water District and sent to San Diego via pipelines operated by the San Diego County Water Authority. The Spanish style building and tower adjacent to the lake are part of a filtration plant that helps to purify water serving approximately 400,000 users within the City of San Diego.

Hikers enjoy 3.23 miles of paved trails around most of the lake's perimeter, with the path to the filtration plant closed to the public because of security concerns. From the trails, numerous waterfowl can be spotted by boaters, pedestrians, and bicyclists. These include many varieties of ducks, heron, egret, geese, and coots, and such small mammals as squirrels and rabbits. Sometimes coyotes are also spotted. The lake is also the venue for fishing and boating. Many photographers have found the reflection of nearby 1,592-foot-high Cowles Mountain in the lake to be an irresistible subject. Cowles Mountain is the highest peak within San Diego's city limits.

While all members of the public enjoy Lake Murray's charms, the lake has particular attraction on Rosh Hashanah afternoon for several Jewish congregations in the eastern portion of San Diego.

Members of Temple Emanu-El, which is Reform; Tifereth Israel Synagogue, which is Conservative; and the trans-denominational Hillel House of San Diego State University, gather on that day for Tashlich services during which—no doubt, to the delight of fish and water fowl — humans, in an act of atonement, cast their bread upon the waters to symbolize the jettisoning of sins and the hope for a fresh start for the New Year.

Over the years, Jews with a keen sense of humor have suggested that certain bread products are best matched with specific sins. *J Weekly*, published in San Francisco, has compiled a list: For ordinary sins: White bread. For complex sins: Multigrain. For twisted sins: Pretzels. For sins of indecision: Waffles. For sins committed in haste: Matzah. For sins of chutzpah: Fresh bread. For substance abuse: Stoned wheat. For use of heavy drugs: Poppy seed. For committing auto theft: Caraway. For tasteless sins: Rice cakes. For ill-temperedness: sourdough. For silliness and eccentricity: Nut bread. For not giving full value: Shortbread. For excessive irony: Rye bread. For particularly dark sins: Pumpernickel. For dressing immodestly: Tarts. For causing injury to others: Tortes. For being holier than thou: Bagels. For dropping in without notice: Popovers. For overeating: Stuffing. For raising your voice too often: Challah. For pride and egotism: Puff pastry. For sycophancy: Brownies. For laziness: Any long loaf. For trashing the environment: Dumplings. For telling bad jokes/ puns: Corn bread.

The Tashlich services are an important outdoor social event for the Jewish communities of eastern San Diego and its bordering cities of Santee, El Cajon, La Mesa, and Lemon Grove. Given San Diego's beautiful weather in the fall, many families combine the services with picnics.

From left, Rabbis Martin Lawson, Devorah Marcus, and Leonard Rosenthal lead Tashlich service at Lake Murray.

From the Lake Murray portion of the Lake Murray/70th Street, Exit 11, proceed on Lake Murray Boulevard, until you reach a traffic light at Kiowa Street. Turn left onto Kiowa and drive into the park's entrance.

-San Diego Jewish World, December 17, 2015

36. Exit 11
San Diego Sexual Medicine Clinic

Alvarado Hospital Medical Center

SAN DIEGO — One might wonder what led to Dr. Irwin Goldstein becoming the head of what is believed to be the first, and perhaps only, hospital-accredited sexual medicine practice in the United States. Was it his undergraduate background in engineering? Or was it the fact that while he was interning in urology, his mentor at University Hospital in Boston, Dr. Robert J. Krane, allowed him to scrub in for a penile implant procedure, which then was a novelty?

Or perhaps it was the fact that an Iranian Jewish acquaintance from his Boston days, Dr. Pedram Salimpour, along with his brother, Pejman, completed the purchase of Alvarado Hospital here in San Diego in 2007 and invited Goldstein to establish the San Diego Sexual Medicine practice in the medical offices next door at 5555 Reservoir Drive, where he could combine his own research with knowledge from numerous fields including urology, gynecology, psychology, pharmacology, and physical therapy.

Goldstein, whose 5,700-square-foot research center and clinic employs a diverse staff, including his wife Sue as program director, says many of the factors were serendipitous that led him to become a recognized authority in the field of sexual medicine, founding editor of *The Journal of Sexual Medicine,* and head of the non-profit Institute for Sexual Medicine.

The doctor had grown up in Montreal, from where he was recruited by Brown University in Providence, Rhode Island, to play college hockey. His major was electrical biomedical engineering, which while fascinating didn't appear to offer many jobs. So, he returned to Montreal and enrolled in the medical school at McGill University. Sue, whom he had met and married in Providence, moved to Canada with him. He did an internship in Montreal, followed by a surgical internship and urological residency in Boston.

With his engineering background, Goldstein suggested, "I had a different perspective than 99.9 percent of all the people working with me. Knowing what was wrong was really important versus saying, 'Tell me how to manage it and I will manage it.'"

In 1976, his two areas of study—engineering and urology—seemed to come together when Krane asked him to assist on a penile implant. "I had never seen one before," he recalled. "A penile implant has a series of devices that takes a man who has erectile dysfunction and by the insertion of the implant, he has a rigid penis whenever he would like. I was totally fascinated by the procedure and at the end of the procedure, I said that 'I have to do this for a living.'"

The amazing thing, continued Goldstein, was that in the 1970s very few people could answer the question, "'How does an erection even occur?' It wasn't studied; it wasn't emphasized" yet male erections occurred "obviously quite often. It's estimated that there are 100 million acts of sexual intercourse every 24-hour period on our planet." When a penis can't become or stay erect, "this is called erectile dysfunction, which happens often in aging, yet in 1976 no one knew the physiology of how that worked."

Assisting Krane, Goldstein learned the field so well that he won a three-year grant from the National Institutes of Health to study erectile dysfunction. "Since then I've been doing nothing else. I was in Boston for approaching 35 years, and as time went on I got more and more involved and more and more specialized, and I really wished and wanted to be separate from urology."

He explained that a sexual medicine clinic needs a "sex therapist, a physical therapist, nurse practitioners, and clinical researchers" in addition to a physician such as himself, and for a department head in the field of urology, these personnel expenditures might seem less important than such other priorities as penile cancer, bleeding, urinary stones and so forth.

Therefore establishing a sexual medicine practice at Alvarado Hospital was "a dream come true," Goldstein said. Realization of that dream became even more profound when he began instructing classes in sexual medicine at UCSD's Medical School. Until then, sexual medicine simply was a subject rarely taught to future doctors.

Elsewhere, "Doctors don't get exposure to this; patients are embarrassed and humiliated and just assume that doctors know, but doctors don't, so it is an uncomfortable condition on both sides of the doctor-patient relationship."

Dr. Goldstein at first was highly skeptical of the drug sildenafil citrate, later commercialized as Viagra. "I was exposed to it in 1994 as a potential therapy. We didn't think it was possible that you could take an oral pill" for erectile dysfunction because "70 percent of the penis is muscle and it sits in a contracted state all day until it goes to a relaxation state, in which case (blood can flow into the penis and) you get an erection. So to induce an erection you need what is called a muscle relaxant. In the usual scenario, we were injecting drugs through the skin of the penis into the tissue to achieve this relaxation. Were these drugs to go systemically (throughout the entire body), they would have caused lowering of blood pressure and fainting, and that is not what you want when you are sexually active."

So, back then Goldstein was of the opinion that an oral pill simply would not be practical. But in 1985, sildenafil citrate was administered for patients with angina, and unexpectedly "Those patients at night would get morning erections. Then it was good science that asked, 'Why did they have the erections?' The enzyme that this drug blocked was specifically located in the penis. Nobody knew that before. So, you could take a pill and although it went everywhere, its effect was more pronounced in the penis where that enzyme was focused. So there is serendipity in science."

Viagra got people talking and joking about erectile dysfunction, and in 1998, on a *Larry King Live* television show on which Goldstein also was a guest, former U.S. Senator and GOP Presidential Candidate Bob Dole mentioned, during a discussion, that following his radical surgery for prostate cancer, he too had developed erectile dysfunction which he counteracted with Viagra.

Goldstein said to have a man of such national prominence discuss openly a sexual problem was a fabulous opportunity to enable others. "It was an amazing event. He got hired by Pfizer (the drug company that produces Viagra) and he flew to different places to talk about it. It was pretty eventful."

As a sexual medicine physician, Goldstein treats both men and women for problems related to healthy sexual intercourse.

"We have something like 26 therapies approved for men, but for women we have only two therapies for sexual pain and one that has been recommended by the FDA Advisory Committee for approval for low desire," Goldstein rued. "We are pre-Viagra in the female world. Hopefully that will change; we have a good chance that will change" with a drug for women.

"The most common female problem is lack of interest," Goldstein said. "Women sort of do duty sex. They preserve the relationship by having sexual relationships, but they don't initiate it. They don't have any desire to have sexual activity. With research, we have found that women who have no interest can have that condition for many reasons. There is a subgroup of women who have that condition because of chemical changes in their brain, much like depression is the result of chemical differences in the brain or that Parkinson's disease involves missing dopamine in the brain. So, in that construct, there is a drug out there (now being tested) which has the ability to rearrange the balance and improve sexual function."

As urologists tended to overlook male sexual dysfunction, said Goldstein, gynecologists often know very little about female sexual problems. He said that when gynecologists do pelvic examinations, they rarely express any interest in the condition of a woman's clitoris, labia or hymen – or anything about a woman's external genitalia – but instead will go focus on the cervix and then will examine the ovaries and the uterus.

Besides not being trained to treat women's sexual dysfunction, another reason for the reluctance of gynecologists may be that "it takes a lot of time" to discuss such matters with patients, "and you don't yet have any therapies for women that are approved by the government."

With all the commercials on television about erectile dysfunction or vaginal itching, I asked Dr. Goldstein if he believed people were becoming less embarrassed by discussions of sexual issues.

He responded that cultural influences, including religion, can have a lot to do with just how candid men and women are willing to be about their sexual problems.

For example, he said, he knows of people from the Indian sub-continent where "their society does not believe in premarital sexual activity. The vast majority of them are in relationships that have been arranged, that they have seen each other naked for the first time only on their honeymoon, so it is challenging. How do you have conversations about sex? I have a patient whose wife left him to go back to India because he was impotent. Her family won't allow her to remain married to him if they can't have any children. Yet, it is a *medical* condition. How often would someone say. 'You can't marry John because he has hyper-tension'? Yet for this medical condition, they say it."

Jews, in contrast, tend to be more open about sexual issues. Goldstein referred to the concept that marital sex on Shabbat is a special blessing, one which makes both parties closer to God. "This concept of sexual intimacy is not espoused in most other religions and cultures," he said. "There is a lot of guilt, and grief, concern and worry that someone is watching over you and you are doing something dirty and evil. That is a more traditional view of sex as opposed to embracing it and saying you are closest to God while doing it."

Our interview concluded with Goldstein offering some general advice for people who have problems enjoying sexual relations.

"I think the best advice that I can give them is 'Go find treatment for it.' It is crazy not to do anything about it. I think the vast majority of people who have some sexual dysfunction can break down relationships because they think they can't do anything about it. There are health providers who can't help them so they think there is nothing that can be done. I would venture that there is a lot that can be done."

Dr. Irwin Goldstein, pioneer in sexual medicine

From 70th Street, Exit 11, turn north onto Alvarado Road (the frontage street) and turn left at Reservoir Drive.

-San Diego Jewish World, December 24, 2015

37. Exit 11

D.Z. Akin's Delicatessen

SAN DIEGO — Thanks to a chopped liver recipe and some bold flirting, San Diego has in D.Z. Akin's one of the county's most popular Jewish delis. Created in 1980 by Zvika and Debbie Akin, the eatery expanded in increments from a 48-seat deli to a 225-seat restaurant, bakery, catering company and gift shop. So often did D.Z. Akin's take over the floor space of a next-door neighbor at the shopping center at 6930 Alvarado Road, it could be thought of as "the restaurant that ate San Diego."

It all started in the late 1970s when Debbie Epstein, who grew up at Tifereth Israel Synagogue in San Diego and moved to Los Angeles to attend UCLA and live with her aunt, was working as a representative for her family's wholesale clothing business. Based at the California Clothing Market in downtown L.A., she called upon men's stores to sell to them shirts, belts, ties, and sportswear. Her aunt noticed that near the intersection of Pico Boulevard and Overland Avenue at G&L Kosher Meats worked a young, single butcher, Zvika Akin, who had immigrated as a teen-ager from a village outside Jaffa, Israel. Check him out, she advised Debbie.

So Debbie did, her pretext being that she wanted to purchase a kosher chicken. Zvika asked if she wanted the giblets too, to which Debbie replied she wasn't sure about the giblets but she wished that there was enough liver in that chicken for her to prepare one of her favorite recipes.

Quick on the uptake, Zvika offered to throw in some extra chicken livers if she would let him taste her creation. That was on a Friday, and the following Monday, Debbie brought some chopped liver for him to sample. He loved it, and she later confided, "It's all in the fried onions. That is what makes it delicious. Most delis don't bother to fry the onions." Today, Debbie's chopped liver is one of hundreds of items on the menu of D.Z. Akin's, popularly known as DeeZee's.

Debbi and Zvika were married in 1977 by Rabbi Aaron Gold of Tifereth Israel Synagogue. After Zvika's rent at the Los Angeles butcher shop was raised $1,000 per month by a lawyer who purchased the property, he decided to sell the business. The couple then decided since Debbie could cook and Zvika knew his meats, maybe they should consider opening a delicatessen. Having no background in the restaurant business, they visited all the well-known delis in Los Angeles, asking for advice, and checking out the pricing on their menus.

The advice was not positive. "'Don't do it, you don't know what you are talking about, you are two stupid kids'—that was basically the advice that we got," remembered Debbie. "Honestly," said Zvika, "they were not very far from the truth. Honestly, other dummies would never have made it."

"Nine out of ten restaurants go out of business," Debbie said. "Of the ten that stay in business most just make a living."

Although Debbie's parents, Bernie and Ethel Epstein and her brother, Steven, were initial investors, after three months of no profits in 1980, they thought they saw the handwriting on the wall and declined to invest any more money. "We had to come up with the money ourselves," remembered Debbie. "Had Zvika's father not passed away in Israel, we would not have had any more money to put into it and we would have gone out of business, just like the rest of the world."

So, they kept at it, seemingly 24 hours a day, setting up in the storeroom an area for their infant son Neil's crib, so they could work at the restaurant night and day.

Growth was not planned; from the original idea of a take-out deli, the restaurant began to evolve in their minds. "If they wanted a pound of corned beef and they wanted to sit down and have a corned beef sandwich, we could put in a couple of tables and let them have a table there," Debbie recalled thinking "From that, it was what if they wanted corned beef and eggs? Well, we'll make corned beef and eggs.

What if they wanted something else?"

"Even though we knew nothing," interjected Zvika.

"We knew nothing. I wasn't a waitress. He wasn't a cook," said Debbie, smiling at her business partner and ex-husband from whom she has been divorced since 2008. "But the restaurant just evolved. We created a monster, we had no idea what we were doing."

Well, what was it that they were doing wrong at first? I asked

"Everything!" said Zvika.

"The one thing we were was good cooks, but knowing how to cook, and knowing when to hold and when to throw away, and to please the customer yet stick to the plan of the menu and not allowing yourself to be manipulated, because you have to stay consistent, all that was difficult. And then, managing employees, not letting them run all over you, dealing with personalities. It was just growing pains, what we did in our first couple of month versus now. I have to tell you, it is easier now with 150 employees, than it was with three. It is so consistent. Now we can practically do it with our eyes closed in comparison to what it was then."

In the first expansion, D.Z. Akin's went from 48 seats to 100; in the second from 100 to 150; and in the third from 150 to 225. Next came a gift shop. And eventually the Akins purchased the entire strip mall, including the building across the parking lot. They make certain to rent to businesses that don't require a lot of parking, so restaurant patrons don't have to compete against their tenants.

Zvika said it was only after the second expansion, to 150 seats, that the restaurant began to make some money. The reason, he explained, is with greater sizes, the restaurant could make greater economies.

"People think this is a gold mine," said Debbie, "but in fact it is a very difficult business."

She said that whereas a steak restaurant can mark up the price of its steaks at a high margin; patrons would never pay such amounts for delicatessen sandwiches and platters. So, Akins has to work within a certain price point. To open potential new profit streams, the restaurant expanded into catering, carry-out delicatessen, carry-out bakery and a gift shop. Debbie says she calls the gift shop "our bar."

"At other restaurants when you have to wait for seats, you can go to the bar. Here, people go to the gift shop."

The secret for the restaurant's popularity, the Akins agreed, was "persistence and consistency."

"I had only one goal, that the customers left with smiles on their faces and rubbing their tummies and saying, 'My God, that was delicious' – like they were coming over for dinner to my house. I never thought about money. To this day, I don't think about money."

"Smiles on their faces" may also explain some of the accoutrements in the restaurant. The wait staff wear T-shirts with Yiddishisms. The wall is covered with pictures of celebrities who have eaten in the restaurant and with cartoons by Ivan Goldstein, who used to publish them in *Israel Today* which metamorphosed into the now defunct *San Diego Jewish Times*. The cartoons transmit some Yiddish restaurant humor, which sometimes consists of customers complaining and waiters responding with a snappy come-back.

Debbie said the cartoons capture the Jewish flavor of DZ Akin's – even though its customer base has been changing. Once perhaps 90 percent Jewish, only about 50 percent of the customers today are Jews – a reflection of changing demographics of the surrounding Lake Murray and La Mesa areas as well as the growing popularity of Yiddish culture among non-Jews, Debbie said.

Which brought to mind two of Debbie's favorite stories about the deli, which serves kosher-style meats as well as non-kosher meats.

"My favorite is the lady who yelled at me. She called up and yelled that we need to put a disclaimer on our clam chowder soup because we put bacon in it, and bacon is not kosher. How dare we serve clam chowder with bacon!"

The woman hung up before Debbie could explain that clam chowder is also non-kosher.

Another lady called before Passover to make certain that D.Z. Akin's served matzo with its meals.

Debbie assured the lady that, in fact, they are happy to put matzo alongside a helping of meats, or any other entrée, if that was desired. The woman was very happy, so happy in fact that she smothered Debbie with kisses when she came in, telling her how wonderful she was to have matzo on hand.

"Later on, I walked by her table, and saw she had bacon and eggs with a side of matzo! It's everything you can do not to laugh sometimes."

I asked when the Akins realized that their restaurant was here to stay and that they finally had made it.

"There is a thing called the Restaurant Association Awards," recounted Debbie. "It is like 1,000 people, and back in the 1990s we were up for 'Best Breakfast' and we won! And I've always been the one who has been pushed to the front because he (Zvika) is shy, so he pushed me, and I said 'you better be behind me because we are going to accept the award, and it was Jack White (a television broadcaster) who was giving out the awards. I was a nervous wreck. I almost didn't want to win the award because I would have to get up before 1,000 people and give a speech, yet. He pushed me and we got up there, and I was stunned. He (White) gives me the award, and the first thing I say is 'Well, I guess I better become a member of the Restaurant Association' and the audience died laughing, thank God. It broke the ice. Then when we left, the Ghios (long-established restauranteurs) of Anthony's, and others were coming over to us, like we won the Academy Award, we couldn't believe it. People were coming up, congratulating us, saying 'We love your restaurant,' and these were all the people who are in the business. It was something else.

"And we got into the car, and he looks over to me and he says, 'It's a long way from Abu Kabir,' his little shtetl in Jaffa, where he's from. He is in his little Mercedes, he has his award, people are congratulating him, he was a super star, and that was the day I knew we arrived."

Now thinking of eventual retirement and someday turning the business over to sons Elan and David (older son Neil went into the real estate business), the Akins were asked if they had ever considered opening delis in other parts of San Diego County, and cashing in on their popularity.

"We can hardly run this one," said Debbie. "That is why you don't really see chains of delis. It is a very hard business. The menus are so big."

"So many items," agreed Zvika. "Very difficult."

"And as we are getting older, who wants that kind of stress? Elan and David think they would like to have another restaurant, but they have no idea," said Debbie.

"They don't know what they don't know yet," agreed Zvika.

"Exactly," said Debbie.

Debbi and Zvika Akin, the D and Z of D.Z. Akin's

From 70th Street Exits, proceed north on Alvarado Road, which is the frontage road, and turn right into the D.Z. Akin's parking lot.

-*San Diego Jewish World, December 31, 2015*

38. Exit 11
The Former
Beth Tefilah Synagogue

The former Beth Tefilah is now a Korean church

SAN DIEGO — Today the structure at 69th and Mohawk Streets houses the Skyline Fellowship Korean Church but when it was constructed in 1971 it was the home of Congregation Beth Tefilah (House of Prayer), a Conservative Jewish congregation headed by Rabbi Samuel Penner, who was known not only as a spiritual leader but as a humorist and a scholar.

Penner worked closely with the architectural firm of Henry N. Miller & Associates to design the 600-seat A-shaped sanctuary that, in its triangular shape, paid homage to the portable Tabernacle that served Moses and the Israelites as they made their way through the Sinai. He was particularly involved in the designs of the congregation's stained-glass windows.

Twenty stained-glass windows, each 20 feet high, had scenes of Jewish history starting with Creation, and working their way through major incidents in the

Torah, through experiences in Europe, to Jewish settlement in America, the founding of Israel, and the plight of Soviet Jews in the days when those wishing to emigrate routinely were refused permission and then treated like enemies of the state.
Another two windows illustrated Shabbat and the cycle of Jewish holidays.

In fact, at the January 3, 1971, groundbreaking ceremony for this edifice, the
Polish-born, Bronx-raised Penner contrasted the joy of Jewish life in the United
States with the misery of Jewish life in the Soviet Union. Beth Tefilah's construc-
tion, he said, "is symbolic of the right to speak out and demand justice in America."

In addition to the sanctuary, the Beth Tefilah complex also contained a library, a facility for kosher receptions, and 10 classrooms. Education was a special
concern of Rabbi Penner, who himself was a childhood protégé, attending CCNY
during his early teens, remembered Marlene Greenstein, who served as Beth Tefilah's religious school principal.

Greenstein said a lower grade school and an upper grade school founded
during Rabbi Penner's administration were forerunners of such communal institutions as the San Diego Jewish Academy and Hebrew High School. She explained
that Penner's Conservative Synagogue was unable to sustain the two schools by itself—particularly when some of its students came from non-member families—
but the enthusiasm Penner had created while they were open helped fuel the movement for permanent community institutions.

"Rabbi Penner was a remarkable, brilliant person," Greenstein kvelled. "His
sermons were so brilliant and inspirational that I tried not to miss any. I always
thought that he should publish those sermons. And he was an excellent cantor as
well."

When she and her husband Herbert first moved to San Diego, she recalled,
they had planned to join Tifereth Israel Synagogue, which was the largest, oldest
and most established Conservative synagogue in the area. However, "Sylvia and
Jerry Weissman, who welcomed us to the neighborhood, came over with a box of
rugelach and persuaded us to come to a service at Beth Tefilah. When Rabbi Penner began to speak, I just knew that this was the right place for us."

That was before the edifice at Mohawk and 69th Streets was built, she said.
The congregation met in a decrepit former church building that was falling apart,
and "He inspired people to build the synagogue that still stands there."

"Oh," she added in an interview, "did Rabbi Penner have charisma! He was
oozing with charisma and personality."

Greenstein shared that "the proudest moment in my life was when Rabbi
Penner introduced me as the principal. I was in heaven. Imagine, I was Rabbi
Penner's principal! I couldn't get over that."

Penner, the scholar, taught a course at UCSD on Judaism, which so captivat-
ed student Mary Soltz with his patient exploration of the stories of the Torah that
she asked him more than a semester later if she could study with him for conversion. Today, in 2015, Mary is the rebbetzin at the Reconstructionist Congregation

Mvakshe Derekh (Pathseeker) in Scarsdale, N.Y. Her longtime husband, Rabbi Ned Soltz, joined that congregation after serving 36 years as the pulpit rabbi at Congregation Beth Shalom (House of Peace) in Arlington, Texas.

Much of Rabbi Penner's teachings were later encapsulated in his book, *The Four Dimensions of Paradise*, published posthumously by his widow, Sheba. He explained in that book that the Torah may be read on four levels: The literal, the metaphorical, the ethical, and the mystical.

A manuscript, now with Penner's other papers in the archives of the Jewish Theological Seminary in New York City, was entitled "A Jet Tour Through 4,000 Years of Jewish Humor."

Although by inclination Penner was a traditionalist, he was not averse to change. Congregant Roberta Dosick persuaded Penner to allow her to have an aliyah, arguing that whereas she had studied Torah for much of her life, the honor of going up to the bima to bless the Torah was denied to her and other women, yet extended to 13-year-old boys upon their bar mitzvahs.

Dosick, and her husband, Hyman, were the parents of Rabbi Wayne Dosick, who has served three congregations in San Diego County: Beth El (House of God), today in La Jolla; Beth Am (House of the People), today in Carmel Valley, and the Elijah Minyan (worshipers honoring the prophet Elijah), in Carlsbad.

Cancer and demographics worked against Beth Tefilah. After Penner was sidelined by cancer in 1985, the synagogue was served by a succession of rabbis, but none was able to attract the following that Penner, who died in 1986, had attracted. This was partially because of Penner's unsurpassed charisma, and partly because the Jewish population of San Diego County was then moving north – up the Interstate 5 to La Jolla, Carmel Valley, and the suburban coastal cities, and up the Interstate 15 to Rancho Penasquitos, Carmel Mountain, Rancho Bernardo, and Poway.

Meanwhile, in rented quarters in Mission Valley, another Conservative congregation – Adat Ami (Congregation of My People) Synagogue – was struggling to attract members. Its membership was an amalgam of people who lived in the downtown, Hillcrest, and Mission Hills neighborhoods, and Mexican-born Jews who traveled from all over the county to be with their Spanish-speaking rabbi, Aaron Kopikis, who had been trained at Argentina's Jewish Theological Seminary affiliate before occupying pulpits in Mexico.

With one congregation having a building to sell, and the other having a loyal core of English- and Spanish-speaking members, merger discussions were complex. Besides allocation of financial responsibilities, negotiations touched on such subjects as what to name the congregation. At one point, the two parties played with finding an acceptable merged name such as Adat Tefilah, or Beth Ami, but ultimately they decided to make a break from the past with a new name. They chose Ohr Shalom (Light of Peace) and, after moving from rented quarters to rented quarters, Ohr Shalom was able to occupy its own building, thanks again to demography.

Al Shelden, a former president of Beth Tefilah who later became a president of Ohr Shalom, said that the 22 stained glass windows remain in the old Beth Tefilah building, but the purchase agreement with the Korean church stipulated that if the church should ever decide to replace those windows, ownership of the original windows would revert to the synagogue.

Asked what he remembers best about Beth Tefilah, he said that it was where he and his wife Marilyn raised their daughters, who are today living in Los Angeles and known by their married names, Gwen Rosenthal and Eileen Katz. "It is where they got the love of Judaism, and it always felt like home. Beth Tefilah always welcomed kids, and our kids benefitted from that a lot."

Another memory: "Rabbi Penner announced his retirement the day I was installed as president." That was just a coincidence. In the 13 years between Penner's retirement and Beth Tefilah's closing, Rabbis Yaacov Rone and Michael Manson served the congregation full time, Rabbi Akiva Gerstein divided his time between San Diego and Los Angeles, and a future rabbi, Israel Vana, who had assisted Rabbi Penner as a Torah reader and b'nai mitzvah teacher, continued in those capacities.

The Reform Congregation Beth Israel (House of Israel), San Diego's oldest and largest congregation, followed its congregants north, relocating from its historic temple at the corner of Third Avenue and Laurel Street, near Balboa Park, to a large campus featuring Jerusalem-style architecture in La Jolla.

Eventually, Ohr Shalom Synagogue moved into the Temple Beth Israel building, in the process helping to save the historic building where many community events had been held between the mid-1920s and the turn of the 21st century. The merged congregation also renovated the interior of the beautiful old building.

The current rabbi of Ohr Shalom, Scott Meltzer, had grown up in the Reform movement in San Diego, so Beth Tefilah's successor congregation has a hometown feel to it.

···

From 70th Street Exit, proceed south to El Cajon Boulevard, turn right, and turn right again on 69th Street. Former synagogue is at the corner of Mohawk Street.

···

-San Diego Jewish World, January 7, 2016

39. Exit 12

Costco

Costo in La Mesa, California
(Photo: Shor M. Masori)

LA MESA, California — As Costcos go, the wholesale warehouse at 8125 Fletcher Parkway in La Mesa is not much different from other Costco warehouses in the United States and around the world. However, by stopping here for a moment (and who doesn't like lower prices on an endless variety of items?), we have the opportunity to reflect on the such people as Sol Price, Robert Price, Jim Sinegal, and Jeffrey Brotman. All but Sinegal are Jewish community members.

The idea of the big box warehouse club started with Sol Price, who developed the concept with his Fedmart chain, and later honed it to a skill with his Price Clubs. In essence, the secret behind his success--which was amplified by his son Robert Price--was keeping the profit margin low and the sales volume high. For consumers, who paid an annual membership fee, the difference between Price Club prices and those at other stores made Price Club membership a highly-sought passport to bargains. Price believed in paying his employees well and he encouraged them to join a union, with which he bargained cordially and worked collegially. The result was that Price Club employees were much higher paid than people in similar jobs at other "big box" wholesalers (Walmart for example) and there was far less turnover.

Sinegal, who grew up here in La Mesa, started learning the "big box ware-house" business at Fedmart, and became one of the executives who developed un-der Sol Price's tutelage. After having served as an executive vice president of Price Club, Sinegal left to form his own consulting company, worked briefly with Build-ers Emporium, and later still, in 1982, he co-founded Costco with Jeffrey Brotman, son of Bernie Brotman, the founder of a Seattle-based chain of clothing stores.

As Price Clubs grew from its San Diego base, so too did Costco grow from its headquarters in Seattle. But Walmart was growing even faster and taking a larger piece of the market. In 1993, Price Club and Costco merged into PriceCostco, but philosophical differences between Sinegal and the Prices led to the latter leaving the company a year later. Thereafter Costco Wholesale, as the successor business run by Sinegal and Brotman was called, focused on sales in the U.S. The Prices meanwhile formed Price Enterprises, which delved into both wholesale sales and real estate development. PriceSmart, under Robert Price, developed new ware-house-style wholesale businesses in Latin America and the Caribbean.

All the men in this story--the Prices, Sinegal, and Brotman--became re-nowned as philanthropists, with Sinegal and Brotman focusing largely on the Pa-cific Northwest and the Prices devoting much of their attention and financial re-sources to the reinvigoration of City Heights, an urban neighborhood in San Diego where immigrants from many countries have lived amid deteriorating city infra-structure.

The Prices helped bring a new police station, library and recreational oppor-tunities to the area, as well as apartment and office complexes. The Prices also part-nered with San Diego State University and the San Diego Unified School District to develop programs for economically disadvantaged students. In Israel, mean-while, the Prices sponsored a similar effort to revitalize the Port of Jaffa, the largely Arab waterfront area serving the city of Tel Aviv. Price Charities also is a major donor to the Biblical Zoo in Jerusalem, a public facility visited by Israelis and tour-ists of every religion and ethnicity.

Up in the Seattle area, Brotman and his wife Susan are major donors to the Seattle Art Museum (SAM), and to the Pacific Northwest Ballet as well as to the University of Washington, on which Jeffrey serves as a regent.

From Fletcher Parkway, Exit 13, proceed on Fletcher Parkway to Costco, which will be on right hand side of the street.

40. Exit 13
The Yiddisher Cowboy

Rob Robboy

LA MESA, California — In the quaint shopping village on both sides of La Mesa Boulevard stands a furniture and accessory store that identifies itself as "Mostly Mission." A plaque further identifies the building at 8340 La Mesa Boulevard as the one-time home of The American Film Manufacturing Company, which was known by its symbol of a winged, flying letter 'A.' The plaque explains that the company produced silent films in 1911 and 1912 under the leadership of director Allan Dwan. A check of the Internet Movie Database (IMDb) reveals that among the numerous films Dwan made in 1911 was *The Yiddisher Cowboy*, although that one was made in Lakeside before Dwan moved to La Mesa.

In the process of researching this one-reel silent movie--in which a brand-new Jewish ranch hand, who is made sport of by "real" cowboys, turns the tables and becomes master of the bunkhouse--I learned that a musician who plays cello with the San Diego Symphony and who also had one of the earliest klezmer bands in San Diego, Ron Robboy, had decades ago encountered the American Film Manufacturing Company in what became a combined quest to learn more about his cultural background, Yiddish literature, and the historic experience of the American Jewish left.

Robboy's story began when he was rehearsing a work by Paul Ben-Haim in 1973 at San Diego's Central Library, then located on E Street in downtown San Diego. Cantor Henri Goldberg, who came to San Diego in his retirement years, suggested to the ensemble that for the performance they dress as Israelis, which may have meant no dress code at all. However, tenor Howard Fried, who was performing as a vocalist, was wearing a Mexican guayabera, and joked that he would wear a similar shirt at the performance and come as a Jewish cowboy. The idea of a "Jewish cowboy" struck many of the musicians as funny, but thinking about it, Robboy wondered whether indeed there had been Jewish cowboys. Maybe the term was not such an oxymoron, he remembered wondering.

As he left the subsequent concert to go to his car, Robboy was hailed by an elderly, Yiddish-accented man who identified himself as Saul Stock. He wanted to know if the cellist was any relation to the Yiddish writer A. Raboy. "What did he write?" inquired Robboy. "Jewish cowboy stories," Stock responded. The coincidence of Fried's and Stock's comments intrigued Robboy, but it wasn't until a year and a half later that his odyssey germinated. One morning in the pre-dawn hours, he awakened from a dream and asked his then companion, Molly, "Whatever happened to Flying-A Gasoline?" She didn't know but later, on that same day, she saw an advertisement in the *San Diego Reader* offering to sell a Flying-A Gasoline sign. Robboy drove from his home near North Park to Ocean Beach to purchase the 4-foot diameter sign for $10.

Why did he dream about 'Flying-A'? Robboy wondered. A friend and composer, Warren Burt, suggested that somewhere in his subconscious, Robboy was launching a quest to learn more about the writer "A. Raboy." The funny thing is that Raboy's first name, in English, was Isaac, but when he spelled it in Yiddish, it wasn't the transliteration for "Yitzhak" but rather one for "Ayzik" starting with the Hebrew letter *aleph* rather than with a *yud*. The *Aleph* thereupon became the "A" in "A. Raboy."

Subsequently, Robboy was alerted by another article in the *Reader* that the Flying A also was the symbol of the American Film Manufacturing Company, and that the company had made movies here. The article mentioned two films *The Yiddisher Cowboy* and *The Cowboy Socialist*. The IMDb website, quoting a synopsis from *Moving Picture World*, describes the plot of that film directed by Alan Dwan as follows:

> Ikey Rosenthal finds peddling a bum business in Wyoming. Consequently he is highly elated when John Darrow, foreman of the 'X Bar' outfit, offers him a job punching cows. He is fitted out at the ranch in chaps, spurs, sombrero, etc., and feels that he is a regular cowboy. On his first appearance in

his new outfit the boys work their game of gun music on him and, in this instance, are treated to a genuine Yiddisher dance. Ikey is very angry, but bides his time until he can even up the score. He learns the work on the ranch and one day succeeds in roping a cow, thinking he has roped a steer. Payday the boys follow their time-honored custom and go to town to celebrate. Ikey, however, with true business instinct, remains at the ranch and, during the cowboy's absence, gets out his old peddling pack and sets up a pawn shop in a corner of the ranch yard. The boys return from town broke and when Ikey shows them his pawn shop they decide to 'hock' their guns. Ikey gets possession of every gun on the ranch and then starts to do a little shooting himself. The boys scatter at his approach and the Yiddisher cowboy is monarch of all he surveys.

No copies of the movie are known to remain in existence, but in the same issue of *Moving Picture World* a still life photo from the movie was featured along with an advertisement that began: "'Yiddisher' and 'Cowboy' do not jibe. There are complications uproariously laugh-provoking..."

In April 2011, one hundred years after the film was made, Robboy delivered to the Western Jewish Studies Conference in San Diego an analysis of the film in which he focused on the perceived "oxymoron" of a Yiddish cowboy.

On the one hand, Robboy wrote, there is:

the cowboy, the weather-beaten icon of self-sufficiency: the leather-faced, rugged individualist; the emblematic strong *silent* type. Yes, the man of few words who knows how to live off the land, he is at home anywhere and everywhere on the land.

On the other hand, Robboy continued:

there is the Jew, the pre-Zionist one, that is, the *goles*-Jew of Diasporic Exile; powerless, puny, pale-faced. And though he or she may be the world's archetype for one who is at home *nowhere* on the land, he or she is anything but the man or the woman of few words.

Looking at the photo, Robboy suggested that it

reveals a short, stubble-faced outsider, hopelessly out of place among the threatening he-men surrounding him. His hat is too small, and his pants are too big, which taken together...would seem to symbolize his sexual inadequacy. In his confrontation with the cowboy to his left, he's offering a paltry and tangled lasso in response to the cowboy's six-shooter (one being the penetrating object and the other the potential receptacle.) The derby, baggy pants, and whiskered near-beard were conventions of the vaudeville 'Hebe' comic, an analog of the blackface entertainer, who was a legacy of

the invidious American minstrel tradition in which (usually) white per-
formers would mimic and exaggerate racial stereotypes of African Americans....

A scholar who briefly considered *The Yiddisher Cowboy* in her book *The Jew
in American Cinema* was Prof. Patricia Erens of the Communications Arts and
Sciences Department at Dominican University. In a telephone interview, she char-
acterized the film to me as one in which an underdog gains his revenge, a "Jewish
revenge" story if you will.

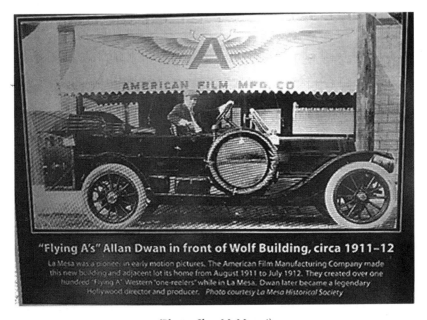

"Flying A's" Allan Dwan in front of Wolf Building, circa 1911–12
La Mesa was a pioneer in early motion pictures. The American Film Manufacturing Company made
this new building and adjacent lot its home from August 1911 to July 1912. They created over one
hundred "Flying A" Western "one-reelers" while in La Mesa. Dwan later became a legendary
Hollywood director and producer. *Photo courtesy La Mesa Historical Society*

(Photo: Shor M. Masori)

Dwan was not a Jew, and his characterization of the Jew is one of someone
who prevails by being a pawnbroker--a stereotype that might be considered anti-Semitic, according to Erens.

Robboy related that he interviewed Dwan by telephone in 1979, two years
before the latter's death. Dwan said he typically went to a location--in this case the
hills behind the now defunct Lakeside Inn, where his company was based before
moving to La Mesa--and would improvise a script based on the surroundings. For
example, if he spotted a rugged cliff, he might have the hero--usually played by J.
Warren Kerrigan--fight with a bad guy up there, then build a script around the
scene for a 10-minute movie also featuring Pauline Bush, whom Dwan later married and divorced.

Asked how he came up with *The Yiddisher Cowboy,* Dwan wisecracked to Robboy that it was "in honor of Kerrigan's nose." Robboy didn't take the snarky answer for fact; for one, Kerrigan played a ranch hand in that movie, not the Jewish cowboy--who was played by a much shorter man, not identified in the credits. Secondly, the size of Kerrigan's nose was ordinary. And third, if Dwan had intended the film as a slur on the Jews, there was a much more likely target. Before joining The American Film Manufacturing Company, Dwan worked for a film company named Essanay--which stood for S and A, the initials of partners George K. Spoor and Gilbert M. "Bronco Billy" Anderson. Bronco Billy starred in 1903 in what is considered the first great silent western, *The Great Train Robbery.* But Gilbert "Bronco Billy" Anderson was a double pseudonym; in reality "Bronco Billy" was Anderson, and Anderson actually was Max Aronson, a real-life Jew who played a cowboy!

Robboy noted that Dwan went on to become a successful Hollywood director of such silent movies as *Robin Hood* with Douglas Fairbanks; and talkies like *Heidi* and *Rebecca of Sunnybrook Farm,* both starring Shirley Temple; *Suez* with Tyrone Power and Loretta Young; *The Three Musketeers* with Don Ameche and the Ritz Brothers; *The Sands of Iwo Jima* with John Wayne; and *Cattle Queen of Montana* starring Barbara Stanwyck and future United States President Ronald Reagan.

∗   ∗   ∗

Robboy's research didn't stop with the Dwan's *The Yiddisher Cowboy,* far from it. He learned that in 1909 another film of similar ilk was made in New York State. In this one, by Bison Films, a Jewish peddler heroically saves a stagecoach under attack by Indians, but we learn it is only a dream; after a hard day, the peddler had fallen asleep against a wall on which there was a poster for a movie western.

Digging into A. Raboy's life, Robboy learned that about the same time that the two *Yiddisher Cowboy* movies were being made, Raboy who had studied agriculture at the Baron de Hirsch school in Woodbine, New Jersey, obtained for himself around 1910 a job on a ranch in North Dakota, where utilizing his knowledge of animal husbandry he tended to the rancher's prize stallion.

This experience was the basis for a Raboy novella titled *Herr Goldenbarg* (1914) in which a Jew from the East comes to work for a successful Jewish rancher and promptly falls in love with his niece. Robboy, who researched the novel, explained that this made the rancher happy because he wanted to pass on the ranch that he built to a Jewish son-in-law. However, it made the non-Jewish son of a neighbor very angry because he also had his eye on the niece. The success of the Jewish rancher also was a cause of envy, resulting in an outbreak of anti-Semitism. The situation was calmed when Goldenbarg gave a speech to his neighbors underscoring their common humanity. But not all the hopes and dreams of the rancher were fulfilled; his niece and the young ranch hand decided to start new lives as kibbutzniks in pre-mandatory Palestine.

The novella, written in Yiddish, was first published in New York with editions following in Europe and even South America, and was made into a play for the Yiddish stage in New York City. Joseph Green, who acted in that play, went on to become a Yiddish film producer, his works including *Yidl Mitn Fidl* in which the great actress Molly Picon posed as a man.

Later in Raboy's career, he wrote an autobiographical novel, *Der Yidisher Kauboy* (The Jewish Cowboy, 1942), in which the plot closely resembled some of the experiences he outlined in *Herr Goldenbarg*. In this book, a Jewish ranch hand from the East makes himself invaluable to a wealthy non-Jewish ranch owner, who nevertheless seems to be pushing him to leave his employ and to file for a homestead. This makes the ranch hand uneasy—why should the man be so anxious to lose his best employee? Perhaps, the rancher was aware that his wife, like Potiphar's wife who threw herself at the biblical Joseph, had been making sexual advances toward the Jewish ranch hand, or perhaps the rancher's eagerness to be rid of the ranch hand was because of something more sinister. The novel did not resolve the issue; it ended with the ranch hand returning to the East to resume his old life, even as Raboy did.

After reading the novel, Robboy--who is of no known relation to Raboy despite the similarity of their name--decided to travel to western North Dakota to see if he could find any document indicating that Raboy had planned to become a homesteader. He couldn't find any such document, but he found something better. By comparing places and descriptions, he learned that the fictional rancher Hildenberg in the novel was based on a real-life rancher named Caldwell, who owned lots of property, but was murdered along with his mail-order bride by a ranch hand.

Meeting with a centenarian who lived at a ranch that adjoined Caldwell's, Robboy heard stories about Stark County, North Dakota, that paralleled stories that appeared in Raboy's Yiddish-language book, which the neighbor never read, nor had he ever heard of Raboy.

After Caldwell was murdered, law enforcement officers found disturbed dirt in his barn. When they dug in the barn, they found the bodies of numerous immigrants who had worked briefly for Caldwell, had homesteaded, and then "disappeared." Their homesteaded properties subsequently were purchased at auction by Caldwell. From this Robboy concluded that had A. Raboy stayed in North Dakota, instead of returning to his family on the East Coast, his might have been one of those bodies.

The question of why the ranch hand killed Caldwell and his bride remains a mystery. The perpetrator was institutionalized for life in the North Dakota State Hospital, and nothing in available records indicated that he had ever homesteaded. So there is no evidence that it was a matter of self-defense against the scheming Caldwell.

Remembering Raboy's story, Robboy suggested a possible solution to the mystery. Perhaps, he said, the mail order bride had made a pass at the ranch hand, even as she had made one at Raboy, and in the ensuing fight Caldwell was killed, but perhaps not before taking the life of his bed-hopping mail-order bride.

The odysseys of Raboy and Robboy were documented by the latter in the 1979 *Der Yiddisher Cowboy — A Film in English*, co-produced by Robboy with his friend Warren Burt.

....

From Spring Street, Exit 13A, proceed on Spring Street to left turn on La Mesa Boulevard.
....

-San Diego Jewish World, January 21, 2016

41. Exit 13

Grossmont Center

Grossmont Center is built on land owned by Adolph Levi's descendants

LA MESA, California — When you see the large "Grossmont Center" sign on the hillside above Jackson Drive, what images come to mind? How about the signs for "Macy's," "Wells Fargo" or "Daniel's Jewelers?"

I love Jewish history, so I think about a quartet of Jewish entrepreneurs--people like Adolph Levi, Nathan Straus, Isaias Hellman, and Joseph Sherwoo--all of whom are represented at the Grossmont Center.

I'll start with Adolph Levi, as he was mentioned in a previous chapter in this book about the Riverwalk Golf Course.

Levi came to San Diego in 1877 and went to work for his brother, Simon Levi, at the general merchandise wholesale firm of Steiner, Klauber and Levi, when San Diego was still a small town with lots of raw acreage for sale at affordable prices.

Eventually, he bought a ranch and established a small general store in Julian—the first one there of brick construction—but his wife, whom he met while attending a family wedding in Austria, felt too isolated in the back country of San Diego County. So Adolph moved to the City of San Diego, opening a livery stable and later investing heavily in real estate. He purchased huge swaths of land throughout San Diego County. Among his holdings were large portions of Mission Valley in which the Riverwalk Golf Corse today is a vestige, and he also owned the 125-acre piece of land in La Mesa on which the Grossmont Center stands.

In 2015, Levi's great-grandson Steve Cushman controlled those properties and announced plans to transform both into mixed residential and commercial developments.

A remarkable thing about Levi was not that he acquired so much land during San Diego's early days, but that generations of his family held onto it for it so long. The profit they may someday realize from that land may be many fold more than Levi ever could have imagined.

Macy's is one of the anchor tenants of the Grossmont Center and although the department store chain was started in Talbotton, Georgia, by R.H. Macy, it was propelled to worldwide fame by two German Jewish brothers, Isidor and Nathan Straus, who originally sold crockery at Macy's store and subsequently became his partners, and eventually his successors.

Isidor had a promising career, having served as a U.S. congressman and as president of the Educational Alliance, which sought to extend education to many underserved segments of society. U.S. President Grover Cleveland offered Isidor a job as his Postmaster General but he declined. Another brother, Oscar, however, would become U.S. Secretary of Commerce and Labor under President Theodore Roosevelt.

Isidor Straus and his wife Ida were among the 1,500 passengers and crew who drowned April 15, 1912, on the ill-fated maiden voyage of the RMS *Titanic.*

In addition to being a co-owner of Macy's, Isidor's brother, Nathan Straus, was an early advocate for the pasteurization of milk and also opened a treatment center in New Jersey for children with tuberculosis. At another of the Straus family businesses, Abraham & Straus, Nathan inaugurated a subsidized company cafeteria to help employees stretch their paychecks.

After the outbreak of World War I, Straus devoted much of his philanthropy to the aid of war orphans. He also was a major benefactor of the New York City Public Library.

A school for girls in Israel also was another of his philanthropies, along with the Nathan and Lina Straus Health Center in Jerusalem, which was later incorporated into Hadassah Medical Center.

The city of Netanya, Israel, was named in his honor, as was Rehov Straus in Jerusalem.

Another of the many establishments doing business in the Grossmont Center is Wells Fargo Bank, which thanks to years of their advertising may conjure up images of stage coaches hurtling through the Wild West--a driver and the "shotgun" guard riding up on the top, and, sitting inside, passengers being jostled by the hooves of teams of horses galloping over uneven, bandit-infested dirt roads.

One can also think of Isaias Hellman, who started his business career with a dry goods store in Los Angeles. Customers who had no other place to store their gold asked him to keep it for them in his safe. This led to him becoming partners with former California Governor John Downey and forming the Farmers and Merchants Bank in 1871, which made loans to such worthies as Harrison Gray Otis for the start-up *Los Angeles Times* and to Edward Doheny for oil drilling operations.

Hellman invested in various utilities, including an electric railroad with Henry Huntington, and also presided in 1872 over B'nai B'rith when that organization was building the Jewish community's first temple in Los Angeles. Like Adolph Levi after him, he purchased large tracts of land. He moved to Northern California to look after an investment in the Nevada Bank, and after he took that bank over, he was joined by such investors as blue jeans manufacturer Levi Strauss and Mayer Lehman, the latter of the Lehman Brothers.

In 1905, Hellman merged his Nevada Bank with Wells Fargo, and just a year later came the great California earthquake. Although some of the bank's buildings were destroyed, its vault was not and Wells Fargo remained open for business, which for a time Hellman transacted out of his home.

Banking *sachel* (know-how) ran in the blood of the Hellmans, three generations of whom directed the affairs of Wells Fargo.

On a smaller scale, but nevertheless impressive, was the success of Joseph Sherwood in creating the chain of Daniel's Jewelers throughout Southern California.

Sherwood had worked in jewelry stores for 17 years until the occasion arose in the economic expansion era after World War II when he was able to purchase another store in Bell Gardens, California.

He and his wife Helene extended credit to local residents who returned the favor with their loyalty. A generous man by nature, Sherwood could be counted on to make donations to charitable causes, increasing the esteem with which he was held. Gradually he was able to expand his operation to multiple locations. His sons, Howard and Larry, followed him into the business and they in turn were followed by Larry's son, David, who became the company's CEO, and by Howard's daughter, Laurie Bahar, who heads the Sherwood Family Foundation.

Under auspices of the Anti-Defamation League, the family established the Sherwood Prize for law enforcement officers in Southern California who promote inter-group understanding and multiculturalism. Additionally, the Sherwoods have been enthusiastic in their support of Jewish Family Service in Los Angeles.

In an interview with JFS, Joseph Sherwood explained: "My parents were always involved in the well-being of our community. We never had much money, but my father in particular, was very concerned with children going to bed hungry and older adults being properly cared for. Some of my earliest memories are of my father collecting food for hungry families. We barely had enough for ourselves, but still, he couldn't go to bed at night knowing someone was in need."

"Even when he was sick with cancer, my father was adamant that it was our responsibility to care for our neighbors – Jewish and non-Jewish. I lost my father when I was young, he was about 45 years old when he died, but what he instilled in me was one of the most valuable lessons a parent could ever teach a child. I learned about the importance of helping others. That advice brought me a lot of luck in my business and it helped me meet a lot of wonderful people but most importantly it brought me a lot of joy. There is no greater feeling than what comes from helping someone in need."

Daniel's Jewelers, the success story of Joseph Sherwood

Exit Grossmont Boulevard, Exit 13B, and turn left to Center.

-San Diego Jewish World, January 28, 2016

42. Exit 13

Chabad of East County

Rabbi Rafi Andrusier at former Chabad of East County headquarters

LA MESA, California — If I were to ask you what a pioneer looks like, perhaps you would describe him as a man wearing a coonskin hat, a buckskin jacket and pants, and moccasins. Maybe you would further imagine he'd have a horn of water at his side, a musket crossed over his chest, and a knife hanging from his belt.

Well, that's one kind of pioneer. The kind I'm thinking about generally wears black pants, a white dress shirt from which tzitzit emerge and dangle below his waist, and a yarmulke or black hat on his head. This kind of pioneer is a Chabad *shaliach*, or emissary, whose job as a rabbi is to reacquaint unaffiliated Jews and their families with Jewish belief and practice, and to offer a menu of supplemental Jewish programming to Jews who already are affiliated with other movements.

Like the Jewish merchants of the 19th century who struck out for the newly forming communities of the American West, moving here and moving there until they found fertile ground in which to put down roots, so too do Chabad emissaries sometimes move here and there, hoping to find just the right place to ignite passion for Judaism among unaffiliated Jews in the neighborhood. One of the places that Chabad of East County found temporary domicile was at 8693-B La Mesa Boulevard in a small strip shopping center. Chabad even had its name on the shopping center's marquis, but the demographics weren't right. An insufficient number of Jews lived within walking distance of the space, and so Chabad held its services in such San Diego neighborhoods as San Carlos and Del Cerro. Having since moved out of the La Mesa Boulevard space, the organization now is hoping to find a new, better located space, while continuing to conduct services in participants' homes.

Meet Rabbi Rafael "Rafi" Andrusier, and his Rebbetzin, Chaya Smoller Andrusier. Together, they have staked out the urban portion of San Diego's east county – specifically the eastern neighborhoods of San Diego, and the cities of La Mesa, El Cajon and Santee as an area in which to make their lives and to spread Jewish knowledge.

The Chabad movement studied this area before giving the couple the go ahead, aggregating its own list of Jews in the affected zip codes with another list supplied by the Jewish Federation of San Diego, and determining that there were at least 1,500 unaffiliated Jewish families in the area, well above the threshold for establishing a Chabad center, according to Andrusier.

At the same time, under the leadership of Rabbi Yonah Fradkin, the regional director of Chabad in San Diego County, the Andrusiers were scrutinized to determine whether their backgrounds as student emissaries and teachers in the Chabad movement indicated that they had the will and the follow-through to make a life-long commitment to the East County. You might say that the Andrusiers had an advantage going into this process: Chaya is the daughter of Rabbi and Rebbetzin Dovid and Rochel Smoller, longtime teachers at the Chabad Hebrew Academy in the Scripps Ranch neighborhood. Rabbi Fradkin had known the Smoller family for a long time, and was well aware that Chaya had come up through Chabad Hebrew Academy and went on to teach in a Chabad school in New York.

As Fradkin did not know Andrusier, he made inquiries about his record during various student assignments to countries such as Croatia, Peru, Greece, Russia and Australia, where Andrusier did such tasks as organizing seders, checking mezuzot to see if they were kosher, and inviting Jewish passersby to strap on tefillin and say a prayer – all part of Chabad's belief that if a Jew can be persuaded to do one mitzvah, he or she will go on to others. One summer assignment brought Andrusier to San Diego as a student, working with Rabbi and Rebbetzen Mendy and Bluma Rubenfeld of Chabad of Poway on a campaign to get people to check their mezuzot, so of course Rubenfeld also was consulted.

Andrusier had grown up in Staten Island, a short trip across the Verrazano Narrows Bridge to Brooklyn and the headquarters of the Chabad movement in that borough's Crown Heights section. His life revolved around the Chabad movement. The last Rebbe, Rabbi Menachem Mendel Schneerson, died while Andrusier was still a young boy, but he remembers those Sundays when the rebbe would hand out dollar bills to Jews who came from far and wide. "I also remember that after he had a stroke, he used to come out on the balcony" of Chabad's world headquarters at 770 Eastern Parkway, known affectionately in Chabad circles simply as "770."

While going to yeshiva, and participating in Chabad outreach programs, Andrusier decided that he wanted to be a *shaliach*, and let it be known that he would like to have a wife with similar ambitions. Through family connections, Rafi and Chaya were suggested for each other, but before they formally were introduced each family researched the child of the other – a process very similar to the one the couple later went through when they applied to become Chabad emissaries.

The reports about Chaya and Rafi were mutually satisfying, and so, in New York City, a meeting was arranged, in the lobby of a New York City hotel. By the time of their meeting, they knew quite a lot about each other, knew that both were serious about marriage, having a family, and establishing a Chabad Center. They talked and talked, and tired of sitting, they also strolled. Walking around, sightseeing, became a typical activity for their dating, during which conversations ranged from light topics to heavy ones.

Rafi didn't drop to one knee and propose to Chaya – that's not the way things are done in the Chabad movement. Before the Rebbe died, couples would go to him and ask for his blessing for their marriage. If he gave it, they were engaged; if not, some remedial activity might be necessary. Following the Rebbe's death, couples went to visit his gravesite or Ohel at a cemetery in Queens. When they emerged from the cemetery, feeling they had the late Rebbe's approval, they would announce their engagement.

In 2010, about 3 ½ months after their visit to the Ohel, Rafi and Chaya were married, a joyous occasion they celebrate on its Hebrew date which coincides with the last day of Chanukah. Having visited the Poway area, and also having a brother, Elly, who is a Chabad rabbi in Irvine, California, Rafi did not require much convincing to move to San Diego, assuming approval for a new Chabad House could be obtained.

While it would not be financially easy to support themselves while simultaneously raising money for a Chabad Center and programming, the Andrusiers had an advantage that many other *shlichim* do not enjoy. Her capabilities being well known, Chaya was appointed as a pre-school teacher at the Chabad Hebrew Academy, working five half-days per week and assuring that the couple had some guaranteed salary.

Chabad Centers do not receive subsidies from either the national or the regional headquarters; it is the duty of the family to develop their own resources through donations and programming. When the Chabad of East County headquarters were in the small shopping mall at 8693-B La Mesa Boulevard, Shabbat services were held there once a month (and on another Shabbat each month at the Andrusier home in the San Carlos section of San Diego). After-school Hebrew classes were conducted once a week; and adult discussion classes were held one evening a week. At the Chabad Center, as well as at offsite locations, individual Jews joined Andrusier for 1:1 studying. Andrusier delights in discussing Torah and the principles of Judaism with adult students, among them, retirees who, after full careers, are interested in reconnecting with their religious heritage.

The distance between the shul in La Mesa and the Andrusier home in San Carlos made the arrangement less than ideal. Because it was too far to walk from their home to the shul on Shabbat, the Andrusiers had to make arrangements to stay nearby. They didn't relocate their home closer to the shul because San Carlos, and not La Mesa, is in the middle of their target demographic area.

There already are non-Chabad Jewish congregations in the San Carlos-Del Cerro areas, including Young Israel of San Diego, a small Orthodox congregation to which Andrusier, himself, sometimes walks to services; Tifereth Israel Synagogue, a large Conservative congregation; and Temple Emanu-El, a substantial Reform congregation.

Andrusier said the intention is not to compete with these synagogues, but rather to supplement current community programming.

One of the first things he did upon arriving in the area, he said, was to introduce himself to Rabbi Leonard Rosenthal, the spiritual leader of Tifereth Israel Synagogue. The two rabbis have been studying Torah, Talmud and Hassidism together in Rosenthal's office, aware that while there are differences between their two movements, they have much more in common as fellow Jews.

More recently, Andrusier said, he participated in a luncheon meeting sponsored by the Jewish Federation of San Diego County which also included Rosenthal, Rabbi Devorah Marcus of Temple Emanu-El, and Rabbi Avram Bogopulsky of Beth Jacob Congregation, whose College area synagogue lies south of the boundary of Andrusier's East County area. Rabbi Chaim Hollander of Young Israel of San Diego also was invited to the luncheon but his duties as a teacher at Soille San Diego Hebrew Day School precluded his attendance.

Among ways that Andrusier has attracted unaffiliated Jews to meet with him on a 1:1 basis has been to walk through residential and commercial neighborhoods looking for doorposts with mezuzot. He will knock, introduce himself, and explain that Chabad's mission is to bring greater understanding of Judaism, without charge or need for membership, to any Jew who is interested.

Additionally, he said, whenever he hears of a Jew throughout the rural portions of the East County – whether that be Crest, Alpine, Blossom Valley, Pine Valley, or even towns and venues within neighboring Imperial County – he will make house calls.

The rabbi and rebbetzin enjoy outdoor ceremonies with school children, and have scheduled events at such locations as Mission Trails Regional Park, Lake Murray, the San Carlos Recreation Center, and Grossmont Shopping Center, where they conduct an annual lighting of the Hannukiah. The Andrusiers have three young children of their own, who, in 2015, were all under 5 years of age.

Public activities--along with a large menorah that sits on the lawn in front of the Andrusier home--arouse curiosity and start a process to bring more Jews back into the fold, Andrusier says. The rabbi also serves as a *mashgiach* (kosher supervisor) for various caterers and is often called to officiate at life cycle events.

The idea, he said, is not to build a new synagogue, but rather to connect and relate to every Jew regardless of level of knowledge or observance.

From Jackson Drive Exit, head south on Jackson to La Mesa Boulevard, and turn right. The former Chabad of East County Center was on the left side, just past Glen Street.

-*San Diego Jewish World, February 4, 2016*

43. Exit 14
La Mesa Cardiac Center

Home of La Mesa Cardiac Center

LA MESA, California — Dr. Ronald Goldberg, the senior of three physicians at the La Mesa Cardiac Center on the campus of Sharp Grossmont Hospital, tells of a woman who periodically and for no apparent reason fainted dead away, but doctors could find no cause for her doing so.

Taken to a hospital, she would be given an electrocardiogram but each time her EKG appeared normal. Similarly, other tests in the hospital indicated no discrepancies. The woman became increasingly distraught. She was afraid to leave her house, and especially to drive a car, lest she faint where she might be most vulnerable, or cause harm to herself and others. She worried herself to the point of being neurotic. Doctors, unable to find any other reason for the fainting, wrote off her episodes as psychosomatic. They concluded that the trouble was not in her heart, but in her head.

Subsequently, Metronic, a biomedical company in Minneapolis, invented a device that could be implanted in a person's chest to enable the patient's heart activity to be continuously monitored. It took about ten minutes of surgery to implant the device inside the woman's chest cavity. A computer inside the device recorded heart rhythms whenever it sensed unusual activity. The recordings could be transmitted to an exterior computer which could relay the information to a printer.

Dr. Goldberg said that only two days after he implanted the device, the patient came into the office and said "It happened again." This time, there was information from the device to analyze and Goldberg learned that his patient "was having periods when her heart stopped for several seconds and this was causing her to pass out. So we put a pacemaker in, and she felt wonderful. She wasn't 'neurotic' anymore because she no longer was afraid to go out."

Patients with cardiac problems do not necessarily exhibit the symptoms on a regular basis; they can occur infrequently, Goldberg said. The purpose of the implanted monitor is to "capture whatever it is that they are feeling" whenever the symptoms occur.

The cardiologist said Metronic subsequently invented an even smaller version of the device, one which can be implanted under the skin in a procedure that takes "about a minute." Currently Medicare requires for payment that the procedure be performed in a hospital, but Goldberg says in reality it's simple enough to implant during an office visit. Goldberg spent two days with Metronic in Minneapolis, along with other cardiologists from around the country, in a seminar suggesting design changes for the newer device, known as the "Reveal."

He said he was one of the first cardiologists in San Diego to perform the procedure with the newer device in 2013, and that since that time he has implanted several such devices per month.

Goldberg was born in Flint, Michigan, and was moved by his family to Phoenix when he was four years old. As a youngster he had "very bad allergies, and I was in the emergency room all the time. A pediatrician would let me look in his microscope" and that, plus his mother's urging, led him to want to become a doctor. Some of the important steps in his life were a bar mitzvah at Temple Beth Israel in Phoenix; college mostly in Arizona, medical school at the University of Arizona, cardiology training at Baylor University in Houston, and moving to San Diego County in 1989, where he and his wife, Ann, reside in the Mt. Helix area of La Mesa. Ann Goldberg volunteers as the president of the Grossmont Hospital Foundation.

The La Mesa Cardiac Center, at 5565 Grossmont Center Drive, Suite 455, takes "care of patients with coronary disease, heart failure, and abnormal heart rhythms," Goldberg said. "My primary specialty is interventional cardiology in which we open up arteries with angioplasty, and put in stents.

"I also do pacemakers, so I tell patients I do 'major plumbing and minor electrical work,'" he quipped.

"I have grown up at the same time as interventional cardiology," he said. "When I was in medical school my father had a heart attack and ended up in the hospital in Phoenix. When he was there, basically all they did was give the patient morphine and put 'em in bed, and basically watched you ... They waited for something bad to happen. As I progressed through my training all these new treatments became available. So now when someone comes to our hospital with a heart attack we rush them to the cath lab (catheterization laboratory); we open up the arteries; and we prevent most of the damage. So it has been very gratifying to see how things have evolved from the time I was basically training. Our death rate from heart attacks is going down because of all that is available."

He also said: "I was really one of the first trained interventionists to come to the program. The program grew pretty quickly after 1989, when we started doing things differently. I would say I am pretty responsible for where the interventionist program at Grossmont is today."

I asked the cardiologist if he had any heart-healthy tips he'd like me to pass along.

"One of the main epidemics nowadays is obesity and that is leading to diabetes and that is going to be a huge health problem in the future because diabetes causes heart disease, causes stroke, causes kidney failure – you name it – and so the key risk for the population is obesity," he responded.

"In terms of diet, unfortunately what has happened is that fats got a bad name and carbohydrates became our way of life, and that is probably what has led to this obesity. It turns out that the FDA (Food and Drug Administration) came up with the low-fat, heart-healthy diet but it was never based on good research. So now they are saying it's okay to eat eggs again. It turns out that eating cholesterol in eggs and eating fat is not the culprit; it is more of the carbohydrates that is causing the problems.

"So I think we are going to see a shift to much lower carbohydrate, higher fat diets," he added. "That will be similar to what we ate a long time ago when we didn't have all these issues."

I asked what is included in his own diet.

"In large part, it's a Mediterranean diet," he said. "Hummus, fish, chicken, a lot of vegetables. My wife is on a similar diet, with no carbohydrates. She tries to keep no bread nor pasta in the house."

No bagels either? I asked crest-fallen.

"Not generally," he said, with a smile. "I try to get those when I go on vacation."

Dr. Ronald Goldberg and tiny implant

From Grossmont Center Drive, Exit 14A, proceed north on Grossmont Center Drive to a right turn at Center Drive and parking lot.

-San Diego Jewish World, February 11, 2016

44. Exit 14
Schumann-Heink Home

Former home of opera star Ernestine Schumann-Heink

LA MESA, California — One climbs the Grossmont—named in the early years of the 20th Century by land developer Ed Fletcher for his partner William Gross—up narrow, curving El Granito Avenue, seemingly only big enough for one-way traffic as it twists past giant boulders and trees that Kate Sessions, the horticul-turalist who also planted much of Balboa Park, chose to accentuate the views of the El Cajon Valley below.

To this hill of enchantment Gross, who was a theatrical agent, attracted as residents some of the world's best-known musicians, including Ernestine Schumann-Heink, the opera star of her day, who built a large home at 9951 El Granito that still stands today. Schumann-Heink was the Maria Callas, Beverly Sills, Leontyne Price, or Roberta Peters of the late 19th and early 20th Century, her contralto voice and generosity of spirit loved by almost all.

Born in 1861 to the intermarried couple of Charlotte Goldmann and Hans Rossler, she was Jewish as a matter of halacha, and counted Jewish War Relief among her many charities. But besides for her roles in German and Italian operas, in which she sang duets at the Metropolitan with such co-stars as Enrico Caruso, she also was beloved for singing in English and German each Christmas Eve the classic carol "Silent Night" so beautifully that to hear it annually was said to be an early 20th Century tradition.

Stories abounded about Schumann-Heink because in the early 20th century, opera singers were the celebrities of their day; their thoughts, their marriages, their divorces, and their babies--of which Schumann-Heink had seven as well as a step-child who made eight--were a constant source of interest and amusement for news-paper readers.

Schumann-Heink's mother was a singer who recognized her child's talent. She arranged for the daughter to study voice with a retired opera singer. When "Tina," as Ernestine was called, became 21 she married Ernst Heink, the secretary of the Dresden Opera, where she had performed in small roles. The secretary and singer were fired for breaking the rules against fraternization. On they moved to the Hamburg Opera, where Ernestine continued to sing in small roles until 1889 when the diva Marie Gotze refused to perform after an argument with the opera's director. Without any rehearsal, Schumann-Heink filled in for her, not only on that day, but for two more days in succession—singing a total of three separate operas. The bravura performances won Schumann-Heink a ten-year contract. In 1893, she and Heink divorced, and she married actor Paul Schumann, who died 11 years later. Her last marriage, which ended in divorce, was to her manager William Rapp, an attorney.

Successful in the opera houses of Europe, Schumann-Heink made her debut at the Metropolitan Opera of New York in 1899, and fell in love with America, a sentiment that was fully returned. In an award-winning article in the Winter 1982 edition of the *Journal of San Diego History*, Helen Ellsberg wrote:

She owed her great popularity to a phenomenal voice with a range from low D to high C and a magnetic personality that charmed everyone from children to grandparents -- that all-important combination of talent and charisma that makes the superstar. She had three husbands and eight children, including a stepson. "Tina" ... barely topped five feet in height, but carried herself with such regal dig-nity that she was occasionally described in the press as looking "tall and stately." Luminous, dark brown eyes were her loveliest feature. She was widely publicized as a Mother figure. But when, dressed in a silver gown, her white hair shining and her arms and ample bosom ablaze with diamonds, she came across the stage with that radiant smile, she generated her own unique brand of glamor. Her rapport with the audience was established before she ever uttered a note.

Yet, not everyone loved her, certainly not Richard Strauss, who invited her to the Dresden Court Opera House, to sing the part of Klytemnestra in the premiere of the opera *Elektra* in 1909. According to the oft-told story, Strauss demanded of the orchestra: ""Louder, I can still hear der Heink."

Kathleen Crawford, in a Fall 1985 article for the *Journal of San Diego History*, noted that in 1912 Schumann-Heink wrote a letter to describe how excited she was about moving onto Grossmont. "I read so much about 'Paradise' well I think I found my dreams realized when I saw Grossmont in our blessed 'California' and I am happy as a child in thoughts of my wonderful future home – Casa Ernestina." A footnote informed readers that "the home of Madame Schumann-Heink included a pantry for a butler, wine cellar, servants' quarters and a secret room. Inside the walls, interspersed among the boulders, orange, olive, eucalyptus, banana. and palm trees grew in profusion."

Although Schumann-Heink's hilltop house was large and well furnished, it was not her only residence. She also had a home in Coronado, and she would commute between the two. An indefatigable performer, she also gave concerts and appeared in operas all over the world, giving her little time to actually enjoy the sprawling casa. Rather than the artist colony that Fletcher and Gross had imagined, Grossmont became more of a retreat, or getaway, for the musicians and artists who settled there.

Still, Schumann-Heink developed a special affection for San Diego, and with such local luminaries as John D. Spreckels, Ellen Scripps and George Marston planned to launch an annual outdoor opera festival at Balboa Park's Organ Pavilion, which she had helped to inaugurate during the Panama-California Exposition of 1915. Generous financial donations were offered in backing for her dream, but before the opening note could be sounded, the United States entered World War I and the idea had to be shelved.

The war was a time of sadness for Schumann-Heink because some of her sons fought in the U.S. military, while another was enrolled in the German military – brothers against brother. She poured her energy into performing for U.S. servicemen and selling war bonds, so excelling in both activities that the soldiers and sailors of America took to calling her "mother."

After the war, Schumann-Heink moved to Hollywood, but her heart—and ultimately her mortal remains—belonged to San Diego. Following her death in 1935, her ashes were inurned at the Greenwood Cemetery off Imperial Avenue.

....

From Severin/Fuerte, Exit 14C, turn right onto Severin Drive,
which becomes Fuerte, then follow to a left on Sunset, and left again
on El Granito Avenue.

....

-*San Diego Jewish World, February 18, 2016*

45. Exit 14
Mount Helix Cross

Bob Lauritzen stands by Mt. Helix Cross

LA MESA, California — The Christian cross atop Mount Soledad in the La Jolla neighborhood of San Diego is 29 feet tall, whereas the Christian cross atop Mount Helix here in La Mesa is 35 feet tall. The two crosses are quite different, and not just by 6 feet.

The Mount Soledad cross has been the object of contention and litigation since 1989, with the case going to the U.S. Supreme Court and back more than once, and still not resolved. On the other hand, the Mount Helix cross was the subject of litigation in 1990, but the issue was resolved satisfactorily in 1999. So what's the difference, and what is the Jewish angle?

When suits were filed, both crosses were located on public lands, raising the constitutional question of whether the City of San Diego and the County of San Diego were showing a preference for Christianity over the many other religions that are practiced in the United States, including Judaism.

One of the plaintiffs in the Mount Soledad case, who has since died, was Philip K. Paulson, an atheist, who said the issue was even broader than that—the government should not show a preference for theism (the belief in God) over atheism. Paulson contended, as did the American Civil Liberties Union, that in order for Mount Soledad to become "kosher"--my word, not theirs--either of two actions could be taken. One: the cross could be removed from the public park on Mount Soledad and placed on private property. Or two, city-owned Mount Soledad park could be sold at auction, and if the purchaser wanted to keep the cross, that could be done, because the land would become private.

Initially, the same choices faced the County of San Diego concerning the cross atop Mount Helix, which towers over the amphitheater where Easter Sunrise services have been a tradition since 1917, when they were initiated by landowner Ed Fletcher. The land was sold in 1923 to Mary Carpenter Yawkey, who had the cross installed two years later. After she died, her brother Cyrus Carpenter Yawkey in 1929 deeded the land to the San Diego County government with the stipulation that the cross be maintained as a memorial to his sister.

After U.S. District Court Judge Gordon Thompson Jr.'s ruling was sustained that the crosses could not remain on public property, the county government concluded that it no longer was capable of fulfilling the terms of the donation. The cross, therefore, needed to be returned to the Yawkey family, or to some organization that represented its interests. It subsequently was ruled that the non-profit Foundation for the Preservation of the Mount Helix Nature Theatre-- which later renamed itself as the Mount Helix Park Foundation--was qualified to be that organization, and could take possession of what was formerly a public park, provided that it received absolutely no public funds to do so.

Indeed, the area around the amphitheater is beautiful to behold, with stunning views of San Diego and the Pacific Ocean to the west, and El Cajon and the Cuyamaca Mountains to the east. Besides being the site of occasional religious services, the amphitheater is utilized by the Christian Youth Theatre to put on various musicals including, you guessed it, *Fiddler on the Roof.*

The Mount Soledad case was not resolved so easily. To tell every legal maneuver in the case would require more space, and time than most readers would be willing to devote.

Suffice it to say that advocates for keeping the cross where it stands eventually persuaded the City of San Diego to auction off the land under the cross, but the maneuver was adjudged in federal court to be unconstitutional because the use the land could be put to, in essence, was restricted to maintaining the cross. It was not like some real estate developer could do anything with such a small patch of land.

The city gave permission for a group to construct a veteran's memorial around the Mount Soledad cross, with granite walls bearing images of fallen members of the U.S. military. This enabled advocates of retaining the cross on Mount Soledad to argue that Mount Soledad was principally a veterans' memorial, not a place of religion, notwithstanding the cross, which was described as a universal rather than a religious symbol. This prompted opposition from the Jewish War Veterans of America who said, in essence, if Mount Soledad is to be a memorial to veterans, it should memorialize all veterans, not just the Christian ones.

The Mount Soledad Memorial Association persuaded local members of Congress to attach a rider to an appropriations bill permitting the federal government to obtain Mount Soledad from the City of San Diego. After the City Council balked at transferring the property, voters, in a referendum, agreed to the transfer by a margin of nearly 3-1. But a San Diego County Superior Court judge ruled that the transfer was an illegal act of preference for the Christian religion. That ruling, however, was overturned by a state appeals court.

Eventually, members of Congress, with the support of President George W. Bush, enacted legislation to have the federal government acquire Mount Soledad by eminent domain. This prompted another lawsuit, with the Jewish War Veterans and a private Muslim individual among the plaintiffs, contending the federal government had acted unconstitutionally to preserve a Christian symbol on public land. A federal district court judge ruled against the plaintiffs, but a federal appeals court reversed that decision, again ruling that the cross on public land was unconstitutional--no matter which level of government owned the land. An effort to appeal the decision to the U.S. Supreme Court was rebuffed, with the high court ruling that further action was necessary at the appeals court level before the case was eligible to be heard.

Congress than acted again, voting to sell a half acre of public land to the Mount Soledad Memorial Association for $1.4 million. As of 2015, a court ruling on the legality of this transfer still was pending.

Like Paulson, the original plaintiff in the case, Thompson, the original judge, has died during what has been a case that, up to this writing, has stretched on for 26 years. Perhaps both sides would agree with the adage that "justice delayed is justice denied."

Meanwhile, the cross atop Mount Helix is warmed not only by the sun but by the fact of no longer being controversial.

....

From Exit 14C, turn right onto Fuerte Drive, then right again on Mount Helix Drive, follow it bearing right on turns to the Mt. Helix Amphitheatre

....

46. Exit 15
Isaac Lankershim
and El Cajon

Home of El Cajon Historical Society

EL CAJON, California — In the early history of the City of El Cajon, two names are particularly well known — Levi Chase, for whom Chase Avenue and the Chase Avenue Elementary School are named, and Amaziah L. Knox, who built El Cajon's first hotel and also served as the city's first postmaster back when El Cajon was known as Knox's Corners. A monument to him is incorporated in the pylons holding up the downtown "El Cajon" sign on Main Street, and his hotel building now houses the El Cajon Historical Society.

Known, but less celebrated, was Isaac Lankershim, the 19th century absentee landowner who retained Levi Chase, an attorney and former U.S. Army major, to evict land squatters and clear the title of a large portion of the 48,800-acre Rancho El Cajon, which Lankershim purchased in 1868 from Mexican land grantee María Antonia Estudillo de Pedrorena.

Historian G. Carroll Rice in the April 2012 edition of *Heritage,* a publication of the El Cajon Historical Society, reported that Lankershim paid Chase for his work with 7,628 acres of land on the southern end of the El Cajon Valley, near where Chase Avenue branches from the El Cajon Boulevard exit on eastbound Interstate 8. Chase shared Lankershim's enthusiasm for agriculture, growing not only wheat but also raisins, which were "dried and packed at the ranch," according to Rice.

Lankershim was also the man who hired Knox to be the manager of his El Cajon property, on which he grew wheat. After gold was discovered in Julian, the area where Knox lived became known as being along the route between Julian and downtown San Diego. With travelers passing in both directions, Knox decided in 1876 to build a combination hotel and residence. He included in the structure a place for a small post office, and was rewarded with an appointment as the area's first postmaster.

El Cajon was only one of Lankershim's investments in California agricultural land. In 1869, he led a group of San Francisco investors who purchased 60,000 acres in what today is known as the San Fernando Valley of Los Angeles. Initially he raised sheep there. But when wool prices fell, he planted over his holdings with wheat. Imagine, the communities today known as North Hollywood, Sherman Oaks, Van Nuys, Encino, Tarzana, and Woodland Hills all one big wheat field!

Lankershim was profiled in the Summer 2013 edition of *Western States Jewish History,* and later on the internet pages of the historical quarterly's online *Jewish Museum of the American West,* www.jmaw.org. It was noted that while Lankershim started his life as a Jew in Bavaria, he ended it as a Baptist in California. This was principally because on his way to San Francisco, he met and married in St. Louis the English-born Annis Lydia Moore, who persuaded him to convert.

Once in San Francisco, Lankershim and his brother James aggregated agricultural holdings in Napa, Solano County, and Fresno.

"In the late 1860's Isaac Lankershim moved to Los Angeles," *Western States Jewish History* reported. "There he had close business and social relationships with Harris Newmark and other Jewish businessmen. They looked upon his Baptist conversion as an idiosyncrasy."

David Epstein, editor of *Western States Jewish History,* recounting how Lankershim was one of the boys in the Jewish circles of early Los Angeles, said, "as far as they were concerned, he was simply a Jew with a quirk."

Newmark was a Prussian-born grocer who dabbled in real estate and with partners subdivided a city that initially was called Newmark but later was renamed as Montebello. A similar fate befell a city initially named as Lankershim, which the landholder had planted over with fruit trees. It was renamed as Toluca, and later still, became known as North Hollywood.

Far more lasting was the name of the city named for Lankershim's son-in-law, Isaac Van Nuys, husband of Susanna Lankershim.

Isadore Choynski, a friend of Lankershim's, commented before the latter's death in 1882, that Lankershim was "a religious eccentric in a family of 'pious Jews.'" He also called him "the richest ex-Jew in Los Angeles."

Like Chase, Lankershim has elementary schools named for him – one in the North Hollywood area, and another in San Bernardino, where he also had real estate holdings. In fact the San Bernardino community northeast of the San Bernardino Airport is known as "Lankershim."

As eastbound cars exit at El Cajon Boulevard, Exit 15, a secondary offramp permits traffic to get onto Chase Avenue. This is the historic area that Isaac Lankershim deeded over to Levi Chase.

-*San Diego Jewish World, March 3, 2016*

47. Exit 16

From junk to recycling

Josh Turchin and electronics ready for recycling

EL CAJON, California — Like peddling, the "junk business" was especially attractive to entrepreneurs because they didn't need a lot of capital to get started. Many Jews, among other groups of immigrants, began their business careers this way.

Jerry Turchin is CEO of California Metals at 297 S. Marshall Avenue and of California Metals Supply next door. He relates the story of his own father-in-law, Mel Klein, who immediately following World War II "used to peddle produce in New York from his pickup truck. He had a problem when he couldn't sell everything because if produce is no longer fresh it is no longer saleable. That is why he got into the scrap metal business. Scrap metal doesn't spoil."

"Mel was very good at what he did," Turchin continued. "He had one employee and himself on a truck. He would get out on the truck at 6:30 in the morning and by 11:30 a.m. they were done with the pick ups. It was a very simple business. They'd buy the scrap in the morning, and sell it in the afternoon. He immediately knew what his profit was."

Turchin trained for a different kind of career. He earned a Bachelor's degree in hotels and restaurant management from Florida State University, then went on to earn a Master's of Business Administration from New York University. He went to work as a systems analyst for the Two Guys Department Store chain. He asked for a transfer to the merchandising department, and was refused, because his father owned three appliance stores, and Two Guys management considered the father a competitor. So, Turchin went to work for Bloomingdales, but didn't love the commuting. That's when his father-in-law asked him to come into his scrap metal business at the same salary he was earning, but without the commute.

So he learned the business, at one time establishing an independent route, and for a while operating both his own business and his father-in-law's after Klein moved from New Jersey to San Diego. Eventually, Turchin decided to sell both Klein's and his businesses and moved out to San Diego County to become a partner with Klein, who had opened another scrap metal business on rented property in El Cajon in 1978.

Turchin decided that the business needed room to grow, and making a leap of faith, rented in 1982 the much larger property at the current address. The decision quintupled the rent to $3000 per month, much to his father-in-law's consternation. Eventually, Turchin was able to persuade the owners to sell the 38,000-square-foot property to him. Turchin also owns Miller Metals nearby, which has 50,000 square feet and handles scrap steel in much greater sizes and quantities.

What used to be called the "junk business" evolved into the "scrap metal business" and today, in an environmentally conscious world, is called the "recycling business."

Turchin's son, Josh, grew up at the scrap metal yard, and when it was time for college, he majored in philosophy at Washington University in St. Louis. He actually had intended to go on to medical school, but "growing up in an entrepreneurial environment like this, I couldn't see paying for 12 years of school," Josh said. "My orientation is to get out and make money. It turned out that I became kind of an expert in electronic recycling. I spoke at national conventions of scrap dealers. I was sent around to speak to the old guard about what it takes to be in this business. It is something the world needs; I had to do this."

Josh, who today is the president of California Metals, escorted me on a tour of the facility, and in the process taught me some of the scrap metal industry's jargon.

"Two functional wings of the business are 'door trade' and 'reverse retail,'" he said. "'Door trade is what we pick up from shops, from machinists who produce scrap metal as part of their regular business function. We do bin exchanges with them. We bring out bins for them to put their scrap metal in and then we pick them up and exchange them for empty bins." California Metal pays these customers for their metal, aggregates the haul with other collections, then sells metal by the ton to foundries to be melted down and recast.

Josh added that "we also do door trade with electronic scrap-generating customers, such as offices and commercial users. We guarantee data destruction and keep the electronic equipment (including computers) from the waste stream."

Old computers turned in to California Metals are disassembled. To protect the privacy of the former users' data, said Josh, "we remove anything that is a circuit board from any kind of electronic equipment." Further, "we have software that meets Department of Defense requirements for data erasure. It writes over all the sectors with 0's and 1's five times, making your data irretrievable. We also have a drill press. Some customers like the pageantry of us putting a hole through their drives. But, in any case, the logic board is separated from the hard drive—which essentially is aluminum platters and housing. You need that specific logic board to make that hard drive work, and they are sent to different countries. The aluminum gets melted as aluminum scrap."

Other components such as monitors can be resold, but "less and less of the electronic scrap that we get is reusable," said Josh.

In addition to those items that California Metals picks up at other businesses, there are additional items that come to the company in what it calls its "reverse retail" business. "That is when people bring things to us, for example bottles and cans, electronic scrap, and commercial scrap metal." Odds and ends come in from people who are cleaning out their garages, spare rooms, basements, or attics.

Josh has created a separate business called One Earth which pays for recyclables at facilities located near two Home Depot outlets, one in Mission Valley (at 5980 Fairmount Avenue), and the other just east of Imperial Beach at 685-B Saturn Boulevard. People also bring their cans and bottles to California Metals.

The One Earth locations near Home Depots are "little storefront operations, like walking into Starbucks," Josh said. He explained that it is not enough to preach sustainability, it is important to make recycling easy for consumers. He said he would like to see people routinely bringing in their cans, bottles and other recyclables every time they go shopping, using the money they receive for the recyclables to partly finance their next purchases.

To enable that, he said, recycling centers need to be attractive and convenient.

Anheuser-Busch, a large customer of California Metals, says it takes only six weeks from the time a crushed can leaves California Metals for it to be back on a grocery store shelf filled with product.

The Turchins' business next door, California Metals Supply, purchases sheet metal from wholesalers to be sold to such customers as machine shops. The idea, explained Jerry Turchin (the father) is to be on both sides of the business: picking up the scrap from machine shops and selling them more metal with which to make their products and to generate more scrap.

Jerry Turchin remembers when he and his late father-in-law Mel Klein had philosophical disagreement over the way the business should expand. Klein was aghast when Jerry first proposed expanding the business. He agonized over the increase in rent from $600 to $3,000 a month, whereas Jerry saw the possibility of having room for larger metal tonnage, which could be sold at far higher prices and margins.

Now Josh, representing the third generation, has his philosophical differences with his father. By combining recycling with other company's retail operations, he sees an opportunity to spread the message of environmentalism, all the while generating source material for the scrap metal business.

Jerry, on the other hand, quotes his own father, who owned the three appliance stores. "When you work with dollars, you make pennies," he said. "When you work with hundreds, you make dollars." According to that philosophy, establishing little storefront operations to collect recyclable materials only makes pennies. Far better, in Jerry's viewpoint, to deal in products worth hundreds or even thousands of dollars."

Which generation of the family is right? The younger Turchin believes success can be measured by "1) benefits to the environment; 2) tons of materials removed from the local waste stream; 3) energy spared as a result of recycling resources instead of mining virgin resources; 4) the amount of money returned to local businesses through recycling, and 5) of course, the spread we make, we want to make a profit on every item that we touch."

While Jerry isn't dead-set against his son's idealistic campaign, he views it with a measure of skepticism.

He said he doesn't believe many people will recycle because they want to save the earth. However, he said, "I believe the best reason to recycle is to make money to pay bills. When legislation passed in 1987, with a nickel redemption value on cans, that gave people the incentive to recycle." The greater the incentive, he suggested, the more people will be motivated.

As a longtime El Cajon businessman, Jerry Turchin has been active on the East County Chamber of Commerce. He served on the membership and government affairs committees, and now is a member of the chamber's overall board of directors. In February 2015, he was appointed by the City Council to the El Cajon Planning Commission.

"I have been in business here since 1978, lived in El Cajon since 1983, I've put kids through college, so I feel that this community has been very good to me, and I volunteered," he said. "Why not?"

....

From Main Street, Exit 16 (east bound), turn right at the bottom of the off-ramp, then right onto Marshall Avenue. California Metals is about 6 doors in on the left side of the street, across from the transit center parking lot.

....

-San Diego Jewish World, March 10, 2016

48. Exit 17
Chains of Success

The Home Depot in El Cajon

EL CAJON, California — Near the intersection of Johnson Avenue and Fletcher Parkway stands the Parkway Plaza Shopping Center, in which the trendy tween-teen-20's clothier Tilly's is one of the tenants. Across the street at 298 Fletcher Parkway, sprawls a Home Depot outlet for fix-it-yourself homeowners. Home Depot and Tilly's appeal to far different demographic audiences, but the stories of their Jewish founders have some similarities.

The older of the two enterprises is Home Depot, which was founded in 1979 in Atlanta, Georgia, by Bernie Marcus and Arthur Blank after they were fired from their jobs respectively as president and vice president for finance of the Handy Dan Home Improvement Centers, which were subsidiaries of Daylin Corporation. Daylin's president Sanford Sigiloff was the man who gave them the axe, prompting them to launch a career which would result in both Marcus and Blank becoming billionaire philanthropists.

Marcus fits the "rags-to-riches" mold that author Horatio Alger made popular in the late 19th century. The son of Russian Jewish immigrant parents, who lived in a Newark, New Jersey, tenement, Marcus earned money while attending pre-medicine classes at Rutgers University by helping his father to build cabinets. But he later said that his hope of eventually attending medical school was dashed when a Harvard University official said a payment—read that bribe — of $10,000 would be required to help Marcus circumvent Harvard's post-World War II quota on Jewish students. So instead, he went into pharmacy.

He soon decided that he preferred working on the retail side of drug stores rather than behind the pharmaceutical counter. Eventually he went to work for Two Guys discount stores, managing the cosmetic departments of the various stores. More and more responsibilities came his way, until by the time he was 28 he was responsible for household appliances, sporting goods and ceramics, a portfolio said to represent some $1 billion in sales.

When he was hired by the Handy Dan Home Improvement Centers in Southern California, the company gained not only a top executive, but one with a very big heart. Influenced from an early age by his mother to give *tzedakah*, he got Handy Dan behind the cause of cancer research and treatment after an employee tearfully disclosed to him that he'd have to quit his job because of a cancer diagnosis.

Shocked, Marcus contacted the City of Hope Hospital to ask if anything could be done for the employee. The patient was successfully treated, and Marcus organized some large fundraisers to help the City of Hope, which began its institutional life as a sanatorium sponsored by the Jewish Consumptive Relief Association.

After Marcus and Blank were fired, they sat down at a nearby coffee shop and figured how to use the large warehouse concept – popularized by Fedmart and Price Club founder Sol Price – in the home improvement business. The two men recognized that shoppers who wanted to fix up their homes needed to shuttle from paint store to hardware store to appliance store. They decided that the tickets to success were large warehouses featuring low prices, one-stop shopping, and personnel who could demonstrate to customers how to execute do-it-yourself projects. With the help of New York investment banker Ken Langone, they raised the money for their first stores in Atlanta, a location they said they chose because of that city's favorable business climate and its huge international airport.

When the first Home Depot stores opened, customers didn't exactly rush to its doors. As the story is told, Marcus and Blank had their children hand out $1 bills to any perspective customer who would go inside and look around. Two years after the 1979 opening, Home Depot went public, initially selling its shares on NASDAQ and in 1984 expanding to the New York Stock Exchange. The company expanded operations to Canada and Mexico, and now has approximately 2,250 outlets.

Marcus had found in Blank a partner of similar upbringing. He and his older brother Michael had grown up in a one-bedroom apartment rented by his parents Max and Molly Blank, in Queens, New York.

Max operated Shelly Pharmaceutical, a small mail-order business, which was taken over by Mollie after Max's early death. Through hard work, she made such a success of the company that Daylin purchased it. After Arthur graduated from Babson College in Wellesley, Massachusetts, he worked as an accountant with Arthur Young and Company, and after joining his mother and brother, transitioned from Shelly Pharmaceutical to Daylin. Initially, he became president of a pharmaceutical division consisting of Elliott's Drug Stores and Stripe Discount Stores, but after Daylin sold that division he moved to Handy Dan to work under Marcus. Handy Dan had $155 million in revenues the day that Sigiloff fired Marcus and Blank in what since has been described as a corporate power play.

The Home Depot partners became beloved businessmen and philanthropists in Atlanta. Marcus collaborated with former U.S. Secretary of State George Shultz to help establish the Israel Democracy Institute, a think tank to promote democracy in Israel. He also donated $3.9 million for the fight against anthrax poisoning to the Centers for Disease Control and Prevention.

Similar to the way he became involved with cancer research at the City of Hope, Marcus responded to the needs of an employee with an autistic child, and created the Marcus Institute, which operates a 16-acre campus for research and treatment of autism. The center has expanded into treatment of patients with brain injuries and neurological disorders, including Alzheimer's.

Returning from a trade mission to Israel, Marcus was sitting on an airplane with then Georgia Gov. Roy Barnes. Marcus expressed an interest to the governor of doing something for the customers in a state where he had such a successful career, and perhaps to find a way to help Atlanta attract tourists who would stay in hotels, eat in restaurants, and thereby contribute to the economy.

The governor suggested a range of projects, including a symphony, but Marcus said that the customers who engage in do-it-yourself projects to fix up their homes were less likely to go to the symphony than to go to some attraction, such as an aquarium. By the time the plane landed, the idea of creating the world's largest aquarium was sketched out. Marcus said he did not want any public money, but would like the project to be fast-tracked in the review process. That it was, and the Georgia Aquarium today occupies 604,000 square feet, houses 10 million gallons of water, and boasts a 30-foot deep exhibit tank measuring 284 feet by 126 feet. An estimated 100,000 animals are on display at the aquarium.

As Marcus had hoped, the aquarium energized Atlanta's tourism economy. The Civil Rights Museum, the College Football Hall of Fame, and the World of Coca Cola soon located nearby.

Blank, meanwhile, was far from inactive. After succeeding Marcus as head of Home Depot, Blank purchased the Atlanta Falcons football team and later added to his sports interests the Georgia Force (an arena football team), and PGA Tour Superstores. He also purchased the Mountain Sky Guest Ranch in Montana.

Of significance is the fact that every Home Depot store, as a matter of company-wide policy, is supposed to adopt some charity or non-profit organization and to help make the world a better place. Comparing the idea to the Jewish concept of *tikkun olam*, or repairing the world, Marcus once exulted, "I turn them into Jews."

Inside a Tilly's store, 2016

Across Fletcher Parkway in the Parkway Plaza Shopping Center is one of the many outlets of Tilly's, initially co-founded as the "World of Jeans and Tops" in 1984 by Hezy Shaked, a former officer in Israel's Navy, and his then-wife Tilly Levine.

According to corporate biographies, the couple worked their way from the East Coast to the West Coast of the United States, with Shaked taking various jobs along the way. One of them was at a garage, where their living quarter was under a staircase, he has said.

After arriving in Orange County, California, Shaked was attracted to the swap meet phenomenon, where for a small fee to the swap meet operator people may set up tables and from them, throughout the day, sell many varieties of goods. Hezy loaded up on clothing, at first bringing a few items for sale, and later buying and selling by the truck load.

Soon he had accumulated enough profits – and sufficient savvy into what kinds of fashions will sell – to open his first store in Los Alamitos, California. "Success," noted his wife, "didn't come on a silver platter. We worked seven days a week for seven years."

Eventually, Shaked renamed the stores "Tilly's" after his wife, which name the chain keeps today notwithstanding their divorce in 1989. Levine, in fact, remains involved with Tilly's; her title being director of vendor relations.

A typical Tilly's store measures approximately 7,900 square feet – large enough to command two or even three spaces in a typical shopping center. The company went public in May 2012, raising $124 million through its initial public offering of stock.

Selling clothing, shoes, and accessories for such activities as surfing, skateboarding, snowboarding, motocross and other sports, each store attracts a variety of shoppers who want such trendy brands as Levi's, Quiksilver, Ugg, Vans, and Tilly's own house brands. The company keeps up with the ever changing fashion preferences of teens and young adults through research that includes ongoing interactions on such social media as Facebook, Instagram and Twitter.

Shaked also has become involved with various philanthropic projects, none more important than Tilly's Life Center (TLC) created by his ex-wife who, in a program known as "I Am Me," seminars with teens about such issues as bullying, drugs, eating disorders, self-esteem; forgiveness; acceptance, and suicide.

As of July 2015, Tilly operated 214 stores in 33 states. Shaked has expressed the hope of surpassing 500 stores by the Year 2022.

From Exit 17 A, Johnson Avenue, use middle lane to turn left onto N. Johnson Avenue, and then turn right onto Village Parkway, which leads into the shopping center.

-San Diego Jewish World, March 17, 2016

49. Exit 17
East County Performing Arts Center

El Cajon Civic Center, home of the East County Performing Arts Center

EL CAJON, California — The East County Performing Arts Center (ECPAC) was the glittering gem of downtown El Cajon's "super block" when it hosted its inaugural performance on September 8, 1977. Many people gave Dr. Sydney Wiener, a retired dentist, credit for being that gem's fine "jeweler."

Wiener was a relatively young man when he retired from his dental practice and the energy that he once put into a career he poured into his appreciation for the arts. After arriving in El Cajon from New York with his wife Charlotte, they became involved in the Grossmont Community Concert Association, which advocated for a first-class auditorium in eastern San Diego County.

Not content just to talk about the idea, Wiener successfully ran for a seat on the Grossmont Community College Board (later to become the Grossmont-Cuyamaca Community College Board) which under an agreement approved by the electorate, became partners with the City of El Cajon in ECPAC's construction and maintenance.

If there were a fundraiser to be put on for the nearly 1,142-seat auditorium, Wiener was among those organizing and contributing to it. If grants for the arts needed to be coaxed out of Washington, D.C., Wiener was the one who jumped into his single engine Beechcraft Bonanza to meet with bureaucrats and elected officials. He also flew the plane as a volunteer rescue worker for the San Diego Sheriff's Office.

Wiener was proud of the acoustics at ECPAC, and said that the seating in 27 continuous rows, with no center aisle, made every patron feel that he or she had scored one of the best seats in the house.

During 17 years of service as a community college trustee, Wiener was elected board president eight times. In that capacity, he not only served on the joint powers agency that created ECPAC, he also served on another joint power agency that oversaw development and construction of the El Cajon Civic Center, which sits across a plaza from ECPAC. The city of El Cajon and the County of San Diego were among the college district's partners. The Civic Center complex includes El Cajon's City Hall and a County Courthouse.

Not surprisingly, some people thought of Wiener both as Mr. Community College and Mr. ECPAC. From his home in the Fletcher Hills neighborhood of El Cajon, he was just a short ride from Grossmont College. And he took pride in helping to create the second college in the district, Cuyamaca College, located in Rancho San Diego. When eventually, he was defeated for re-election, his shocked colleagues on the board voted to honor him as a "trustee emeritus" bringing him life-long invitations to district events.

Wiener's daughter, Laura Mills, today a clinical psychologist in Maple Bay, British Columbia, said music and culture were always revered components of her parents' lives. When she and her sister, Barbara Hanawalt, were children, Sundays typically meant an outing to a New York City museum. Laura played the viola, Barbara played the cello, and one summer their proud parents enrolled them both in the National Music Camp in Michigan.

"Our father enjoyed and valued culture, particularly music and the visual arts," Mills said. "He loved listening to classical music. Our mother played the piano and had a beautiful singing voice. He greatly admired that. They ensured we learned how to play music. When asked if he played anything, Dad would say he played the record player!"

Hanawalt, who teaches visually impaired children in Portland, Oregon, suggested in an interview that her father's interest in creating the ECPAC not only was cultural but also was technical.

She explained: "When he was a young child, his parents bought a player piano for his older sister. He loved to listen to the music from that. Years later he recalled how the piano had to be hoisted up on ropes because his family lived on the 5th floor of a six-story walk-up in what is today Spanish Harlem in Manhattan. No elevator! He also recalled the many opera melodies and classical music themes he absorbed from the music on the piano rolls. This was the start of his interest in music."

When the drive began to build ECPAC, Hanawalt recalled, "he was interested in creating a building with good acoustics. He and our mother enjoyed going to concerts and the opera in New York, and Dad had an ear for good sound in a concert hall."

In that he was a pilot, Weiner "saw his involvement with building the Performing Arts Center as an opportunity to go places in the plane to visit different halls and experience their acoustics," his daughter said. "He and mom took a trip to Roseburg, Oregon, to the community college there because that school had an auditorium known for its good acoustics. They went to Seattle to meet acoustics expert Paul Veneklasen, and were pleased to have his input. Also, Dad liked the world of finance, so raising the funds to build the Performing Arts Center was fun for him in its own way. He liked putting together the bond funding for it. He consulted with lots of people about the acoustics of the new hall, including my father-in-law, Clare Hanawalt, who was the chief engineer at KGW TV in Portland."

Stan Flandi, who capped a 33-year career at Grossmont College as the dean of its evening division, recalled "Dr Wiener," as he always called him, with fondness. "He was a professional person, a dentist, a fun-loving kind of guy, always smiling and laughing," Flandi said. "He always looked for the positive and not the negative. I have a lot of respect for him and what he tried to do for the arts in the East County."

Del Hood, the retired longtime reporter and editor of the now defunct *Daily Californian*, said he admired Wiener because "he was pro-education doing what he thought needed to be done for the college district and sustaining ECPAC as long as he could. He was a good guy who had the best interests of the college district at heart."

When Wiener died in 1995 at age 76, after 50 years of marriage to Charlotte, he was eulogized by Rabbi Leonard Rosenthal of Tifereth Israel Synagogue as a "modern-day Renaissance man," who invested all his projects "with his characteristic verve and enthusiasm."

Wiener's other interests, Rosenthal noted, included collecting old Edison phonographs that he was "expert at repairing and restoring." He proudly displayed them at his home along with a fine collection of art works that he and Charlotte had collected, and photographs that Wiener himself had taken on his trips with his wife to many countries all over the world. Charlotte lived nearly 20 years longer than her husband.

Unfortunately Wiener's enthusiasm for culture could not be mass-cloned. Filling up a large auditorium far from San Diego's downtown cultural center was not easy. A Google review of productions prior to 2010, when the facility was shuttered, indicated that operators did their best to bring a variety of offerings to the East County public.

For example, ECPAC had musical programs such as a Patti LuPone concert in 2003, Steve Lawrence & Edye Gorme in 2005, and a "Mozart mania" program bringing together the Grossmont Symphony Orchestra, Helix Charter High School Advanced Choir and String Orchestra and the San Diego Children's Chorus in 2006. Stage productions included *Little Shop of Horrors* in 1987 and a revival of *Thoroughly Modern Millie* in 2008. Among dance programs was an exhibition of csardas, "the tango of the east," staged by the Budapest Ensemble from Hungary. There were also community gatherings, such as a large fundraiser in 2004 for SPRITES, a mother-daughter organization that focuses on volunteering. And for the Jewish High Holy Days, the East County Performing Arts Center annually served as the venue for the Reform services of Temple Emanu-El.

But the Center had major problems during economic hard times. Rather than being a revenue source, ECPAC meant expenditures for the Grossmont-Cuyamaca Community College District. Flandi said that "supporting ECPAC became a drag on the district's budget." Why did ECPAC struggle so? "In some cases ECPAC was too big for some types of performances and in other cases it was too small," Flandi said. "Critics always talked about insufficient fly space, the area in the back for staging and scenery. So there were some problems with the ECPAC."

Editor Hood said initially the community college district and the city of El Cajon, acting as a joint powers agency, had the right to impose a "community service tax" to finance ECPAC, but when that right was repealed, ECPAC began to struggle. The development of Indian gaming casinos, offering fine entertainment at low ticket prices, added to ECPAC's financial woes, Hood said.

Eventually the college district relinquished its ownership of ECPAC to the City of El Cajon, which in a cost-saving move later shuttered the facility. If Syd Wiener were alive to see what had happened to ECPAC, "I think he would have been heart-broken," said Flandi. "He was the advocate for it; he was really in support of it. He thought it would be best for the community, a source for the arts in East County. Yes, we have the arts in San Diego, but, hey, this is El Cajon. We need some place for the performing arts."

In 2015, efforts to revive ECPAC, which needs some physical repairs including new roofing, led to leasing the facility on Sundays and one weekday evening to the Rock Church, a non-denominational Christian megachurch.

Dr. Syd Wiener and family

From N. Magnolia Avenue, Exit 17C, make a right turn on N. Magnolia Avenue, and follow it to a left turn on E. Main Street. The Performing Arts Center at 210 East Main Street will be on the left.

-San Diego Jewish World, March 24, 2016

50. Exit 18

Refugee resettlement

Grounds of St. Michael Chaldean Catholic Church

EL CAJON, California — With millions of refugees lingering in camps around the world, receiving refugee status in the United States is a difficult process – only a fraction of the refugees ever make it. And for those among the lucky few, the road to rebuilding their lives and gaining economic security is strewn with obstacles. But working in rented quarters at St. Michael Chaldean Catholic Church at 799 E. Washington Avenue, staff members of Jewish Family Service –some of them Jews, others Christians, others Muslims – are helping to ease the way for numerous refugees from Iraq.

And why shouldn't there be such inter-religious cooperation? comments Husam Salman, an Iraqi Muslim who now is on the JFS staff. If one reads history, one knows that there were periods when Jews and Muslims, working together, excelled in learning and sciences in places like early Spain. He said that from his perspective, all religions teach about peace, love, and helping one another, but somehow governments and their politicians are able to turn people of one religion against another. This shouldn't be, and thankfully, he says, for the most part it doesn't occur in his new adopted country of the United States.

Jenny Daniel, employment coordinator for Jewish Family Service's refugee resettlement program, said that she has never heard a single Iraqi refugee express concern or unwillingness over working with a Jewish organization, or vice versa. A Jew of Syrian and Mexican background, Daniel would have sensed hostility if it were there, but it simply isn't, she said. The refugees are war-weary people who fervently want to get on with their lives, and are glad for all the help that they can get.

Etleva Beijko, an Albanian who directs the JFS Refugee and Immigration program in San Diego – and who professes no religion whatsoever – said often neighboring countries, such as Jordan, to which Iraqi refugees flee, don't have the resources to absorb all the people who are running from sectarian violence. So the United Nations High Commission for Refugees becomes involved, negotiating with third countries to take in those refugees and give them a new chance at productive lives.

The United States, Australia, New Zealand, and several countries in Europe are the nations that consistently agree to accept refugees. A presidential proclamation determines the number that will be accepted each year in the United States. Priority is given to those refugees who have skills needed in these destination countries, as well as to refugees who are seeking to be reunified with family members already in those countries.

Once each country tells the United Nations High Commission for Refugees how many people it will accept for resettlement – the total being only a small fraction of the number of refugees who would like admittance – the winnowing process begins. Refugees with severe health problems or criminal histories often are rejected by destination countries. Refugees with little likelihood of being employed may be rejected in favor of those who are ready to join the workforce.

In the United States, there are nine national agencies that help to resettle refugees, many of them at least nominally affiliated with one faith community or another. Especially active are Catholics and Lutherans, who have large organizations and networks throughout the United States. The smallest of these nine agencies, handling 4.7 percent of the total number of refugees coming to America, is HIAS, which got its start in 1881 as the Hebrew Immigrant Aid Society helping Jews from Eastern Europe fleeing anti-Semitic pogroms.

HIAS was again active when there were influxes of Vietnamese refugees in the 1970s, and Jewish refugees from the Soviet Union in the 1980s and 1990s. Since the First and Second Gulf Wars, HIAS has been involved with the many Iraqis streaming to San Diego County. In 2015 it was also settling groups of refugees from Burma and from the Congo.

El Cajon, within which St. Michael Catholic Chaldean Church occupies the southwest corner of Mollison and E. Washington Avenues, has a large population of Iraqi immigrants and refugees, second only to Detroit. With Michigan experiencing a downturn in its economy, more and more Iraqi refugees have been directed to San Diego, where Jewish Family Service serves as the HIAS affiliate.

In 2014, JFS resettled some 447 people in San Diego County comprising 193 family units, according to Beijko.

Well before a refugee family arrives in San Diego, JFS is advised that they would like to come. It is up to JFS to decide whether it is able to accept sponsorship of that family based on such factors as their family composition, their medical backgrounds and their employability "because we know that San Diego is an expensive city to live in and housing is not cheap," Beijko said. "We have to make our decision as well on language ability and staff. If we accept a case, then we tell HIAS, and at that point the case is placed with us. A couple of months down the road—perhaps two to six months—when the family is ready to travel, we receive notification that they will arrive in two to three weeks. Then we start finding housing, furnishing their apartments, making sure that we have the paper work done..."

"We make arrangements for airport pickup, make sure that they have a first meal, make sure that they have enough food in their refrigerator," Beijko continued. "Right away we need to start services. There is a core service list, certain services that we have to provide within very specific time frames. The intake needs to happen within five days. They need pocket cash within 24 hours. A home visit needs to be done; orientation; enrollment in programs; referrals; connections with the county; schools; health care providers – and that is just the initial stage, which we call 'R&P' for 'reception and placement.'"

In addition to "refugees," JFS sometimes is also assigned responsibility for "asylees" – that is people who have come to the United States on their own and have asked for asylum based on fear of persecution. Only after a determination is made by the government that the people in question are eligible for asylum are they able to receive government-funded services such as those that JFS provides to the refugees.

A small building on the grounds of St. Michael Chaldean Catholic Church is a good place for JFS staff members to meet with refugees living in El Cajon because for the refugees, who often have limited access to transportation, it is easier to get to than the administrative offices for JFS's Refugee and Immigration Programs on Mission Gorge Road in San Diego, near Exit 8 of Interstate 8.

In Beijko's office is a large flow chart detailing the steps JFS must make in the refugees' five-year journey between arrival in the United States and their eligibility to apply for U.S. citizenship.

One of the most important responsibilities is to help the refugees find jobs so they can support themselves. This program is funded under provisions of the Wilson-Fish Act, named for Pete Wilson and Hamilton Fish, Jr. Wilson was a mayor of San Diego, U.S. senator and later a California governor, whereas Fish was a congressman from New York. While the act is called "Wilson/ Fish" here in San Diego, in New York the names of the two sponsors are reversed.

Daniel's responsibility includes coordinating matching grants under the Wilson/ Fish program, which covers single refugees as well as couples without children. Another federal program provides matching grants for families with children.

To find work, refugees usually need to speak English, so they are enrolled in English-as-a-Second-Language (ESL) classes. "We also do job readiness training within the first two to three months that they are here," Daniel said. "We prepare them on how to write a resume; how to prepare for an interview; what is appropriate to wear for an interview in the U.S. The level of experience our clients have varies. There are clients who never have worked before and are illiterate, even in their own language (Arabic), and there are clients with PhDs. Some clients come with high expectations of re-entering their careers as soon as they get here–so it is harder to place them because both programs (those for families, and those for singles and couples) are entry-level employment, the goal being to get them that first job. We will get them into the American work force in order to help them grow their careers."

Most, but not all, these jobs are as food and beverage workers, or as hotel workers, because San Diego County has a voracious appetite for laborers in the tourism sector. The refugees also receive assistance payments calibrated to their wages to make certain they have enough to house, feed, and clothe their families.

Before he became a caseworker for Jewish Family Service, Salman, a Baghdadi with a law degree, went through the program, working at a recycling center in San Diego, and later as a cashier at Walmart.

Whether the refugee was a doctor, lawyer, or other professional in the old country, said Salman, "the thing is that you are new in this country. The most important thing is that you need to start with something, so that you can have work references, something."

Helping to place the refugees in jobs, he said, "we help them to stand on their own legs."

Ilena Gudino, who helps to supervise the employment program, said that a majority of the refugees "want to get a job and to become more involved in San Diego society and understand how everything works here. Even if they were doctors, they want to get into the process of building a livelihood and getting integrated into society."

Salman is a believer in the American dream: "If you work hard; if you study; if you think for yourself; then the more you work, the more you are going to succeed," he said. "It is like a race. You can't just reach your goal without doing something."

He contrasted the hope of America – that people who work hard can make something of themselves – with what he described as the desperation of Iraq, where people who work hard still may end up nowhere because the way up is blocked. "Here," he said, "it's a better life."

Beijko said that seeing refugees settling in this country and working hard to give their children opportunities often resonates with members of the Jewish community, who find emotional parallels to the experiences of their own immigrant parents, grandparents or great-grandparents. Among the largest group of people to donate furniture, household items, and even money (which always is needed) to the program are members of the Jewish community, Beijko said.

She said that such donations can account for important differences in the quality of the lives of refugees.

For more information, Beijko may be reached via

etlevab@jfssd.org

Jenny Daniel and Etleva Beijko

....

From Mollison Avenue, Exit 18, head south on Mollison to Washington Avenue, and turn right. The church is on the left hand side.

....

-San Diego Jewish World, March 31, 2016

51. Exit 19
Danielle Van Dam Overpass

I-8 Sign honoring slain 7-year-old Danielle Van Dam
(Photo: Shor M. Masori)

EL CAJON, California — One of the most painful murder trials in San Diego County was that of David Westerfield for the February 2002 murder of 7-year-old Danielle Van Dam, who lived two doors away from his home in the Sabre Springs community of San Diego off the Interstate 15.

The Second Street Bridge over the Interstate 8 is named in Danielle's memory. Second Street via Jamacha Road and East Washington Avenue leads to Dehesa Road, where the little girl's naked body had been dumped, about 25 miles from her home. Danielle's partially decomposed body was discovered among weeds about a month after her kidnaping.

The prolonged search for Danielle, followed by allegations that the murdered little girl had been raped, stirred up a lot of outrage in the community, most of it against Westerfield, who at the time of this writing still was appealing his 2003 sentence of death for the murder. The case took months to litigate. It mainly turned upon forensic evidence that little Danielle had been in Westerfield's recreational vehicle and his home coupled with evidence that on the day of Danielle's disappearance, Westerfield had behaved very erratically—driving his RV to the beach and then to the desert. There was also testimony that Westerfield had child pornography on his computer.

The "Jewish connection" in this fiercely emotional case was the fact that Steven Feldman, a highly respected defense attorney, drew the assignment along with Robert Boyce as co-counsels for Westerfield's defense. Some of the outrage against Westerfield spilled over against Feldman, who tried unsuccessfully during the trial to persuade the jury that the case brought by District Attorney Paul Pfingst and other prosecutors against Westerfield was circumstantial and not conclusive.

For example, Danielle was not the only member of the Van Dam family whose DNA was found in the recreational vehicle; so too was that of other members of her family, so it was possible, Feldman argued, that the trace amounts of Danielle's blood and hair might have been left on Westerfield's clothing and in his home and RV on other innocuous occasions.

Furthermore, Feldman suggested, someone who knew of the "swinger" life styles of Danielle's parents – Brenda and Damon Van Dam – might have snuck into their house and kidnapped Danielle during the party they had held the evening of Danielle's disappearance. Evidence indicated that the parents had not looked in on their daughter's bedroom until the following morning.

When emotions run high, anti-Semitism can come to the surface. Feldman said he suffered anti-Semitic slurs for doing his job, which was to try to provide a defendant in a criminal case with the best possible defense.

A staunch opponent of the death penalty under any circumstances, Feldman argued prior to sentencing that the San Diego and national news media had turned the trial into "entertainment" that had led to a "lynch mob" mentality. Nevertheless, Judge William Mudd concurred in the jury's recommendation that Westerfield be executed.

When Feldman retired as a defense attorney in 2013, he told the local CBS television affiliate that during the Westerfield trial he received letters, including one that said "if a bus should kill you, I would say thank you God." At one point the *San Diego Union-Tribune* even referred to him as the most hated man in San Diego next to David Westerfield. "As I said at the time, 'what about Osama bin Laden?'"

In the CBS News 8 (KFMB) interview, Feldman said he didn't want to be remembered solely as Westerfield's defense lawyer, but rather as "someone who can be remembered as giving his clients the best possible defense, as being an ethical and honest person, as someone who has made a difference to the criminal defense community and dead-set against the death penalty."

Attorney Steven Feldman

So who is Steven Feldman really? What makes him tick?

He consented to an interview with *San Diego Jewish World* in September 2015 in which he told of his upbringing, his motivation to become a defense lawyer, some of his more famous cases, and his thoughts about the Westerfield case.

Born in Culver City in 1947 the son of a World War II veteran and grandson of a World War I veteran, his family moved during his boyhood to the San Fernando Valley, where he had his bar mitzvah at Temple Beth Hillel of Studio City. Afterwards, however, he did not become involved with Judaism; "it didn't sink in. I was not raised religious, neither of my parents were religious." A big Bruin fan, he went to UCLA for the first two years of college, then, following a girlfriend, transferred to UC Berkeley for the last two years. He and the girlfriend soon broke up, but Berkeley during the late 1960s was for Feldman a transformative experience.

"I arrived at Berkeley in September 1967, the beginning of the Vietnam War," Feldman related. People were getting drafted and it was pretty intense. My first week at school, there were demonstrations. My girlfriend got sick and at the hospital I started seeing students coming in with head wounds. It was during 'Stop the Draft Week' and the students got turned on. That a little bit opened my eyes." The following year, 1968, Feldman met his future wife Linda, who would become a teacher.

One day Feldman purchased a gas mask for protection during an anti-war demonstration. It didn't work. Subsequently, he was caught up in a mass arrest of students during a protest at "People's Park." Prior to the demonstration, his speech professor told students in his class that they should not go to the demonstration and "if we did, we would flunk the class. I didn't think that was reasonable, so I went to the demonstration, and that was the day (May 15, 1969) James Rector got killed. He was the guy who was shot and killed when he was a spectator upon the roof of a building in the area of the demonstration. That opened my eyes."

Rather than being defended in the "disturbing the peace" case by an overworked, underpaid public defender, Feldman retained Penny Cooper, an attorney who though just starting out was considered to be a brilliant defense lawyer. She got the case against Feldman dismissed. Admiringly, Feldman began to think that perhaps he would become an attorney too. He was accepted at Loyola Law School in Los Angeles, where one of his professors was Gerald Uelman, who later would serve as one of O.J. Simpson's defense attorneys in that celebrated murder case. Feldman was among Loyola students who traveled to the Watts neighborhood of Los Angeles periodically to provide free legal services.

While Feldman was nearing completion of law school, Uelman brought in a representative of the Los Angeles County District Attorney's staff to interview students for potential jobs. "Much to my shock he offered me a position, but I couldn't do it; I just couldn't do it," Feldman said. He said he knew he wanted to be a defense attorney, not a prosecutor. "Professionally it might have helped me to learn from the prosecutor's perspective, but in terms of what's right, it wasn't the right thing — that is just inside of me."

Instead, he took a job with the Riverside Public Defender's Office after being interviewed by his future boss, Michael F. Flynn, who called him after the interview to announce "You're in like Flynn." It was an office with a small staff, and "they started me trying drunk driving cases. Two weeks afterwards, I got my first trial. How I picked my first jury I don't know. It was totally frightening." And yet it was "fun, challenging, intense, focused, and mattered so much."

Feldman said he is adamantly opposed to the death penalty, contending it is morally wrong and economically foolish for the state to kill. "Too many innocent individuals have been sentenced to death, and in some instances executed, based upon false or insufficient evidence," he said.

"The reality is that the state's behavior is more premeditated and deliberate than any case of murder where people are getting the death penalty," he said. "Our government, its elected officials, are premeditating deaths. Murder is a premeditated, deliberate and illegal crime, and they think about it, and then the go ahead and do it. To me that is murder."

Besides believing that life imprisonment without possibility of parole is punishment enough, Feldman argues that such a penalty "is tremendously cost-effective. The amount of money the state spends to try a capital case is astronomical. There are two prosecutors in the case, each being paid somewhere in the neighborhood of $150,000 per year. There is a judge sitting every single day at his salary. There are bailiffs in the plural because there is extra security. There are court reporters who charge by the page. There is all the security that moves the defendant to and from the court. In 75 to 80 percent of the cases, the defendants are willing to plead guilty in exchange for life without parole."

Another reason for abolishing the death penalty in his view is that "every single time something happens with the case, it is in the news, which means that the surviving victims are again publicly confronted with their loss which is extraordinarily painful to them. Then there are people such as myself in the appellate sphere who will do everything ethical to make impossible the imposition of death. These cases average 10 years and in California the average is more than 20 years. So as a practical matter it saves the family having to be reminded again and again that their loved one was killed–on the front page.

"Also it saves the excruciating costs of the appeal," Feldman said, pointing out that death penalty cases are automatically appealed to the California Supreme Court, which has to hear every one of them. This means they have to pay to get them prepared, they have to get their clerks working on them, and this explains too, why it is blowing up the civil justice system." Because capital cases take priority, civil cases "languish as resources for the justice system have consistently declined and courts simply do not have time to hear civil matters."

Feldman spent 5 1/2 years as a public defender in Riverside, during which time his first murder case involved a woman on an Indian reservation who had killed her boyfriend. "They had been out dancing," Feldman recalled. "They had too much to drink. They went home. She was cutting up a steak. He threw a right cross at her. She said she saw stars. She said she instinctively went like that (Feldman pantomimed thrusting a knife). He looked at her, said 'Goodbye, Sugar' and went down. "

When the deceased hit his girl friend he broke her nose. Feldman put on the stand Dr. Rene Modgelin, a forensic pathologist who had performed autopsies for the Riverside and San Bernardino Counties for many years. Feldman asked how much force it would take to break a nose. The pathologist using a hammer provided by Feldman, tapped a skull with a hammer. "Like that?" he was asked. Harder, said the pathologist. "Like that?" asked Feldman after the pathologist struck it with more force. Harder still. The pathologist hit the skull harder, causing it to shatter with pieces flying toward the jury. Feldman told the jury that thrusting the knife was a reflex action in response to being hit so hard. "She didn't have control over her actions," he said. The jury agreed, acquitting her.

In 1979, Feldman moved to San Diego County to work with Defenders, Inc. Not long afterwards, he was able to win an acquittal in a capital murder case in which members of the Imperial County Board of Supervisors had been so certain of defendant Robert Corenevsky's guilt in the murder of jeweler Tom Wood that they refused to authorize funds to pay for an attorney, forensic pathologist, licensed investigator, and other necessary defense experts. Ultimately the California Supreme Court ordered that Corenevsky's defense be funded. The case subsequently was moved to Orange County, where a jury found Corenevsky not guilty.

"When the jury acquitted him, they hugged him... and we literally went out to dinner the next night in Orange County. At that party, the jurors presented me with photographs of them, complimenting my work on the case."

His next big case was that of carpet cleaner David Allen Lucas, accused of throat-slashing, serial murders. Lucas was found guilty in the 1979 deaths of Suzanne Jacobs, 31, and her son Colin, 3; murdered in 1979, and USD student Anne Catherine Swanke, 22, killed in 1984. Likewise, he was found guilty for the attempted murder of Jody Santiago-Robertson, 34, of Seattle, who was choked and had her throat slashed in 1984. He was found not guilty in the murders of Gayle Roberta Garcia, 29, a realtor who was found with a slashed throat in 1981, and in the 1984 deaths of Rhonda Strang, 24, and Amber Fisher, 3. After a mistrial in the Strang-Fisher case, another jury returned a death penalty verdict in August 1989 nearly five years after Lucas's arrest in December 1984.

For the defense, Feldman handled three cases and Alex Landon handled the other three. Both attorneys had co-counsels, meaning four attorneys in all for the defense. The prosecution, said Feldman, "brought in every DNA expert in the United States. I spent nine months on my feet questioning people about electrophoresis, a system of identification of blood types before DNA. "

In 2014, the California Supreme Court upheld Lucas's conviction, 25 years after his conviction. "Now the case is headed for federal court and he hasn't exhausted his administrative remedies in state court. So in a circumstance when a jury is convinced that a guy has death coming, look at the delay in imposition."

There still would have been an appeal process if Lucas had been sentenced to life imprisonment without parole, but it would have been handled by an appellate court and not by the Supreme Court, "so it distributes the volume," Feldman said.

In another celebrated case in which alleged prosecutorial misconduct resulted in convictions being set aside for the accused killers of San Diego Police Officer Jerry Hartless, Feldman grilled Deputy District Attorney Keith Burt for several days over the treatment that life prisoner Darren Palmer received in exchange for testimony against San Diego street gang members Stacy Butler, Daryl Bradshaw, Kevin Standard and Clifton Cunningham.

Palmer was brought to the district attorney's office where, on several occasions, he was allowed to have sex with his girlfriends who were transported there by representatives of the DA's office. In addition, Palmer was permitted to make collect calls to the district attorney from his prison cell and then be connected via the D.A.'s office to his girlfriends with whom he spoke for hours, running up some $5,000 in phone bills, according to Feldman. Burt testified that the treatment accorded to Palmer was not out of the ordinary, but he subsequently was disciplined with a demotion. Eventually, Burt was permitted to retire with full benefits, which Feldman called a travesty.

So Feldman's reputation as a defense attorney was well established when he and attorney Bob Boyce, with whom he co-owned a building, were contacted by David Westerfield and asked to represent him in the Danielle Van Dam case. Westerfield had not yet been arrested, but knew he was under suspicion.

The first meeting was at a coffee shop in Mission Valley, and Feldman recalled that police were all around, keeping Westerfield under surveillance. Wherever Westerfield went, so too did the police. Feldman offered to have Westerfield privately surrender, but instead they arrested him outside Feldman's office.

Feldman said he made it a practice not to discuss the case with the news media, while police and the district attorney's office did just the reverse, leaking information throughout the trial.

Knowing that the district attorney had set up a special crime laboratory just to process evidence from this case — perhaps in reaction to the O.J. Simpson murder case in Los Angeles in which evidence had been mishandled — Feldman and Boyce decided to seek an immediate trial, which, although unusual, is the constitutional right of any defendant. Most defendants in capital cases prefer to waive that right in order to have more time to prepare a defense. But the other side of that coin is that it gives the prosecution more time as well, and Feldman thought the prosecution's case at that point in time was weak and circumstantial. "I wanted to insure Westerfield was provided with all of his constitutional rights without unnecessary delay," Feldman said.

In opting for an immediate trial, Feldman gave up the opportunity to have a change of venue. Later when breathless news coverage of the trial created a tense atmosphere not only for Westerfield but for his defense team as well, Feldman wondered whether holding the trial elsewhere would have been a better strategy. But the die was cast.

Early polling indicated that the public was divided on who might be responsible for little Danielle's murder. Some people blamed the Van Dams because of their swinger life style and their apparent lack of concern for their daughter's welfare. Some even went so far as to suspect the Van Dams themselves. But as the trial progressed, opinion shifted, and in the public mind Westerfield and his defense team became the villains. Feldman, whose courtroom style can be abrasive, became a lightning rod for criticism.

A newspaper cartoon depicted Feldman in a manner reminiscent of the anti-Semitic cartoons of Jews one finds in Nazi propaganda. Feldman was depicted with ears like wings and a giant nose–almost fiendish looking.

Television commentators resentful that Feldman wouldn't talk to them during the trial, invited other "experts" to be their talking heads, heaping scorn on Feldman and his effort to cast doubt on the prosecution's case.

At one point after the verdict, District Attorney Paul Pfingst said that in pre-trial negotiations, Feldman had offered to plead Westerfield guilty if the death penalty were taken off the table.

Without conceding that was what occurred, Feldman said that plea bargaining sessions between the prosecution and the defense are supposed to be completely off the record, and that Pfingst breached that ethical practice with such comments.

"All I want to do is to save someone's life, so what may be discussed in those circumstances needs to stay confidential," Feldman said. If what Pfingst alleged were true, he said, "one might legitimately ask why did the community have to go through nine months of that 'bloodshed'? Why did the Van Dams have to be put through that? Why did the county taxpayers have to eat the costs of this?"

He noted that by 2015 Westerfield had been on death row for 12 years, and that his opening brief on appeal had just been filed. "It will be easily 5 to 10 years before his case is finally resolved. Had a plea bargain been offered and accepted, none of that would be occurring today."

When the death penalty verdict came down, there was great cheering for the prosecutorial team and the district attorney (who nevertheless was defeated for reelection by Bonnie Dumanis) and lots of anger expressed towards Westerfield and his defense team.

A letter to Westerfield written at that time conveys the mood. "They and their children did not deserve the fate you dealt them and as for that pig lawyer of yours, well when they stick you with the lethal poison I hope to hell they do it to that pig Feldman. No one deserves a defense, least of all you."

Another letter, to Feldman, said: "I wish you no ill but if a truck should hit you in the ass causing your demise I would consider it God's will."

At first, Feldman's practice was hurt by the public vilification that he drew, but eventually, he said, he started receiving referrals again and was rebuilding the practice, when he started having tingling in his arm –"like when you hit your crazy bone." Shortly afterwards, he ran up the stairs of his house to get a telephone call and "I was out of gas. I had indigestion that wouldn't go away. I called Kaiser and said 'these are my symptoms' and they said 'come down immediately! Don't drive!' So I went down. They did tests. They told me to come back and I got on a stress exerciser and they tackled me off it."

Wheeled into surgery, Feldman had an emergency quadruple bypass.

In 2013, Feldman sold his portion of the building in which he had practiced for the previous 23 years, closed his law practice and retired. Since then, he and Linda have traveled to Europe and other parts of the globe, and have been actively involved in raising their granddaughter.

....

Follow Interstate 8, to Second Street in El Cajon.

....

-San Diego Jewish World, April 7, 2016

52. Exit 19
Jack and the two lady mayors

Jack in the Box and Union Bank are neighbors on El Cajon's Second Street
(Photo: Shor M. Masori)

EL CAJON, California — There are numerous Jack in the Box restaurants, and nothing other than convenience made me pick the one at 495 N. Second Street over any of the others to tell the story of two partners—one Christian, one Jewish—who made a fortune selling Jack-in-the Box to Ralston-Purina and wound up both marrying ambitious politicians who, one after the other, became mayors of San Diego.

This particular Jack in the Box outlet is right off Interstate 8 at the 2nd Street exit.

The Christian partner was Robert O. Peterson, a restaurateur who had founded a drive-in diner called Topsy's in 1941, which he operated along with Oscar's restaurants following his service as a naval intelligence officer in World War II. The Oscar's located at 6270 El Cajon Boulevard in San Diego he converted in 1951 to a

Jack in the Box, the first in the nation. Unlike the original McDonald's Restaurant in Downey, California, the first Jack in the Box restaurant – complete with a rooftop clown on a spring popping out of a box — was torn down to make way for other commercial development.

The Jewish partner, Richard T. Silberman, was brought into the Jack in the Box restaurant chain to utilize his financing savvy to help grow the chain to 265 restaurants before the Ralston Purina sale, which was reported at $58 million. Millionaires and still relatively young men, Peterson and Silberman became involved in banking and in politics. They took over First National Bank, renaming it California First Bank and later selling it to the Bank of Tokyo, which renamed it again to Union Bank.

However, the pursuit of politics eventually drove them apart, according to lengthy and well-researched articles by the investigative reporter Matt Potter of the *San Diego Reader*.

Maureen O'Connor, San Diego's first female mayor, was a Democrat. Susan Golding, the city's second female mayor, was a Republican. Their ambitions to advance even higher than the mayor's office spelled rivalry. Peterson married O'Connor in 1977, midway through her second term as a member of the City Council. Peterson and Silberman both helped O'Connor win election in 1986 as the 31st mayor of San Diego, a position in which she served eight years.

Meanwhile Golding served on the San Diego City Council and briefly as a Deputy Secretary in California's Business and Transportation Agency. Daughter of former San Diego State University president Brage Golding, Susan Golding used her maiden name after her divorce from attorney Stanley Prowse, and her children, Sam and Vanessa, also became known as Goldings.

All this while, Silberman was climbing the political ladder, appointed in 1977 by Gov. Jerry Brown as Secretary of Business and Transportation, and later, around the time when Brown was opposing President Jimmy Carter in the Democratic primaries of 1980, as the State Director of Finance.

Golding and Silberman began dating in 1982 while she was serving in Silberman's former agency in the gubernatorial administration of Brown's successor, Republican Gov. George Deukmejian. Silberman became Golding's confidante and in 1984 her husband as well, in what wags referred to as the "great political *alloyance*."

Although Silberman was a Democrat, he supported his Republican wife to the hilt, crushing the hopes of attorney Lynn Schenk of having his support in a race for a seat on the County Board of Supervisors.

Schenk was a Brown loyalist who had been Silberman's former deputy and protégé in the state Department of Business and Transportation. Some years later she would serve a single term in Congress, and later still would serve as chief of staff to Gov. Gray Davis, who himself had previously been a chief of staff to Jerry Brown.

Winning that election for county office in a bruising battle against Schenk, Golding went on to serve two terms as a member of the County Board of Supervisors, which oversees land use for the unincorporated areas of the county and is responsible for providing health and judicial services, among other services, throughout the entire county. On many issues, particularly in the realm of regional planning, the city and the county governments could cooperate or clash, and with both O'Connor and Golding eyeing higher office, the tension between the two former partners' wives became palpable.

In the middle of her second term, as Golding was pondering running to succeed Mayor O'Connor, Silberman was indicted on a charge of money laundering. The FBI had been wiretapping the phone of Chris Petti, a San Diegan with reputed mob connections, and were amazed when they heard Silberman offer to launder some money for the mob. That led to Silberman's phone also being tapped, and then to a sting operation, and, in 1989, Silberman was placed under arrest. At one point, he reportedly attempted to commit suicide prior to his trial, conviction, and sentencing to 46 months in a minimum security federal prison. Golding filed for divorce in 1991.

Issuing a contrite apology from prison via a son by a former marriage, Silberman said that "unfortunately I was not always truthful with her regarding critical and vital aspects of my life, and I know I am responsible for the changes in our relationship. We have been separated over a year now, and the obvious strains and difficulties have led us to mutually agree that it is time to end the marriage. I will always be grateful to her."

In December 1992, over spirited opposition from Democrat Peter Navarro, Golding was elected as the city's first Jewish mayor, the 32nd person to hold that office. Golding served two terms, for a total of eight years. A highlight of her term in office was having the 1996 Republican National Convention in San Diego – which erased the sting of the Republicans pulling their convention out of San Diego in 1972 in the midst of Richard Nixon's ITT scandal. One of the 1996 presidential debates between incumbent Bill Clinton and challenger Bob Dole also was held in the city, on the University of San Diego campus.

Many of Golding's political allies believed that this chance to be in the national spotlight as the host mayor would position the mayor well to run for higher office – or to receive a highly visible Cabinet post in the event that Dole should win. But Clinton easily turned back Dole's challenge, and a ticket guarantee deal with the San Diego Chargers in which the city agreed to make up the difference in revenue for any home football game not sold out was quite controversial, and cost Golding political support.

In 1998, Golding was an early entrant in the Republican contest for the U.S. Senate seat held by Democrat Barbara Boxer, but her campaign never caught on and she decided to drop out of the race.

Ironically neither Golding nor O'Connor advanced beyond the mayoralty, leaving former San Diego Mayor Pete Wilson, who became a U.S. Senator and later a governor of California, the only San Diegan in recent memory to win election outside what some have described as California's political cul-de-sac.

In a sad footnote, O'Connor developed a bad gambling addiction, losing millions of dollars over the years, some of which she financed through a charitable trust left by Peterson. She told the court that a brain injury had influenced her errant behavior, and was put on probation, provided that she return the money to the trust. Eventually, the case against her was resolved without jail time.

Golding went on to become president and CEO of the Child Abuse Foundation in San Diego.

....

From Second Street, Exit 19, turn north on Second Street. Both the Jack in the Box and the Union Bank are a short distance but on opposite sides of the street.

....

-San Diego Jewish World, April 14, 2016

53. Exit 20
California Highway Patrol

CHP Kevin Pearlstein shows site of horrific crash at I-8 and State 79

EL CAJON, California — Most of the 31-mile stretch of Interstate 8 between Greenfield Drive (Exit 20) and Buckman Springs Road (Exit 51) is known to California Highway Patrol officers like Kevin Pearlstein as Beat 83. Amid its climb to an elevation over 4,000 feet are beautiful views and vistas that the tourist can see. But, for Pearlstein and the 110 other officers assigned to CHP's El Cajon station, this road also prompts vivid memories of wasted lives.

I met Pearlstein, who celebrated his 18th anniversary with the CHP in June of 2015, for a media "ride-along" from the CHP offices at 1722 East Main Street in El Cajon, where by appointment, motorists may receive free instruction on the proper way to install an infant car seat. Here, too, motorists may bring their cars in to show that they have complied with vehicle "fix it" orders issued by any law enforcement agency in the state. There is no charge for either service.

In different parts of the United States, there are stories of "speed traps" where law enforcement officers wait to catch speeders in order to raise revenue for their towns. Nothing like that happens with the CHP, commented Pearlstein, because "CHP receives no money" from the tickets it writes. "We don't get a penny, and that is the way the governor wants it. We don't want anyone to think it is a revenue generator. We write tickets because tickets save lives."

In fact, commented Pearlstein, who went through a pre-drive check of his snazzy assortment of radios, lights and siren, computer, weapons (a Remington 870 shotgun and an AR-15 rifle), and radar, just by the CHP "showing the door"— that is, making their marked patrol cars very visible on the area highways—lives are saved because motorists are reminded to slow down and do the right thing.

A gate with a sign telling how many days (42 days when I visited), it had been since a CHP officer was in an accident opened to allow us to leave the CHP yard. Pearlstein guided his cruiser up the eastbound Interstate 8 ramp, and, as we got to know each other, he shared a story of growing up with his father's Chanukah and his mother's Christmas celebrations. Still today, his family celebrates both holidays. Additionally, he has attended a lot of family *bar* and *bat* mitzvahs, and one of his cousins—Elise Pearlstein—is a film maker perhaps best known for the documentary *Food*. Additionally, for family use only, she interviewed their common grandmother about how she had to hide out during the Holocaust, "kind of an Anne Frank story."

Kevin Pearlstein had grown up in San Diego, graduating from Patrick Henry High School and from San Diego State University where he majored in political science and minored in sociology. A relative who had worked for the San Diego Police Department suggested he consider a career in law enforcement, and the idea grew on him. It took two years before he was accepted into the CHP Academy, and over six months of intensive training before he earned the right to be called an officer. His first assignment was in northern Orange County, but later he was able to be transferred to his home turf, San Diego County.

After his 16th year with the CHP, he accepted a tour in the public relations department, which involves teaching students in public schools about safety and serving as a spokesman to the media in the event of newsworthy cases in the East County. He enjoys the assignment, okay, but he said he hankers to get back on patrol, where every day is different, and challenging, and where law enforcement officers enjoy a special camaraderie.

Some people mistakenly think that the California Highway Patrol's jurisdiction is only on highways, said Pearlstein, but out in rural, unincorporated portions of San Diego County, it also divides responsibilities with the San Diego County Sheriff's office. Sheriff's deputies investigate criminal matters, while the CHP is responsible for traffic. If you're driving drunk, or over the speed limit, a CHP officer can pull you over, whether you're on a highway or a back-country road. They also are there to help if your car is stalled or you're in an accident. Sometimes, Pearlstein said, officers from other law enforcement agencies will deride the CHP as "Triple A (Road Service) with a badge" but they make such comments out of jealousy. The CHP is harder to get into than most law enforcement agencies. "We have 20,000 applicants and out of that maybe 50 will make it." In East County, he said, such inter-agency rivalry is at a minimum. Most of the people serving there have been with their respective agencies for long times and are happy with their careers, according to Pearlstein.

As we approached Dunbar Lane, Exit 27, Pearlstein recalled the time that a mother who was taking her son westbound to Valhalla High School lost control of her vehicle, and rolled her car on that particular stretch of highway. "He wasn't wearing a seat belt and was ejected and killed. She survived. The dad was so distraught later in the day that he got on the freeway the wrong way at Tavern Road (Exit 30) and he was trying to go head on with vehicles and he finally did it and he hit this young girl head on. Fortunately she survived, but he didn't. That was right here."

I barely had time to picture the suicidal incident before Pearlstein gestured to a sign up ahead marking the Jimmy A. Arevalo Memorial Highway. "There was a young girl," Pearlstein related. "She was a valedictorian student in high school, and she was graduating from UCSD summa cum laude. She was just a week away from graduation. She went out dancing and she got drunk, the alcohol in her blood testing at .12. She crashed and came to rest in the fast lane on her roof. A Good Samaritan, Jimmy Arevalo, a teacher from El Centro, pulled his truck up, got out, and was trying to assist her. He was on 911 talking to our dispatcher, and while he was doing that, another drunk driver doing 80 miles an hour, with no braking apparatus, killed both Arevalo and the girl. The dispatcher heard it all on the radio. 'I'm over here – Oh my God!' and the lights went out. The driver who killed them had moved here from Washington, was here only a month, had no license, no insurance, and several drug convictions. She was driving to a casino. Now she is serving 9 ½ years in state prison on a plea bargain. Mrs. Arevalo says her husband was killed by two drunk drivers: the first being the girl who started the whole chain of events, and then the next driver."

When Pearlstein stops a motorist on suspicion of drunk driving, he conducts a number of "field sobriety tests" always in the same order. Sometimes, if a person is elderly, "they obviously can't stand on one foot, so I am not going to give them that test, but if a person is in his or her 30s, I will do the same tests that I always do. A lot of what we do is routine, and that helps us if ever the arrest is challenged in court. Someone might say 'How do you know you did the Romberg Balance Test as your second test?' I answer 'Because I always do; I have made one thousand DUI stops…'"

If the motorist is arrested on suspicion of drunk driving, he or she will be asked to take either a breath test or a blood test. One or the other must be chosen, because "when you signed for your driver's license, you said if ever you were arrested for drinking and driving, you would submit to either a blood or breath test. The breath test is immediate. Once it is done, it can't be done again; there is no way to retest it, whereas blood can be retested. The crime lab does it for us; a defense lawyer can have it done independently. We used to have to offer urine as well; thank God, they don't do that anymore."

If a motorist takes a breath test and it shows an alcohol level of over .08, "then I'm going to read a Trombetta Advisement to you explaining that a breath test cannot be tested by another agency, however if you wish to provide an additional sample at no charge to you, we can have a blood sample drawn and sent to the crime lab for evaluation. And then we check a box that Trombetta was offered."

I asked at what point does a drunk driving suspect need to be read his or her Miranda rights—the right to remain silent, or to have an attorney present during questioning. "Arrest plus interrogation equals Miranda," Pearlstein replied. "So if I arrest you for drunk driving, I have already made up my mind that you are drunk and I don't need to ask you further questions. Some people do; I don't. I don't need anything else from you... but if I were to ask questions because there was a hit and run in the same area, with a car fitting the description of the person who I've arrested, then I would Mirandize him, and if he waived his right and wanted to talk, then I would ask him, 'hey were you on that road, and could you have hit that car?'"

At East Willows Road (Exit 36) Pearlstein said "whenever we have to shut the freeway down, maybe because of high winds, we will always shut it down here at East Willows, and people will turn around and go back or park on the shoulder and wait for us to reopen it. We have had 75 to 85 miles per hour winds at the Pine Valley Bridge (Exit 45), Sunrise Highway (Exit 47), and Crestwood (Exit 67). Once the first big rig or RV overturns, it's over. We shut it down. We shut down traffic for high profile vehicles and that is the time when we will run escorts for passenger vehicles."

In an escort situation, he explained, "I will be the lead vehicle and we will start going and people will start following me. I don't have to zig zag, I straddle the lanes, with my (flashing) lights on. Motorists usually get the point. I will go 20 miles to 30 miles per hour, trying to get someone over the Crestwood summit. On the other side, in El Centro, the CHP will close the grade so no one can start (westbound) up the hill."

The winds being normal, we drove at regular speed to the Ellis Wayside Vista Point (Exit 37), named for the family of pioneer Charles Ellis who came from Norway in the 1880s and settled in the Descanso area in the 1900s. He was the surveyor of the Viejas Grade Road, which made travel easier between the Imperial Valley and western San Diego County. In the past a plaque marked the spot, but vandals pried it off its cement pedestal as well as a facing plaque describing the viewpoint which is 40 miles inland from the ocean. A copy of the plaque, which can be found on line, informed that "the land around you is a portion of the Sweetwater Watershed, which is protected by the Forest Service to supply water from winter rains." The brush, the plaque further explained, is chaparral, which in dry conditions can be quickly ignited, resulting in "large, extremely hot brush fires" that damage the watershed, and result later in "floods, mudslides and severe erosion." The plaque concluded with a plea to "please protect this watershed. Be careful with fire at all times, and use your ashtray as you continue your travel."

Pearlstein said the vista point also is the place where the driver of a big rig, distraught that his wife had left him, drove the rig as fast as he could from a parking area "and launched it down the hill. He ended up way down there, and it took three or four days to pull the truck up, with three or four tow trucks pulling it up piece by piece. It was a major headache."

Suicides, alas, are not confined to the vista point. The Pine Valley Bridge, at Exit 45, is another structure that attracts the terminally depressed. "I worked the San Diego office of CHP and the Coronado Bridge is the same thing. People do it; it is just crazy. The thought of suicide has never popped into my head; I can't imagine what they were dealing with that they thought that was the best option."

We got out of the car and stretched at the vista point. Pearlstein said that drivers should take constant breaks, at least every two hours on long trips. Furthermore, he advises people who will be traveling long distances on the highways to "make sure your tires are good, and if it is the winter season make sure your wipers are good. Before I go on a trip, I always make sure the tires are balanced and rotated, and I get the oil changed. Make sure that your vehicle, first and foremost, is going to make it. Get plenty of sleep the night before, and if you have two people who can drive, split the driving up. And give yourself time! What we find on a Friday afternoon, coming west, a lot of people from Arizona are doing 85, 90, 95 miles per hour, just flying out here, in such a hurry to escape the heat, and Sundays they are out of control trying to get back."

He said that in 2014, the El Cajon office of the CHP made 72,000 traffic stops. "We didn't write 72,000 tickets. A lot of them were at night, drunk driver checks. You check them and if they are sober they go on, but it is still an enforcement stop."

What does he say about the oft-repeated charge that law enforcement officers single out minorities for tickets?

"Say we are sitting here (at the vista point) watching traffic and that truck goes by right there, can you tell who is driving that truck, or that car behind him? You have no idea. I'm sitting on the side of the road, and I am running my radar and watching my mirrors and I see a car. I think he's doing maybe 85, and I lock on the radar, and he's actually doing 87. I have no idea who that person is until I am walking up, looking through those windows, absolutely no idea."

Whether he gives a ticket, or issues a warning, can depend upon the attitude of the driver. The speed limit in this area of the freeway is 70 miles per hour. "If you are doing 95 miles per hour, you are getting a ticket. If you are going under 80 and I stop you and you're respectful, and you say something like 'it got away from me, my kid was crying,' I might say, 'hey, try to slow down a bit, and drive carefully.'"

On the other hand, "if I say you were doing 85, and you smack your hand on the seat and say, 'I was only doing 80!' that's a ticket. But if they have a good attitude, 'sorry it got away from me, my fault, I'm sorry, officer,' that person is so much likely to get his stuff (driver's license and registration) back."

The law permits such discretion, he said. "There are three words in our policies: 'may,' 'should,' and 'shall.' 'May' is you 'may do it; 'should' is you probably should do it, and 'shall' means you must do it, and if you don't you are in violation of policy. If someone is going five miles over the speed limit, it is 'shall' stop and 'should' cite. It is not 'shall' stop, 'shall' cite, so it's our discretion. It all depends on the interaction with the driver, what their attitude is toward law enforcement. I don't care if they are Hispanic, white, African American, male, female, I don't care. I don't care if they are Jewish and wearing a yarmulke — 'Pearlstein? you're going to give me a ticket? I'm Schwartz' – that doesn't matter, it means nothing."

We continued to Exit 40, which is the junction of Interstate 8 with State Route 79. This, said Pearlstein, was the site of "the biggest crash I ever had. It was a truck loaded with illegal immigrants from Mexico. They loaded up down by Tecate and came up State Highway 188 and as they turned onto Highway 94, the U.S. Border Patrol attempted to stop them. They attempted to run over one of the agents, and so a huge pursuit ensued, and there were 17 people in the back of this truck and three in the front: the driver, an innocent young lady, and the smuggler or coyote. They ended up crashing into the bridge abutment here over the 79, and all 17 people in the back got ejected onto the 79 state route down below. Three of them were killed, eight or nine had major injuries. Fortunately, the driver and the coyote were trapped in the cab; they wanted to run but they couldn't, so we were able to prosecute them. Each of them got 25 years to life per each death, so they'll be locked up forever. They will never be out."

We continued to the exit at Buckman Springs Road (Exit 51), marking the beginning of the territory which four resident CHP officers are responsible for patrolling. From their homes, they cover the Interstate 8 from this point to Exit 77, In-Ko-Pah Park Road, which sits on the border of San Diego and Imperial Counties. They also are responsible for Highway 94 to Tecate. They fax their reports from a sheriff's substation, and twice a week receive mail and notices from the home office, brought to them by senior volunteers.

As we headed back to the El Cajon station, I asked Pearlstein whether there were any driving tips he'd like to pass onto readers.

He said if people want to avoid injury accidents, they should be sure to follow four rules:

(1) Drive the speed limit

(2) Wear seat belts

(3) Don't drink and drive

(4) Don't talk or text.

The last one caught me by surprise. Weren't we, in fact, talking at that very moment?

Yes, he said, "but we are both paying attention to the road. That is called 'shared awareness.' We are both watching the traffic conditions. If there is some traffic stopping up there, and you see it, you would say 'Whoa, look out!' But if I am by myself in a car, and I am in a perfectly legal conversation (that is with a cell phone hooked up to a speaker/microphone), I have lost shared awareness. Fifty percent of what I am seeing, I have lost because I am focused on the conversation. My focus isn't driving. You are four times more likely to crash if you are talking on the phone compared to someone who isn't on the phone. When you are texting, you are 23 times more likely to crash. Texting involves three separate distractions: your eyes are off the road (as you look down at the screen of your cell phone); you have one hand off the wheel, and your mind is off the road."

During our outing, we had the chance to schmooze about Pearlstein's perceptions of TV dramas depicting law enforcement. He said that when he was a boy, he used to love to watch the television series *CHiPs* starring Eric Estrada as trainee "Ponch" and Larry Wilcox as his more seasoned partner Jon Baker. The TV series influenced Pearlstein's desire to become a California Highway Patrolman. Now when he sees reruns, he laughs, he just has to roll his eyes at some of the unlikely plots. A far more realistic portrayal of law enforcement, he said, was the television series *Southland*, which no longer is on the air. As for the various *CSI* (Crime Scene Investigators) shows, "I can't get into that, I mean, people in the crime lab out there doing interviews? You think, 'where's the rest of them? Where's the police force?' I mean really, these two people are doing everything. I used to like *Law and Order* back in the day, especially when Jerry Ohrbach was in it."

....

From Exit 20, turn north on Greenfield Drive, and left on East Main Street. CHP station is on the left.

....

-San Diego Jewish World, April 21, 2016

54. Exit 22
Lindo Lake

Old Boat House at Lindo Lake

LAKESIDE, California — This small unincorporated western-flavored town is known for its rodeo and for the former automobile track around Lindo Lake where pioneer race driver Barney Oldfield set a speed record a century ago, covering a mile distance in 51 and 4/5 seconds. It is not a town one normally associates with Jews, but here (and as we suggest, everywhere) some Jewish threads are included in the tapestry of local history.

One of the first Jews to make an impression on Lakeside was Edgar Klauber, great-grandson of a rabbi and son of pioneer Jewish merchant Abraham Klauber of San Diego. He used to travel from San Diego to back country towns to take orders and deliver to stores such merchandise as groceries, tobacco, boots, shoes, dry goods, hardware, and farm implements.

The Lakeside Historical Society reported in its book, *Legends of Lakeside*, that Klauber had recorded a sales trip on behalf of Klauber-Wangenheim Co: "My first day took me through Lemon Grove, Spring Valley, then by way of Sycamore Canyon to El Cajon, where I had lunch at the Knox Hotel. At El Cajon, I had three customers: my old friend John Burgess, who was doing a thriving general merchandise business in those days; Al Brower, the druggist, and Harry Hubbell, who I believe was the town constable in conjunction with his saloon business. In the afternoon I left for Lakeside, via Bostonia, stopping at Lakeside overnight.

"There was no store at that time in Lakeside, but I remember a fellow named John Ike ran what he called a 'club'—you signed your name to a register, and after paying $1.00 for dues, you automatically, as it were, became a member in good standing. You could buy drinks as long as you could stand up and stand the drinks, as no saloons were allowed in Lakeside. John Ike's club had a big membership."

Edgar Klauber subsequently recalled in an article of his own in the *Journal of San Diego History* that he had attended a grocer's picnic near Lakeside during the Depression year of 1893. A Republican, Klauber blamed economic hard times on Grover Cleveland, who was then the occupant of the White House.

"Suddenly I saw the manager of the Lakeside Hotel coming toward our Retail Grocers' Picnic of 29 grocers, 29 wives, and a lot more children. He was running and when a manager of a hotel runs, there is something wrong. At first I thought he was going to have us arrested for not eating in his hotel, but, no, it was even worse than that. He called me aside and broke the news. He had just received a telegraph message from San Diego. There had been a run on the three San Diego banks and all three had closed their doors."

Klauber went on to write that he made the following announcement: "Ladies and gentlemen, little boys and girls, and various innocent relatives, please stop eating and give me your attention. This man at my side is the manager of the Lakeside Hotel. You can see by his face that he carries bad news. All three banks in San Diego have closed their doors. I advise you to continue your picnic for two very good reasons. First, I happen to know that very few of you have any money in the closed banks. Second, even if you did have any money on deposit, you could not get it out with a crowbar. So please sit right down and go on eating before the ants set in…"

The Lakeside Hotel was a resort property which long since has been destroyed. However, the boat house which was a popular place for guests to row to still graces Lindo Lake, which to this date attracts various kinds of water fowl including ducks, egrets, geese, herons, and pelicans, among others.

A denizen of Lindo Lake.

Eventually the Klauber-Wangenheim Co. purchased property in Lakeside. According to the Lakeside Historical Society, "In 1903, Klauber-Wangenheim bought the Lakeside Store and C. W. Ross was sent to Lakeside to manage it in 1904. Mr. Ross brought with him his wife, Mary Annie, his daughter Josie, and Mrs. Ross' mother, Josephine Mansfield. They occupied the upper story of the Lakeside Store (over the Meat Market) while they built their house next door, and moved there in 1905. There were only 16 dwellings in town at that time, including the Church, Inn, and Lindo Hotel."

Legends of Lakeside also noted: "In 1919, Lakeside's first high school classes were held upstairs in the Klauber-Wangenheim Building on the southwest corner of Maine and Sycamore, with Alice Gibson its teacher. In 1920, Riverview H.S. was built on Woodside Avenue...."

In 1911, the silent movie industry produced in San Diego County some 45 short films between May 25 when it made *A Trooper's Heart* and October 2 when it filmed *The Love of the West*, according to a compilation by Gregory L. Williams in a 2002 edition of *The Journal of San Diego History*. As was noted in the earlier chaper concerning Exit 13 A, Spring Street, one of the films that Alan Dwan made in Lakeside was *The Yiddisher Cowboy*.

Lindo Lake always has been a pleasant destination for San Diegans. During World War II, Sam Sloan, a U.S. Marine, took Ruth Ann Trupin, whom he met at a USO dance at Temple Beth Israel in San Diego, on a spin in his car out to this lake. They liked what they saw, and in the 1950s, after Sam earned an optometry degree and they were married, the Sloans moved to Lakeside where Sam opened a practice, Ruth taught school, and they raised two children, Iris and Tom.

The Sloans became active civic boosters, Sam in particular. Lakeside's chamber of commerce, its historical society, and its Kiwanis Club all, at one time or another, elected Sloan as their president. He is credited with helping to start the annual Lakeside parade, an occasion for which the former leatherneck recruited the Marine Corps Band, and attracted as a participant another former Marine—and a future U.S. senator and California governor— Pete Wilson.

Another Jewish professional in Lakeside was Robert Siegel, a dentist who arrived in the mid-1950s. His widow, Paula, once recalled that Bob had intended to practice in El Cajon, where a medical/dental center was being constructed. In the meantime, he participated in a San Diego County program to bring dental and medical services to areas of the county where there were no resident physicians and dentists.

"The county had a trailer for places without professionals," Paula Siegel recalled. "So, he would go there once a week and to other places. Some members of the Town Council came to him and asked if he would like to start practicing in Lakeside. They offered to set him up in a building. Bob's feeling was that if they needed a dentist in Lakeside, it would be better to go there than to El Cajon where there were already dentists."

Eventually, Siegel purchased a piece of land and built his own dental offices. He practiced there for approximately 28 years, until his death in 1983. His wife, Paula, outlived him by 21 years. Like Sloan, Siegel was a member of the Kiwanis Club and "we went to Chamber dances," Paula once said. She also recalled that for a while the Kiwanis Club had a piano that no one seemed to be able to tune. "It was like an old Jimmy Stewart movie—someone playing the piano out of tune."

Although Lakeside was considered the back country, that didn't stop Siegel from becoming a leader among California dentists. He regularly lobbied the Legislature for bills affecting the field of dentistry, among them one which called for the computerization of dental records. That program helped Siegel perform his work as a forensic dentist, particularly in identifying victims of the Pacific Southwest Airlines (PSA) airplane crash in San Diego in 1978 that claimed 144 lives.

One of Lakeside's most famous residents was a girl who lived to be only 12 years old, Heather Michele O'Rourke. As the story goes, the little blonde girl and her mommy were visiting the commissary of MGM Studios in Hollywood. A man asked her name.

Reluctantly she told him, but added: "You're a stranger; I can't talk to you." The man waited for Heather's mother to return so that he and Heather could be properly introduced. It was Steven Spielberg, and there was something about Heather that made the famous producer think she might be just perfect in a movie about the supernatural: *The Poltergeist*. After two auditions—the first not having gone so well—5-year-old Heather got to act in the movie, and also to utter one of cinema's most famous lines: "They're here."

Heather, who won election as president of her 5th grade class, starred in two *Poltergeist* sequels. She died of cardiopulmonary arrest brought on by a chronic intestinal condition before the completion of *Poltergeist III*, which was dedicated to her memory.

....

From Exit 22, head north on Los Coches Road until it becomes Maine Avenue. Turn right on Woodside Avenue or Lakeshore Drive to access Lindo Lake.

....

-San Diego Jewish World, April 28, 2016

55. Exit 23
R.M. Levy Water Treatment Plant

R.M. Levy Water Treatment Plant
(Photos courtesy of Helix Water District)

LAKESIDE, California — I have a saying that "there's a Jewish story everywhere" but who would have thought that it would take a former governor of Illinois to put me on the search for one right in my own back yard in San Diego County, California.

Back in 2005, I was reading *Thirst for Independence: The San Diego Water Story* by Dan Walker, who had grown up in the Encanto neighborhood of San Diego before moving to Illinois where a career in the law and politics led to his serving as that state's governor.

After leaving office, Walker became a principal in a savings and loan association, and engaged in what the federal government contended were illegal loan practices. After pleading guilty, Walker spent 18 months of a 7-year-sentence at a minimum- security prison in Duluth, Minnesota. He decided to rebuild his life in his boyhood San Diego County, where he has been redeeming his reputation by writing solid books of local interest.

I met Walker at a party for authors thrown by our mutual publisher, Sunbelt Publications of El Cajon. We exchanged books—I being quite pleased that Walker was interested in reading my *Louis Rose: San Diego's First Jewish Settler*. Reading Walker's book resulted in my learning about the various dams on San Diego County rivers, our county's dependence on imported water from the Colorado and Feather Rivers, and—not surprisingly, given the background of the author—some of the behind-the-scenes forces governing the politics of water.

On page 88, I was startled to read that in the Helix Water District—which old timers know as the former La Mesa, Lemon Grove and Spring Valley Irrigation District— "all water goes through the district's $50 million state-of-the-art R.M. Levy Treatment Plant at Lakeside that uses the advanced ozonation process to improve taste and color."

"All state and federal standards for quality and safety are met and the plant's capacity is 106 million gallons per day," Walker wrote. "The San Diego Chapter of the American Institute of Architects recently granted its coveted Orchid Award to the plant as an outstanding Environmental Solutions Project. The plant is hailed not just for its physical appearance but also for being the first in San Diego County to provide such clean, fresh-tasting, ozone-treated water that there is, as the boosters say, 'no need to lug jugs of bottled water home anymore.'"

I had thought that I knew of all the Jews for whom public buildings in San Diego County had been named. "Levy, who was Levy?" I wondered.

Kate Breece, public relations director at the Helix Water District, told me R.M. "Rube" Levy had been a longtime director of the district, a man who had led a colorful life before he died in a 1959 traffic accident during a hunting trip in Imperial County. At one time, he had played professional baseball, she understood.

Breece directed me to Bob Friedgen, a former general manager of the Helix Water District, who added that Levy's father, Henry, had owned Levy's Hardware Store in La Mesa. Friedgen said he thought, but could not be certain, that the Levys were members of the Jewish community; that prior to World War I, Levy had played second base perhaps in the Detroit Tigers organization, and that Levy had won medals for his World War I military exploits in Europe.

Friedgen, in turn, referred me to Norrie West, a retired journalist and sports publicist, who recalled that as a 17-year-old in 1933 he bought his first baseball glove at Levy Hardware, located on what then was called Lookout Avenue, and today is known as La Mesa Boulevard. He also remembered that a principal of Grossmont High School, Carl Quicksall, had been gravely injured in the accident in which Levy had died. He recalled that Levy, then 70, apparently fell asleep at the wheel.

R.M. Levy inspects the bottom of Lake Murray in 1947
(Photo courtesy of the Helix Water District)

Paul Engstrand, a retired principal of the law firm of Jennings Engstrand and Henrikson, which represented the Helix Water District, remembered that Levy was a strong water board chairman, who when running a meeting, "kept on top of things." Levy at one point became an advocate for putting a traffic signal on La Mesa Boulevard—and when he heard that a decision would be based upon traffic counts—"drove back and forth over that route all afternoon to get the count up," Engstrand remembered.

I also called George Bailey, the former mayor of La Mesa who later became a member of the county Board of Supervisors, but Bailey, alas, couldn't recall much more about Levy. Bailey's mayoral successor, Art Madrid, only knew him by name, and some longtime members of Tifereth Israel Synagogue, the San Diego congregation closest to La Mesa, also couldn't remember Levy. As a point of interest, however, I did learn that the La Mesa neighborhood in which Levy had resided had been named "Mount Nebo" by the developers—making me wonder if they considered the area between their mount and the Pacific Ocean to be the western "Promised Land."

Via phone and email, I put out queries about R.M. "Rube" Levy to baseball and military historians, to the Jewish Historical Society of San Diego, the San Diego Jewish Genealogical Society, Jewish War Veterans, and to various longtime residents.

While I waited for a break—something that would definitively tie Levy to San Diego's Jewish community, other than his surname—I learned from a CD thoughtfully sent to me by Breece what makes the R.M. Levy Water Treatment Plant near Lake Jennings so special. Built about four years after Levy's death, it more recently underwent modernization. The "ozonation" process that Governor Walker mentioned involves passing electricity through oxygen to create ozone and then injecting that gas into the water supply. Highly reactive, the ozone bonds with various organisms that might be in the water, forming solids that can be filtered out of the water. Ozonation is followed by chlorination.

Roberta Berman of the San Diego Jewish Genealogical Society subsequently messaged me that a Reuben Martin Levy, whose birth and death dates matched those of the man I was seeking, was buried in plot S 1268 at Fort Rosecrans National Cemetery, and that after serving as a 2nd lieutenant in the infantry, he had been demobilized at Camp Kearny, California.

Other genealogical records found by Berman indicated that Levy's mother's maiden name was Wingate. Given that Wingate is not usually a Jewish name (but then again, neither is my surname "Harrison"), I wondered whether Levy perhaps had been the child or descendant of an inter-marriage, who was raised outside the Jewish religion. This might account for why he was so unknown in the Jewish community.

A phone call to Fort Rosecrans National Cemetery substantiated this hypothesis. Delia Fernandez, noting that Levy's gravesite was not far from her office at the cemetery, took a quick walk outside to look it over. According to the markings on the stone, Levy had won the Distinguished Service Cross and the Silver Star during his World War I service. The religious icon on his stone was a Christian cross.

So after all that, I had to wonder had I really been embarked on a "Jewish" story? Yes, I decided, but the story in question wasn't Levy's. Instead, it was a story about the interesting byways one can travel in the process of Jewish historical research.

....

From Lake Jennings Park Road, Exit 23, turn left and the plant at 9550 Lake Jennings Park Road will be on the left.
....

-San Diego Jewish World, May 5, 2016

56. Exit 23
Eddy Pump

Brothers Peter and Ben Weinrib stand by a submersible Eddy Pump

EL CAJON, California — A pumping system estimated to save the U.S. Navy millions of dollars over the equipment's lifetime was invented by a Jewish surgeon with a PhD in fluid dynamics and a master's in electro-optics who defected from the Soviet Union in the 1970s to become an American citizen.

Today, Dr. Harry P. Weinrib and his family operate the company, Eddy Pump Corporation, and all four of his children are deeply involved in building upon his legacy, both in business and as active members of the community.

Ben, who has a degree in mechanical engineering, is the executive vice president; Peter is the chief financial officer; Rebecca is chief legal counsel, and Kathy, who lives in Northern California with a husband she met on JDate, manages the company's web presence. Eddy Pump Corporation is located about three miles from the Lake Jennings Park Road exit of Interstate 8 at 15405 Olde Highway 80.

Why did they locate there? I wondered. Peter told me that initially the company had located in Santee but when the Olde Highway 80 property became available, it was purchased because it was close to the family home in the Blossom Valley neighborhood.

Peter said that after his father immigrated to the U.S., and did a surgical residency at UC Davis, his father practiced reconstructive and micro surgery at Rush Presbyterian Hospital in Chicago and tinkered, during his time off, in the basement of his home developing a pump that harnesses the eddy effect of a tornado instead of centrifugal force, which then was the most common technology.

After his father perfected the design in 1987, Peter said, he decided to retire as a surgeon. "Around the same time my parents (Harry and Eileen) took a vacation in San Diego and as they were driving out here in the mountains they found a piece of property for sale and decided that this is where they wanted to build their dream home."

The residential property covers over four acres in the Blossom Valley area, which so delighted Eileen's green-thumbed father, Carl Weinshenker, that he and his wife Esther traveled as often as four times a year from their retirement home in Florida to visit their daughter's family. Carl planted 50 fruit and nut trees on the property.

"Today, there are only between 20-25 trees left on the property," said Peter, adding that in the years since then he personally has planted numerous fruit trees at his own home in Santee. During his boyhood, Peter reminisced, he and "Zayde" Carl often fished at nearby Lake Jennings. Peter confided that one of the best ways to catch a bass at that lake is to use a Carolina rigging with an inflated night crawler as a power bait on a treble hook. "Ask at the bait shop at what depth they are hitting, and then set the leader and your power bait."

Not long after the Weinribs settled in their "dream home," a friend put Harry in touch with the U.S. Navy, which determined the Eddy Pump to be ideal for pumping sewage, grey water, and brine. Over 20 years later the Eddy Pump could be found in 2015 on almost all classes of U.S. Navy ships. An abstract of a research paper published in the *Naval Engineers Journal* stated that "the use of the new transfer pump system has been estimated to result in life cycle savings of about $3,000,000 per aircraft carrier.... Pump performance is noticeably improved as the new pump system can achieve flow rates three times as fast, with less power, than the previously installed centrifugal plant." The report went on to say that using the Eddy system to pump brine for cooling nuclear reactors aboard the aircraft carriers would result in an estimated life cycle savings of about $2 million per aircraft carrier.

Asked to explain the difference between the Eddy Pump and a centrifugal pump, brother Ben, the mechanical engineer, gave a technical explanation. "The Eddy Pump uses hydrodynamic forces that are similar to the eddy current of a tornado. So the eddy pump creates a synchronized eddy current which agitates the material and brings it into the intake and out the discharge of the pump."

"The advantages of an eddy pump is that it can move higher viscosity material, higher specific gravity material, a high percent of solids material, and higher corrosive material while having less negative effects on the pump. That means the pump requires less corrective action and less maintenance costs over its life," Ben added. "So when you are pumping oil, or heavy mining materials, or corrosive chemicals, the Eddy pump will last significantly longer than a displacement pump or a centrifugal pump, and be able to do it at a higher production, thus saving the customer significantly more money in the long run."

The Eddy Pump, I learned, has been used in a variety of locales for an interesting array of projects. Viewers of the Discovery Channel may be familiar with one of its shows, *Bering Sea Gold*, which follows miners on their quest to mine gold from the bottom of the Bering Sea in Nome, Alaska.

Eddy Pump was contacted by the show in order to demonstrate the capabilities of its remote-operated submersible dredge (sub-dredge), which is equipped with lights and cameras and can be operated by someone watching a monitor. As portions of the Bering Sea were frozen over in March 2015, a hole was carved in the ice and the sub-dredge was lowered to the bottom of the sea to begin pumping. An Eddy Pump engineer was on site to observe. After a month's use, the sub-dredge outperformed all other equipment, according to Ben. It will be returning to Nome for the spring/ summer season.

The pump pulls up "rocks to a certain diameter, the dirt, everything that can be sucked up," said Peter. The material is piped up to the barge, "where there will be a sluice box. The heavier gold will be collected and everything else will be shot back into the ocean."

Another notable example of how the Eddy Pump can be utilized came after a mysterious black "blob" appeared in 1985 at the bottom of the St. Clair River which demarcates the border between Sarnia, Ontario, Canada and Port Huron, Michigan.

The "blob," as the phenomenon became known, had resulted from a spill of 35,000 liters of perchloroethylene—an industrial dry-cleaning solvent—into the river, where it mixed with other chemicals that had layered over the years on the river bed. The mixture resulted in the creation of tarry blobs, and traditional hydraulic and mechanical dredging only served to disperse the mixture over a longer portion of the river. Subsequently, Eddy Pump's former subsidiary company, Tornado Motion Technologies, was awarded a contract for environmental dredging services.

"We customized our dredge for the application," said Peter. "We went in there and it took three years, but when it was done, they were very happy with the job and it was a big success."

Closer to home, said Ben, there was a project funded by the state and federal governments for a habitat restoration in Imperial Beach, a project that involved dredging a former salt mine to very strict specifications. "We needed to cut 8:1 slopes underwater, which is an impossible thing for conventional dredging equipment to do but with our Programmable Logic Controlled (PLC) ground pressure technology, we were able to pre-program it so that the head of the dredge would exert only x amount of ground pressure. Essentially we automated it for the operator to make those cuts without over-gouging into the material."

The company also works with some of the largest irrigation districts in the U.S. Eddy Pump has completed projects for Imperial Irrigation District (IID) and many others. Currently it is working with districts all through Arizona and California.

"There are concrete-lined canals," said Ben, "and there is sediment built up, so they want to remove the sediment without having an effect on the concrete liner and not wasting too much of the water. So with our remote-operated submersible dredge, you don't need to put anybody into the water, and you don't have to shut down operations. You essentially lower this dredge on its own and it drives itself into the canal and with an operator on shore using cameras and acoustical positioning, he can precisely move around the canal and pump the material out."

On the other side of the world, in Abu Dhabi, the pump was utilized to transfer sand used in the construction of an artificial island.

I asked if the fact that the Weinribs are Jewish raised any issues in Abu Dhabi, which is an Arab emirate. "None at all," responded Peter. The three non-Jewish engineers who were sent on that job were treated royally. The Weinribs were too busy with other business to even consider participating in the project on site, Peter said.

The company currently engineers, manufactures, sells, rents and provides turnkey project solutions.

In what Ben described as "completing the circle," in reference to his father's surgical career, the company now is developing a miniature pump which cardiovascular surgeons hope will be able to break up and remove plaque buildup and blood clots in veins and arteries.

While Eddy Pump does not have any projects in Israel, family members have traveled there several times. Ben, who serves as president of the Young Leadership Division of Friends of the Israel Defense Forces, recently went there with about some 20 representatives of other non-profit organizations. His sister, Rebecca, also attended. She is the co-founder of "The Animal Pad," an all-breed dog rescue operation that helps dogs from all over Southern California and Mexico. Organized by the Next Gen division of the Jewish Federation of San Diego County, the mission's goal "was to do collaborative work together and get a better understanding of what everyone is doing in the community, and hopefully create new ideas."

During the trip, in which the group also visited Berlin, Germany, the leaders met with an Israeli non-profit organization called "Save a Child's Heart" which offers surgeries to children with congenital heart defects in the Palestinian territories, African, and other third-world countries. Save a Child's Heart transports the children and one parent to Israel, where it has "a facility to take care of them and house them, and then provides surgeries that would otherwise cost $100,000 to $300,000 in other countries."

Touched by the project, Ben and Rebecca and some of their travel companions decided to raise $10,000 to pay for the surgery needed by a one-year-old Ethiopian girl. For the FIDF meanwhile, Ben is planning another mission to Israel in which two members of the U.S. Congress will be escorted to Israeli military bases to meet with generals to get an up-close look at Israel's security preparations.

Peter said he supports both the FIDF and AIPAC, and while he didn't go on that mission, he's been to Israel twice and expects to go again in 2016 to attend a friend's wedding.

The Weinrib Family

From Exit 23, follow Olde Highway 80 about three miles to Eddy Pump plant.

-San Diego Jewish World, May 12, 2016

57. Exit 27
Harbison Canyon

Melissa Stroh keeps a Shabbat candle holder in her kitchen window.

HARBISON CANYON, California — In this small community in the back country of San Diego County, the 4Ms of the Stroh family—Marty, Melissa, Mason, and Max—are known for keeping the flame of Judaism burning bright inside their home, and for helping neighbors stave off the destruction of the massive October 2003 Cedar wild fire that killed 15 people, destroyed 2,820 buildings, and consumed 280,278 acres throughout San Diego County—up to then the largest fire in California history.

Located between the City of El Cajon and the unincorporated community of Alpine, Harbison Canyon gained fame in the 19th century for the thousands of beehives owned by John Stewart Harbison, who was one of the largest producers of honey in the United States of America.

According to *A Brief History of Alpine* authored by Carol Morrison for the Alpine Historical Society, the differences in elevation within the canyon area offered honeybees "a wide choice of plants within easy bee range. These include white sage, black sage, ceanothus, manzanita, columbine, collinsia, verbenia, wild rose, honeysuckle, and wild buckwheat."

Changes in elevation also result in some spectacular open-air scenery, and that is what attracted Melissa and Marty Stroh to purchase a home in the area. "It was the farthest east I could get him to move," said Melissa in a 2015 interview. "We've been here 27 years" on a side street above Harbison Canyon Road.

Living in the Harbison Canyon area meant residing in a neighborhood where very few people are Jewish. Melissa was constantly on the lookout for people with whom to carpool their children to religious school and to bar mitzvah studies at the Reform Temple Emanu-El in San Diego. Additionally, she took it upon herself to acquaint Mason's and Max's public school classmates with such Jewish holiday customs as making latkes and playing dreidel at Chanukah time, and eating matzo during Passover.

"When the boys were at Shadow Hills (Elementary School), I would go to their classrooms at Chanukah and make latkes and give each child a dreidel and some gelt and teach them how to play and talk about what it is," Melissa recalled. "To this day, how many years later, kids will say, 'I remember you. I still have my dreidel.'"

"Every single person asked for my mom to make latkes," Max recalled. His mother would send the potato pancakes to school and "they'd take them and eat them so fast. I would go to school with 50 latkes and they would be gone by the second class."

When Max first was starting school, Melissa remembered, he was asked to identify pictures of well-known persons and objects. A picture of Santa Claus stumped him. "He didn't know what it was, and the woman was shocked," Melissa recalled. "I said, 'Honey, we're Jewish –so he doesn't know that.'"

Every Erev Shabbat, after lighting the Shabbat candles, Melissa puts them in her kitchen window so neighbors can see that they are burning and that the family is Jewish. Chanukah is even a bigger deal, as Melissa collects hannukiahs and puts candles in every one of them, and sets them in front of their living room's large picture window. To underscore their pride in Judaism, the family also strings blue and white lights on their house for the holiday.

Marty, who was raised to "respect" all religions, but practiced none, said he has learned quite a bit from his Jewish wife. "She keeps me well grounded" he said. "Our kids have been bar mitzvahed, but sometimes I get the days mixed up. Like when do we open the door for Elijah and drink wine, that kind of stuff."

On a Sunday in October 2003, a neighbor was carpooling the boys, who are three years apart, to religious school at Temple Emanu-El in the Del Cerro neighborhood of San Diego when she called to say "you know there is a fire down here by the highway (Interstate 8). I think it is probably not good to have the kids so far away." Melissa agreed: "Okay, okay, bring them home."

Marty, who drives a UPS truck, said not long after that phone call, a law enforcement officer "came through with his loudspeakers telling everyone to evacuate, which they called 'mandatory,' which means that if you leave you can't come back, but not that you have to leave. We started gathering up the stuff, figuring we had a

20-minute time frame to get out of there, instead of two minutes. We went through the house and gathered a file cabinet, computers , hard drives, a cedar chest, and some photos. We loaded this up in the car and Melissa left with the kids for Granny and Papa's. I had another car in the garage, and I thought if the house burned, I don't want the car to burn too, so I moved the car outside.

"So I was taking care of that, putting the car at the bottom of the hill, when I looked up and saw that the hill behind our house was burning," with the flames working their way up the hill, away from the house. "The wind was blowing pretty good, 20-25 miles per hour, and I thought, well in that case, I will stay because if things go sideways here, I can run up the hill because it is not going to burn twice. So I formulated a plan. I got a sleeping bag out, soaked it with water in case I had to cover up (which I never had to). I called Melissa on the cell phone to try to explain what I was doing, but things weren't going well with the cell phone conversation. Especially back then, they weren't very reliable. All she heard was "under a sleeping bag."

Said Melissa, who had driven to her mother's house on Mt. Helix in La Mesa: "All I heard was that 'I have beer and a wet sleeping bag.' And I thought, how will either one of those save him from a fire like this?"

"I think I said there was fire all around," Marty recalled. On the back hillside, the flames had come within 15 to 20 feet of his house. Down the street "when the flames came through the canyon I watched the houses, one after the other, burning down, but it stopped about three houses away, and didn't transfer to the next home."

He related what he did next:

"I had a three-wheeler back then, and I was running around, doing what I could do. I found out that most of the homes burned down because stuff caught on fire around the home. It's only a factor of time before the fire will transfer to the home. You are not going to put a home out with a garden hose, but you can put out a fence, or lawn furniture, or a pile of wood, or whatever it is that is burning next to the house. So I think I kicked down a couple of fences, put them out, put out some shrubbery that was burning, and did what I could. I went across the street where they have a detached garage, which was completely involved. I tried to put some water on it, and it wasn't doing any good, so I put some water on the side of the house and left because I didn't want to get hurt if something went wrong."

Most of the time, he concentrated on his neighbors' homes, because "my house was fairly safe because it burned the back hill, so that created a fire break."

Asked if professional firemen eventually arrived, Marty responded: "I have nothing but high regards for the fire department. I am sure that none of them were sitting on their butts doing nothing that day. There wasn't a single fire person in this neighborhood."

Did his actions make a big difference?

"Who is to say? Who knows? I thought I did some good, but if I weren't there, who knows? But I did see some homes that caught on fire because no one was around." A large cone-shaped hill within view of his front door was entirely engulfed in flames.

While Marty was running around the neighborhood, putting out small fires, Melissa and the children worried about him from their evacuation point at her mother's home. "We were watching the glow across the valley and thinking, wow, I hope that is not my house."

Marty said that even after the wildfire had passed, "the houses burned all night long, like giant bon fires. There was not probably an hour when they weren't burning." At 10 p.m., he recalled, he "saw the houses burning and propane tanks going off. It was like a rush of rocket fuel that was released; you would see a flame like a giant pilot light, and it would go away in about 20 seconds when it would consume all the fuel.

"At 1 a.m, I heard footfalls on the street below, and I thought 'wow! The looters don't wait long' but it turned out that the man who had moved in next door, a deputy sheriff, was able to get out here and check on his home. He let me use his cell phone about 1 a.m. in the morning and I was able to contact her for the first time."

Not surprisingly, Melissa had been in a near panic about his safety. After a gasp of relief and thanking God that he had survived, she gave him a piece of her mind for risking his life the way he did.

According to Marty, she said something like, "I'm glad you survived, now I'm going to kill you!"

He laughed.

On his motorcycle, Marty then navigated his way out of the Harbison Canyon area, dodging downed power lines, passing car carcasses along the side of the road, and enduring a "fog of smoke hanging about 20 feet off the ground."

Today in 2015, Mason, like his father, works for UPS. He showed up just after our interview in time for a photo session. He plans on joining the Marines. Max is in his second year at community college, studying to be a veterinarian's tech. Melissa works for a merchandising company, which arranges and rearranges product displays on grocery shelves.

So, having gone through the Cedar fire experience, what does the family do differently today in preparation for a possible wildfire?

Melissa said even before the Cedar fire, "we had a plan, we made it a practice to make our property very defensible by planting greenery on the property in front of their house." Marty said the "biggest changes were installing a fire-proof safe in our home, refining our exit strategy, and keeping more bottled water on hand."

Twenty-seven years after moving in, and twelve years since the fire, the Stroh family confides it is planning to move from their first home.

Oh, not because of the threat of wildfires.

They said they were negotiating to buy a house across the street, which has more acreage and a swimming pool.

The Stroh Family

....

From Exit 27, at Dunbar Lane, go straight to Arnold, make a right, and then turn right again on Harbison Canyon.

....

-San Diego Jewish World, May 19, 2016

58. Exit 30

Dream Rider Equestrian Therapy

Catherine Hand, in gray overshirt, supervises volunteers leading
Alisa Yamamoto in equestrian experience.

ALPINE, California — A head-on automobile collision near her home in this mountain community alongside Interstate 8 put Catherine Hand into a wheel chair and ended her first career as a set and costume designer for major productions of the ballet and the opera. But riding a horse got her out of her wheelchair and into the profession of therapeutic horsemanship—using horses to help people overcome both physical and mental disabilities.

No longer needing a wheelchair, Hand today walks around the arena adjacent to her home on Anderson Road, offering instructions and encouragement to children with disabilities as well as to survivors of breast cancer for whom bonding with horses can be a pathway to wellness.

With the permission of 16-year-old Alise Yamamoto's mother, Samantha, I recently attended an hour-long session designed to improve the girl's sense of balance while strengthening her memory and ability to follow instructions.

"My daughter is developmentally delayed," Samantha Yamamoto told me. "She speaks in one and two words, not even sentences. Sometimes, if prompted, I can get her to speak in full sentences. She is orthopedically impaired, and she is about a third-grade level in reading. Her comprehension and receptive language is there, but it is very hard for her to get across what she needs. But you talk to her and she understands every word."

Alise's brother Ryan, 11, is a natural athlete, good at golf, good at soccer, and very comfortable on a horse. On the day that I visited, he rode in the same arena as Alise--a first--and the experience of doing the same thing as her brother obviously delighted Alise. "I think that is why she is so giggly today," her mother said.

Hand, a Jewish American who learned many of her teaching skills at the Wingate Institute, Israel's National Center for Physical Education and Sport located in Netanya, set out a program for Alise and Ryan that included, among other activities, performing stretching exercises on their horses; reaching for rings on posts alongside the arena and depositing them into low buckets; knocking a ball into a net with a field hockey stick, and leaning over to withdraw letters from a mailbox.

Alise, who had been riding off and on for nearly 10 years, was aboard a 21-year-old mare named "Ginger Sparkles." Previously she had ridden Hand's personal horse, the late "Treasure." Ryan was mounted on a young mare named "Daisy Mae." They performed their tasks accompanied by their favorite music. For Ryan and his mare, it was Ennio Morricone's theme for the movie *The Good, the Bad and the Ugly* that starred Clint Eastwood, while for Alise, it was Carmine Coppola's theme from the movie *The Black Stallion* that starred Kelly Reno.

Turning on a boom box with *The Black Stallion* tune, whenever it was Alise's turn to perform, was one of the jobs that the children's mother volunteered to do during the hour-long session in this picturesque setting.

Other volunteers included two teen girls who are approximately the same age as Alise – which gladdened Alise's heart – and four local women who were attracted by the opportunity to do volunteer tasks that involve helping a child with special needs and working with horses. The girls were Katelyn Mangum, 16, and Bea Wygant, 15, while the adults included Bea's mother, Christina; Stacey King; Marilyn Bach; and Nancy Edwards. A couple of them told me they learned of the volunteering opportunity through nearby churches, while another saw a notice on a bulletin board at the Alpine Community Center.

The volunteers walked alongside the young riders; made sure their horses were positioned properly near a stand for mounting and dismounting; modeled the stretching exercises; and generally offered encouragement to the riders under Hand's watchful eyes. You could include Ryan in the corps of volunteers as well because he demonstrated on a barrel the exercises that Hand teaches her clients to familiarize them with the muscle groups needed in horseback riding.

Hand told me that "Alise started coming here when she was 6 years old. She had fused feet requiring multiple surgeries and wore leg braces before she was brought to Dream Rider Equestrian Therapy, the non-profit organization that Hand heads. "She had to be carried here and was wearing diapers," Hand said.

"After six lessons she was no longer incontinent. The reason for that was that I had her doing exercises on the horse that stimulated the nerves in the pelvic area, awakening her sense of when she needed to go. Before that she didn't have that. She was non-verbal but responded to music. In the womb she had "Baby Einstein" played for her, and she loves "Fur Elise" by Beethoven.

"At the age of 13, Alise experienced a major setback when it was determined that her skeletal frame was not developing properly and she had to spend a year in a full body cast," Hand said. "We have been working on developing her flexibility since that operation."

Alise initially "couldn't button her clothes, tie her shoelaces or do anything with her hands, and she didn't have to because her family took very good care of her. Now at 16, she is riding, controlling the horse, holding the reins, making the horse turn to the right and turn to the left. In order to exercise her brain, we do a lot of left and right, left, right, left, right to stimulate both sides of the brain, to cross the midline between the two hemispheres in order to get the communication going."

Though a typically developing pre-teen today, Ryan had difficulty adjusting earlier in his life to all the attention that Alise required from their parents. According to his mother, he was quiet, hard-edged, and uncommunicative, but like his sister, he benefitted greatly from therapy with horses. He came to accept that although younger, he was Alise's "big brother" and today cheerfully accepts extra duties.

I asked Samantha whether she felt the therapy with horses had helped her daughter physiologically. She said it has made a difference in "the way she moves and walks. She gets off the horse and she is more comfortable in her own skin. She can move better. She has had several orthopedic surgeries, and this is helping. It has been the best thing for us." Furthermore, "she is more verbal on the horse, more animated, although she is not usually so giggly. When we come home from a lesson, she will be talking in the car, not full sentences, but more engaging. It just brings that out in her. She is excited."

Alisa Yamamoto and aides make their way around the arena.

As the lesson ended, the children reached into the mail box and found addressed to them letters with presents inside – a blue ribbon and stickers for Alise and a "million horse dollar" bill for Ryan. Once the Yamamotos and the volunteers headed for their respective homes, Catherine and I sat down for an interview in which she told me of some of the high points of her life.

She said that up until age 6, she lived in Toronto, Canada, with her mother, the former Bertha Shoichet, who came from a shtetl in Poland, and father Louis Coldoff, an aspiring sculptor. Later the family moved to Orange County, California—a culture shock for her mother who had been a labor organizer and felt out-of-place in the politically conservative area to which they relocated. Her mother and father were divorced before Catherine went off to study music and literature at UC Berkeley.

Catherine married and divorced young—her first husband George Hand, and father of her son Peter, was related to the famed jurist Judge Learned Hand and was a descendant of immigrants who came to America on the *Mayflower*. She said she retained the surname Hand because "it suited everything about me. I always loved my mother's hands. She was a very distinguished woman, but she had the hands of a stevedore. She worked hard all her life. I don't have those hands; I have little hands. I thought 'I am going to work so hard in my life someday my hands will be like hers." Aged 73 in 2015 when I interviewed her, her hands still were not particularly rough, but she said, "I think I'm getting there."

She graduated from UC Berkeley and moved to Pennsylvania where her then-husband taught history at a private college for boys. There she became involved in helping to paint sets for the drama department. In the summer of 1967 she went to New York for an opportunity to work under New York Public Theatre director Joseph Papp as an apprentice at the New York Shakespeare Festival in Central Park. In New York City, she met actor Stacey Keach and set designer Ming Cho Lee, each of whom positively influenced her career. Returning to the San Francisco Bay Area, her work with Ming Cho Lee helped win her a job as a stage and costume designer for the Marin County Shakespeare Festival.

"The designs got great reviews so I was on my way," she reflected. "I met Davis West after being hired as a junior designer and draughtsman by the San Francisco Opera. When I saw opera paintings for the first time, I was so excited by the scale and grandeur of these paintings, I had to learn to do that... and I did." Fifteen years after West and Hand began working together, they were married.

Hand flipped through a photo album in which she showed me various backdrops that she had designed for opera and ballet, pausing lovingly over the designs for *The Nutcracker*, which instead of in Bavaria or Victorian England, she set in an imaginative interpretation of Russia, in which the onion domes of the Kremlin were transformed into strawberry finials atop a strawberry shortcake Kremlin wall. This was the era of Ronald Reagan's presidency, and little jelly beans fly through the painted sky. Other backdrops included a *Doctor Zhivago*-esque dacha and a horse and carriage reminiscent of one that had been painted on a lacquer box her mother had brought back from Russia in the 1930s.

During the early 1980s, Hand traveled extensively, even moving to Israel for an extended period, where she sampled kibbutz life and worked in Israeli television as a set designer. Career opportunities persuaded her to return to California, where Hand's reputation for designs reached the ears of rock singer Jon Bon Jovi. He asked her to design a set of 40-foot high curtains to drape in front of the large speakers he would use in his group's 1989 appearance at a "peace concert" in Moscow. She said he asked for a design showcasing famous American movie gangsters as portrayed by actors Edward G. Robinson, George Raft, Jimmy Cagney, and the like. Bon Jovi sent Hand a deposit check, which she picked up at her post office box in Alpine. On the way home, her car was hit head-on by a car driven by a speeding teen driver. The force of the collision broke her jaw as well as both ankles. She thought her productive life was over.

She said she messaged Bon Jovi that she would have to send back his deposit; she didn't believe she would ever design another set. But the singer demurred. She could use her hands, couldn't she? She could still see? Keep the deposit, he said, and work on it when you can. He asked her to send him faxes showing the progress of her work. So with the help of husband Davis West, she placed a door on top of a couch and, wheeling alongside the couch, created a gangster collage that Bon Jovi liked and subsequently had transferred to lightweight scrim curtains through which sound could travel and that could be seen, or seem invisible, depending on the lighting.

Hand said remaining in a wheelchair for months was physically and psychologically painful for her. When you are in a wheelchair, she said, "people will shout at you because they think you are deaf. They will stoop very low because they think you can't see well, and they will speak in baby talk because they think you are simple-minded sitting down there. I made up my mind after that experience that I would never talk to anyone who is handicapped that way."

Although her ankles were held together with plates and screws "and still are" Hand said "I had to get out of the wheelchair. My husband would bring the horse to the front door and wheel me down a ramp, and lift me onto the horse, and let me walk up the mountain behind our house on the horse. What that did was stimulate the spine; it kept me from atrophying. It built up the muscles in my legs so that I could support my weight despite the damage to my ankles."

She would ride the horse and then be lifted off by her husband. "One day, I said 'don't put me in the chair. I want to try to stand.' I did, and I was able to stand. And the next day, after he put me down, I said 'I want to take a step.' It was one baby step at a time. When I could finally walk, all I wanted to do was run. And I went back to Israel (Netanya) to take a two-year-course to study therapeutic riding."

In the meantime, Hand and West decided to divorce, agreeing that their marriage was a mistake. "His 1950s idea of a wife was not me," Hand said later. "We were better off as colleagues and best friends."

In 1995, while still in Israel, West had a stroke, and Hand flew back to Alpine to take care of him and to remarry so she could have the legal right to speak for him to obtain treatment. "We were still best friends," she said. Besides, he had taken care of her after the accident, and now it was her turn to reciprocate.

"He couldn't paint, he couldn't talk, he was paralyzed," she said. "I discovered that if music was playing, and it was a song that he knew, he could sing the words of the song, and so we started to sing to each other. I sang to him to the tune of "Row, Row, Row Your Boat" a question, and he sang back to me his answer. There are two parts of the brain where speech resides: the left-hand hemisphere where we have the spoken word, which was damaged, but on the right-hand side of the brain, there are words, if they are connected to music. That is why I use music in the horse therapy program."

Singing questions to her ex-husband "triggered an awakening in the brain and the synapses began to regrow in his brain, eventually to the point where he could read and paint again but he still had to do it with one side of his body. He could drive a car, but he had to pass the (usually written) test with 'yes' or 'no' answers, which I asked them to do. He was rehabilitated with the music" and had several productive years of life before he died.

Hand went through another crisis of her own in 2007 when she had a mastectomy following the discovery of breast cancer. Hooked up to an oxygen tank, on hospice, weak, and believing she would die, she wheeled herself out to her horse, "Treasure."

Forcing herself to stand up from the wheel chair and to remove the oxygen mask, she climbed up a mounting block and lay down backwards upon her old friend Treasure's back. "As I lay there taking shallow breaths, I felt her taking deep breaths, her barrel expanding and contracting as she inhaled and exhaled," Hand wrote in an article prepared for a therapy journal that she shared with me.

"Instinctively, I matched her breathing. I stayed that way for about a minute. I pushed myself up from her back and inexplicably discovered that I could breathe on my own and was able to walk back to my house without using the oxygen tank.

"The next day the hospice nurse came to take my vital signs. Amazed, she said, 'all your vital sign readings are normal. What have you done?' I answered, 'I went out to say good-bye to my pony, lay down on her back and hugged her.'"

Hand and the nurse compared the phenomenon to a premature baby with respiratory and circulatory problems being laid on its mother's chest. "Through skin-to-skin contact, nerves in the skin transmitted the mother's respiratory rate and heart rate to the infant brain to regulate and kick-start those systems thus eliminating the need for incubation."

Having survived, Hand and her therapy horses work with other breast cancer patients. She explains her work in a pamphlet entitled *Your Guide to Equine Assisted Rehabilitation for Breast Cancer Patients*, which can be ordered from her at catherineh@prodigy.net

In 2015, once-a-week lessons over a six-week period cost $210 paid in advance. Because lessons require considerable advance set-up time, and coordination of volunteers, this fee is non-refundable, Hand said.

Dream Rider Equestrian Therapy seeks tax-deductible donations for clients who can't afford that amount, and also seeks donations to defray such expenses as insurance and the $4,000 annual cost of maintaining a therapy horse. Those wishing to donate may do so via the website, www.dreamriderequestriantherapy.com, or by check to Dream Rider Equestrian Therapy in care of Hand at 543 Anderson Road, Alpine, California 91901.

From the I-8, Exit 30, at Tavern Road, turn left to Victoria Drive, and continue to a left on Anderson Road. The horse arena may be visited by appointment only. Hand may be reached via info@dreamriderequestriantherapy.com or 619-445-2576.

-San Diego Jewish World, May 26, 2016

59. Exit 33
Viejas Indian Reservation

VIEJAS INDIAN RESERVATION, California — I wrote the following story for the Sept. 19, 1997 edition of the *San Diego Jewish Press-Heritage*, of which I was editor. The sentiments expressed in this excerpt still apply today, and provide background for any visit to the Viejas Casino or Outlet Center at the Willows Road exit of the Interstate 8.

Indian honoree turns tables on his Jewish hosts

The American Jewish Committee tribute dinner at the downtown Hyatt Regency Hotel was to be a salute to Anthony Pico, the chairman of the Viejas Band of Kumeyaay Indians, but Pico decidedly turned the tables, speaking so earnestly about the parallels between Native Americans and Jews, that he moved many in the audience to tears.

"We have both faced extermination and survived a holocaust," Pico said after being presented the AJC's David and Dorothea Garfield Human Relations Award.

"Indians were not sent to gas chambers; our prisoners-of-war camps came with blankets infected with disease that were more lethal than even bullets," he said.

"In their zeal and greed to reach their manifest destiny," the strangers took our land and took pride in the slogan that "the only good Indian is a dead Indian," Pico added.

"In California, it was legal to shoot an Indian on sight, to purchase homeless Indians in auctions for slave labor, and steal Indian children from their parents to 'save' them from their primitive ways. Our religious ceremonies were banned as satanical and many have been lost from our memory as a result."

Pico said that as a Native American, he can "sympathize with the ferocious love and militancy Jews bring to protecting Israel. We know the value of having a homeland, a place where you are free ... to exercise your own destiny and be a family."

"How Jews have managed to survive as a people amidst strangers in strange lands without a land for so many centuries is an absolute miracle as far as I am concerned," Pico said. "Our reservations aren't as grand as our original lands but they represent the continuation, security and a future to us. ... Native Americans, like Jews, will always rise to fight when our homelands are threatened."

"Tonight it seems appropriate for me to return the honor and pay tribute to the gifts that the Jewish community shares with all the world," the Viejas chairman said. "One of the most important is showing how our people, struggling to be free, can preserve our humanity when the world chooses to treat us inhumanely," he added.

"Jews have always been the first to speak out against injustice and inhumane practices in the United States," he said. "I know the greatness in your heart and spirit comes from the terrors of the past. I also know from experience that it is not an easy thing to do to maintain tolerance and empathy for others when your own life is at stake. Living defensively takes a toll on the human spirit."

"Too often the poverty of Indians takes on a romantic mystique. There is nothing romantic about being poor and powerless, scratching daily to eke out an existence that can bring out the worst as well as the best in people," Pico said.

"It is a temptation for those who are oppressed to take on the cruelty of the oppressor."

But Jews have chosen to turn the suffering into compassion, he said. "You have turned the pain of persecution into a crusade for the rights of others. And we commend you."

"For Native Americans, this is a historic time ... shaping a new future between our peoples, and the rest of America," he said. I hope that this evening is the beginning of an alliance that will serve the cause of justice."

"Tonight," he added with rising emotion, "the tribes of Israel and the tribes of America have reached across their history and their experience to share something rare and wonderful. Tonight we honor the power of the human heart to love even when faced with hate. Tonight we celebrate the ability of people to rise above evil and cruelty. Tonight we honor the victory of dignity and pride over ignorance and prejudice. Tonight we honor humankind's most noble cause and greatest challenge: living as a humanitarian."

Pico thus brought to a crescendo an evening designed to forge a sense of unity among two diverse peoples. After Kumeyaay elder Tom Hyde offered a prayer in his language which he explained was to thank the Creator for arranging for his people "to be here among our friends the Jews," Rabbi Lisa Goldstein of Hillel of San Diego responded with an invocation that told of the Jewish tradition of *tikkun olam* (repair of the world) as well as the saying of Rabbi Nachman of Bratslov "that each plant, each tree, each blade of grass, each has their own melody of praise that they sing to God."

"So too does each nation, each people, each tribe, each community have its own role in repairing the world, to return the world to that state of perfection that God had intended," she added before intoning *ha motzi*, the traditional Hebrew prayer over bread.

U.S. Sen. Barbara Boxer (D-Calif.), the keynote speaker for the event, emphasized what the Viejas Band has been doing to help repair the world since the operation of a gaming casino on the reservation enabled the band to become economically self-sufficient.

"Here are a few of some of the diverse organizations they have supported," Boxer enumerated: "The American Indian Women's Center, Urban League of San Diego, San Diego Chinese Center, Chicano/ Chicana Youth Leadership Camp, Vietnam Veterans of America, Senior Women's Basketball, Women's Auxiliary of the San Diego Hebrew Home, San Diego Hospice, American Heart Association, San Diego Chamber Orchestra..."

The senator said "the very foundation that makes all these good works possible is under attack" with legislation pending in the United States Senate to strip Indian reservations of some degree of sovereignty, and efforts in the state of California to sharply curtail the kinds of games that Indians may offer in their casinos.

Boxer won applause when she alluded to a fellow member of the Jewish community, who was not present at the event: "Fortunately here in San Diego County," she said, "we have a U.S. attorney who respects tribal sovereignty, who has done everything in his power to resolve the dispute fairly and equitably. I am proud to say that I nominated Alan Bersin to be San Diego's U.S. attorney."

Under federal law, Indians are permitted to offer at their reservations only those games which are legal in the states where their reservations are located. Differences in interpretation of that law have caused disputes. For example, how different are automatically-dispensed California State Lottery tickets—in which the numbers are randomly assigned to the purchaser—from a video slot machine?

Bersin had resisted calls from the California state government to seize the video games on the reservations, and instead negotiated an agreement with the Indians that they would not expand such gaming pending a court decision in the dispute.

When the courts ultimately ruled against the Indians, Bersin and the Indians began implementing an agreement to phase the devices out--a phase-out that may result in considerably reduced revenues on the reservation.

Meanwhile, the Pala Band of Indians (which currently has no gambling on its reservation) has been negotiating with the state of California a "model" compact, but the negotiations have dragged on for a long time, and fewer games then are now offered at the Viejas, Barona, or Sycuan reservations are likely to be included.

Boxer suggested there is a perfect fit between the American Jewish Committee and the Viejas Band of Indians. Both "have had the wisdom and generosity of spirit to see that we are all in this together, that the best way to safeguard the rights of our community is to preserve an America where all groups can reside in peace and with mutual respect," she said.

"The core mission of the American Jewish Committee--safeguarding the rights of their own people while nurturing a diverse America--is very much the credo of the Viejas," she said.

Another highlight was an announcement by four members of the State Assembly from San Diego: Republican Jan Goldsmith and Democrats Susan Davis, Denise Ducheny, and Howard Wayne that the Legislature adopted a resolution calling for the renaming of a stretch of Interstate 8, east of El Cajon, passing the Viejas Reservation, as the Kumeyaay Highway. Said Wayne: "Chairman Pico, on behalf of the state of California, I say mazal tov."

Take Willows Road, Exit 33, cross over freeway, and turn on Willows Road. Follow until you arrive at the Viejas Casino.

-San Diego Jewish World, June 2, 2016

60. Exit 36
Viejas Outlet Center

Kumeyaay art and sculpture grace Viejas Outlet Center

VIEJAS INDIAN RESERVATION, California — I grew up watching cowboys and Indians in the movies and on television. Cowboys and Indians were enemies back then, but not anymore. Especially not here.

Levi's, which today we know as "jeans," are one of the clothing brands that many people associate with cowboys, although in truth they were invented to serve a multiplicity of laborers who earned their bread outdoors, among them, cattle ranchers, sheep herders, miners, and railroad workers. Today Levi's has a factory outlet store here on the Viejas Indian Reservation, amid sculptures of wildlife and designs evoking earlier ways of life of the Viejas Band of Kumeyaay Indians.

The origins of the popular Levi denim work pants can be traced to Buttenheim, Bavaria, where Loeb, later "Levi" Strauss was born in 1829, and to Riga, Latvia, where Jacob Youphes, later Davis, was born two years later.

Strauss and Davis, both Jews, separately immigrated to the United States. Strauss arrived in New York in 1848, and went to work for his older brother, Jonas, who had crossed the ocean earlier and had established a wholesale dry goods company called J. Strauss Brother & Co. Eventually it was decided that Levi, as he was by then known, should immigrate to the West Coast to open a sister branch of the business in San Francisco. He went by way of the Isthmus of Panama.

In 1854, Youphes came to New York City, and with his tailoring skills, he found work in such far-flung locales as Augusta, Maine; San Francisco; Weaverville, California; Victoria, British Columbia; Virginia City, Nevada; and Reno, Nevada. It was in Reno where the career paths of the two men first crossed. Davis, as he was then known, purchased off-white cotton duck cloth from Levi Strauss & Co., beginning in 1870, for the fashioning of tents and wagon covers.

Off-white cotton duck cloth was just one item (or stock keeping unit as they now are called) among many hundreds that Levi Strauss & Co. supplied to small stores all over the west, including Davis's tailor shop in Reno. After receiving goods by ship, sent by his brother and other suppliers, Strauss would put together wagon loads of such goods as fabrics, umbrellas, underwear, handkerchiefs, and clothing and transport them to the small general stores then common throughout the west.

On the Levi Strauss & Co. website, the story is told about the birth of Levi's jeans, then known as "waist overalls."

Sometime in 1870 a female customer came to Davis's store in Reno, complaining of a problem. Her husband, who was a large man, kept ripping his pants. She asked Davis to make a new pair of pants as strong as possible. Davis decided to fasten the pockets of some white duck pants with the same kind of rivets he used to attach straps to horse blankets.

The pants held up, and soon Davis was making them for other customers. Rivets were added to the base of the button fly as well. And eventually denim was substituted for white duck.

Davis sent samples to Strauss in 1872, telling him about the popularity of his invention. He wanted to patent the process because local tailors in Reno were beginning to imitate him. But Davis didn't have enough money to patent these new strengthened work pants on his own; he needed a business partner.

Strauss not only agreed to partner with Davis in obtaining a patent for these "waist overalls," he invited him to San Francisco to oversee their manufacture. They began business together in 1873.

It was not the first time that Davis had applied for a patent. In the past, he visualized a steam-powered canal boat and a steam-powered ore crusher, but this was the first patent which brought him and a partner great success.

Levi Strauss
(Photo: Shor M. Masori)

While for Davis, the manufacture of riveted waist overalls was a great preoc-
cupation, for Strauss it was but one of several business ventures in which he was
engaged. A biography written by historian Lynn Downey reports that:

> He became a charter member and treasurer of the San Francisco Board of
> Trade in 1877. He was a director of the Nevada Bank, the Liverpool, Lon-
> don and Globe Insurance Company, and the San Francisco Gas and Elec-
> tric Company. In 1975 Levi [who preferred to be called by his first name]
> and two associates purchased the Mission and Pacific Woolen Mills from
> the estate of silver millionaire, William Ralston, and the mill's fabric was
> used to make the Levi Strauss & Co. "blanket-line" pants and coats.
> He was also one of the city's greatest philanthropists. Levi was a contributor
> to the Pacific Hebrew Orphan Asylum and Home, the Eureka Benevolent
> Society, and the Hebrew Board of Relief. In 1895 he and a number of other
> prominent San Franciscans provided funds to build a new railroad from
> San Francisco to the San Joaquin Valley (a project which unfortunately
> failed). And in 1897 Levi provided the funds for twenty-eight scholarships
> at the University of California, Berkeley.

Strauss died in 1902, and Davis died in 1908, a year after selling his interest in
the patent to the firm that he and Levi Strauss had made famous throughout the west.

··

Take East Willows Road, Exit 36, turn left, and then left again to
Viejas Outlook Center across the street from Viejas Casino.

··

-San Diego Jewish World, June 9, 2016

61. Exit 40

Raising Alpacas

David Kabbai, "Vanessa," and Amy Alyeshmeri

DESCANSO, California — While operating his DaMar Plastics business in San Diego, and later El Cajon, David Kabbai often dreamed of living a quieter, simpler life, somewhere where the air is clear, the nights are starry, and where he could raise gentle alpacas for their fleece. Seven years before he retired, he purchased a 14-acre ranch in this eastern San Diego County hamlet, whose name translated from the Spanish means a "rest" or a "break."

A rest or a break was just what Amy Alyeshmerni needed. Her real estate consulting company specializing in shopping center leasing took her on fast-moving business trips all over the country, and one day, after watching her sister undergo medical treatment for breast cancer, she had an epiphany. If the disease had interrupted her life instead of her sister's, would she have lived the life that she really wanted? When a cousin called her and said there was a guy, who raises alpacas, whom she should meet—a Persian Jew, like her own father (both families left before the Iranian Revolution in 1979)—"I said, 'A what rancher? Set it up! ' I thought if it was a man who cares for animals, he would have the right moral center that I was looking for, and I was totally right."

Alyeshmerni gave up her consultant company, and took a job as a leasing manager with Westfield Shopping Centers, and when I met her in 2015, she was focusing on the redevelopment of Horton Plaza Shopping Center in downtown San Diego, about 40 miles away. Although she was a "city girl," who grew up in the Jewish neighborhood of St. Louis Park, Minnesota—a suburb of Minneapolis—she fell in love with Kabbai and his bucolic life style. She is also very fond of the alpacas, especially one named Venessa, who at first considered Alyeshmeni to be a rival for Kabbai's affection.

"It took a while for her to accept me," she recalled. "When I would stand next to David, she considered David hers—she thought she was David's girlfriend—and when I first came on the scene she would come right between us and push us apart. She was literally jealous of me." Subsequently Venessa could see that "there is a connection between me and David, and now we're okay. Over time, I won her over."

Venessa is one of 65 alpacas at the Kabbai ranch, some of them owned by a friend who also is in the alpaca business. Alyeshmeni's man "who cares for animals" also owns 11 chickens, one rooster, two female cats, and two Anatolian Shepherds, the latter being very large guardian dogs that protect the alpacas against such backcountry predators as mountain lions, bobcats and coyotes.

Tika watches over a group of alpacas

One of the dogs is named Tika, and the other, not yet full grown, is Caleb. When Caleb reaches adulthood, Kabbai told me, he will weigh approximately 155 pounds and will be a formidable opponent for any mountain lion that might consider alpacas a potentially tasty treat. "He might get hurt in a fight with a mountain lion, but he will outweigh the lion by some 30 pounds. Rather than jump over our 8-foot fence and encounter two large dogs, a mountain lion would prefer to go after somebody else's chickens."

Originally, said Kabbai, Anatolian Shepherds were brought to the United States from Turkey. "They are trained by herders to think for themselves. They are problem solvers. If there is a problem that has to do with the animals, they will solve it on their own." At the Kabbai ranch, that tendency has manifested itself in chasing crows away from the alpaca's water supply, and in saving an alpaca from drowning during the rainy season.

One day while Kabbai still was working at DaMar Plastics, "it had been raining all day, and we have a ravine that was clogged up. There was an alpaca there and Tika, standing up to her neck in water in the ravine, kept putting her head under water to pick up the leaves that were clogging the ravine and throwing them behind her... just to save that alpaca. She must have done that for an hour; she did not give up. When I went in with a shovel, she stayed out until the ravine's water level went down, until she knew that the alpaca was safe, before she went inside to dry off." Alpacas are taller than the Anatolian Shepherds; at the time of its rescue, that particular alpaca was in water "up to its belly."

Alyeshmerni said the Anatolian Shepherds "will do anything they can to guard what they consider to be their territory" and its occupants—whether those be alpacas or human children. "Tika taught the (human) babies next door to walk," she added. "They would crawl around and grab ahold of Tika's hair and as the baby would stand up, Tika would stand up too. As the baby took a step, Tika would also take a step. As baby would sit down, Tika would lie down next to the baby until it was ready to get up again. Tika is incredibly intuitive."

There is money to be made in the alpaca business, which Kabbai conducts under the name of Atlas Alpacas. The best part of the alpaca business, he says, is that it doesn't result in any animals being slaughtered for their meat or for their hides. Once a year, the alpacas are shorn of their fleece, which, depending on its softness, density, and its crimp (the number of bends per unit) can sell for $8 to $10 per ounce. From 65 alpacas, Kabbai said, he can realize between 350 and 400 pounds of fleece.

Kabbai and other U.S. breeders are working hard to produce alpacas whose fleece is well crimped, very soft, and as appealing to the finest clothing manufacturers as the fleece now produced in certain South American countries that is sold to top-of-the-line Italian clothiers.

Male alpacas with top quality fleece potential can sell for hundreds of thousands of dollars, while females sell for considerably less, Kabbai said. That is because less than one percent of alpaca males qualify for breeding, whereas a much higher percentage of females are considered suitable.

Another market for alpacas is people who want them for pets – who, like Kabbai, enjoy watching them graze as the sun is setting behind the western hills.

Kabbai has family in La Jolla, where he grew up after migrating to this country from the Iranian capital of Tehran, and, likewise, Alyeshmerni has family in Los Angeles. Respectively the two families are members of Congregation Beth El in La Jolla and Sinai Temple in Los Angeles. The couple enjoys family reunions for the various Jewish festivals and alternating Shabbats.

Still, compared to La Jolla, Los Angeles, or St. Louis Park, Descanso is well off the beaten path for Jewish life. In the back country areas of Lakeside, Harbison Canyon, Alpine, Descanso, Guatay, Pine Valley, and Laguna Mountain, there are isolated Jewish families, most of whom, like Kabbai and Alyeshmerni are animal lovers. Every once in a while, usually by serendipity, they find each other and compare notes about what it is like living on the frontier of Jewish life.

This need to find people of similar backgrounds who know a challah (Sabbath bread) from a kallah (bride) was an element in the friendship that formed between Kabbai and the late Bob Howard, a Pine Valley resident who was the son of a Catholic mother and a Jewish father.

"When I moved up here, he was very helpful," Kabbai recalled. "I didn't know anything—for example, the drinking water here comes from 200 feet underground. I didn't know anything about wells, and he helped me set up. I had no real idea what ranch life was about. Because he was half Jewish we spent quite a bit of time together. He was much older, 70 something years old at the time, so when we had to move him out of his house to a smaller place, he stored his belongings here. Sometimes, he would come over and go through the things, and he found letters that were written to his father from Europe."

The letters were from two different families, both desperate to get out of Nazi Germany and Austria. In the first, dated February 2, 1939, Dr. Emilie Bondy of Vienna said of her husband, Dr. Emil Bondy: "Since August 1938, ie, since half a year, he is in prison in a concentration camp. When he will get free we must leave the country and we do not know where to go. I am therefore addressing myself to you with the request if it would be possible for you to help us. If you would be so kind and give us the possibility of going to U.S.A. by sending us affidavits we would be immensely thankful to you. Once arrived in America, we surely would not trouble you anymore. My husband, a skillful and expert doctor of medicine, will certainly find an occupation very soon. As for myself, I have studied Anthropology at the University of Vienna, and have published scientific works; I hope to get in a short time an employment in a museum or institute. ... I beg your pardon for addressing myself to you, but there is really no other way left to me."

The second, dated June 3, 1939 from Vienna, came from Ernst Katscher, an attorney who said he was born in Moravia on Nov. 27, 1881, the son of Jakob and Henriette (Horowitz) Katscher. His father owned a brewery and later a factory before the family moved to Vienna where Katscher received his law degree. "The change of affairs in Austria, however, as well as the introduction of the race-laws forced me, like all the other Jews, to give up my profession, whereby I lost my means of living and the fruits of 26 years hard work. In this way I undeservedly got into distress and there is nothing else to do for me but to build up a new existence abroad. I hope that with the aid of friends in America, I shall succeed in doing so, especially, as I am a bachelor and thus need care only for myself but not for a family as well."

Both letters were written to Howard's father, whose surname also was Horowitz, in the hope that some family relation could be assumed.

Kabbai and Alyeshmerni were touched by the letters and took them to Yad Vashem on a recent trip to Israel, where they were logged and entered into that Holocaust Museum's extensive collection. Thus far, the couple has not been able to learn what the fate was of the Bondy and Katscher families.

"These letters are heart breaking when you read them," Alyeshmerni observed.

"Amy and Bob would sit and talk for hours about this stuff," said Kabbai. "His father was in the garment business and because I was getting fleece, he was interested, and he would come here and spend hours staring at those animals out there."

....

From SR 79, Exit 40, turn left to Riverside Drive, which will become Viejas Drive, and then left at River Drive. Atlas Alpacas is located at 9718 River Drive.

....

-San Diego Jewish World, June 16, 2016

62. Exit 45

Kashrut in a Catholic home

Judy Hunter Osterberger feeds her chickens

PINE VALLEY, California — Although she was raised as a Catholic, Judy Hunter Osterberger felt a certain restlessness about religion as a young woman. "I wanted to get to the genesis of things and read the Bible for myself" she recalled. She investigated several different faiths, but found herself drawn to Judaism. Her family always had felt comfortable among Jews. Her mother had many Jewish classmates at Hoover High School in San Diego and her aunt had a Jewish boyfriend. But perhaps the most compelling reason for the attraction were the things that her maternal grandmother did.

"Cracking eggs for instance," Osterberger related in an interview. After Osterberger became acquainted with the rules of kashrut, "I'd ask, 'Grandma, why do you do that? Cracking them separately into a bowl, instead of putting them into one bowl together?' She'd say, 'You've got to make sure there is no blood in them.' I didn't understand. Most store-bought eggs didn't have blood in them, but that was her habit. And she never mixed milk with any meat, ever. 'You just don't do that!' She ate lamb almost all the time. And if she ate chicken or meat, I would find heavy salt on the counter. 'What are you doing that for?' I'd ask. And she'd say, 'You can't have any blood in the meat.'"

Clearly, grandma was following some of the practices of keeping kosher, but why? Her great-grandma long had been rumored to have had Jewish roots. She may have converted from Judaism to Catholicism when she married Osterberger's great-grandfather. Great-grandma's name was "Engesser" or "Engasser," and one can find both Jews and Christians today with that name.

When Osterberger asked her grandmother directly about it, she was told that whereas there had been a lot of speculation that Great Grandmother Marie Engasser Warlop was Jewish, it never could be substantiated. Wanting to satisfy herself on this point, Osterberger had her DNA tested by 23andMe, a genetic testing company whose name refers to the number of pairs of chromosomes in a human cell. The test revealed that among Osterberger's matrilineal genes was one that was very common in Syria, Lebanon and among the Druze. Additionally, the test found that Osterberger had DNA relatives who were Jewish, including one third or fourth cousin whose name is Engesser.

Fascinated, Osterberger began delving further into online genealogical research. Initially, she made informal inquiries of Rabbi Samuel Penner of Congregation Beth Tefilah, and later undertook formal study with Rabbi Leonard Rosenthal of Tifereth Israel Synagogue. Eventually, she converted to Judaism. In fact, she became so involved with Tifereth Israel that she became a member of the board of directors of that Conservative synagogue. She also is affiliated with the downtown San Diego Chabad.

Her husband, Les, who has remained devoutly Catholic, was accepting of Judy's religious quest. Mezuzot went up in their house, where no hanging crucifix is to be found. On the other hand, Les, who grew up as an outdoorsman, likes to decorate other portions of their home with the mounted trophies of animals that he has successfully hunted. While Judy enjoys shooting skeet and other forms of target practice, she personally does not like killing animals, not since she once wounded a rabbit and heard its screams. "They sounded like a baby's," she confided with a shudder.

The couple met through the heating, ventilation, air conditioning and plumbing business. Judy, whose degrees from Cal State Humboldt are in political science and environmental engineering, went to work for University Mechanical Engineering, where she met Les briefly before he left that company to work at A. O. Reed. Subsequently at industry conferences she would run into her future husband. It caused quite a stir when they became engaged, because A .O. Reed, in which today he is a partner and a vice president, was the major competitor for University Mechanical. Avoiding conflicts of interest, Judy resigned from University Mechanical to focus on the couple's rental properties.

While Les likes to hunt ducks, Judy raises a half dozen or so chickens for home use.

That started one spring day on a visit to a nearby feed store where she went intending to buy some outdoor pottery. She spotted in the store some baby chicks "and they were so cute. They were itty bitty, just three days out of their eggs. I picked out six or seven, which all looked alike. I got white leghorns and some ar-aucanas, which are the ones that lay the blue eggs. One little itty bitty one charged my hand and I said, 'Oh, you charged my hand, you must like me.' I kept them in the kitchen with a heat lamp. One day, when I was out there building with chicken wire, I realized that one that had been charging me was a rooster," a Rhode Island Red.

One of her white leghorns was a brooder, who would sit on her egg, hardly ever moving. Judy said she gathered three other eggs and put them under that hen, and the four were later hatched. Back then "we named our chickens, but you should never do that," not if they might end up on someone's dinner table--and it would never on mine! We have given the chickens away but we have not sold them."

The Rhode Island Red, named Jimmy, "was the meanest thing. My step-daughter would run from him in the yard, yelling to her daddy (Les) that Jimmy was bothering her. "Our neighbors had a bright light, a motion light, and whenever it would come on Jimmy would think it was the sun and cockadoo-dle-do. I had to take him from the roost and put him into a dog kennel kept in the garage every night. He got habituated to being in that dog house." One day, when Judy came back from an errand, she found the rooster all alone, going crazy. The hens had been given to a neighbor across the street. "I had this candle holder in the shape of the hen, and I put the fake hen in the kennel, and when I went out there later, Jimmy had cuddled up next to it."

The Osterbergers keep their hens during the few years which are most productive for laying eggs. Judy and Les both love to have fresh eggs in the morning, and Judy is particular to the blue ones because "they taste so good."

In fact, "I only eat the blue eggs," said Judy. "The reason is the other ones are usually fertilized and they have blood on them, and it gives me the creeps."

Shades of her grandma and great-grandma!

Take Pine Valley, Exit 45, and follow the road into town. The Osterbergers live in a private residence on a street off the main road.

-San Diego Jewish World, June 30, 2016

63. Exit 47

Historians and the Kwaaymii

Sylvia Arden, second from left, and volunteers

MOUNT LAGUNA, California — Jackie Lucas dropped in on the Serra Museum in Presidio Park, San Diego, in 1975, to look around the museum that focuses on early San Diego history. She saw on display a photo of a Kumeyaay woman. She walked into the offices of the San Diego Historical Society, which then was headquartered at the Serra Museum, and told chief archivist Sylvia Arden that the woman pictured in the photograph was none other than her grandmother, Maria Alto.

So pleased, excited and engaging was Arden—who is our "Jewish connection" to this story—that Jackie decided to invite her father, Tom Lucas, to return with her to the museum to see the photograph and to talk about the old days. Tom Lucas was a member of the Kwaaymii band of the Kumeyaay Indians, a band whose territory is near Mount Laguna, which is accessible from the Sunrise Highway exit 47 of Interstate 8. Sometimes the Kwaaymii are called the Laguna Indians.

Lucas brought with him a scrapbook of photographs and other documents pertaining to the lives of his family and that of the Kwaaymii, which he later donated to the historical society. Arden and Michael Carman, then the society's curator, conducted a preliminary interview with Lucas. A month later, Lucas engaged in a more formal interview with Richard Carrico, who then was just beginning to make a name for himself as this area's leading ethno-historian. "Not only was I delighted at the chance to conduct such an interview, I was complimented," Carrico wrote in a 1983 *Journal of San Diego History* article describing the encounter. "Mr. Lucas agreed to an interview at his home in Pacific Beach on November 4, 1975 and to a later informal talk and tour of his ranch in the Laguna Mountains."

Dennis Sharp, today the curator of the San Francisco Airport Museum which focuses on commercial aviation, trained at the San Diego Historical Society after Arden had retired. The story of how Arden arranged the interview between Lucas and Carrico, he said, was "so typical of her--all those little connections that she made. She was always so selfless about promoting history for the community."

Dan Arden, a Hollywood-based producer of television documentaries, recently told me that his mother Sylvia's passions were the museum's oral history program, which she had helped to develop into a nationally recognized art form, and chronicling the history of San Diego's minority communities -- for which, as a Jew who had experienced anti-Semitism in the Poconos of New York, she felt great empathy. The Lucas-Carrico interview, in a sense, was a "twofer" for Arden, both an oral history and about minorities, while for Carrico it was a decisive step in his career.

Working from known facts, Carrico, through the interview, incrementally extended his (and our) knowledge of the customs and practices of the Kwaaymii. First, he asked, how old Maria Alto was, and although Lucas didn't know exactly, he figured she must have been over 90 when she died in 1924. That would mean that she would have been at least a teenager, and possibly an adult, in 1850 when California became the 31st state of the United States. Lucas said that his mother often worked as a live-in domestic, traveling to ranches in San Bernardino, and possibly in Santa Barbara, from her home on what is now the Laguna Indian Reservation. Next, Carrico introduced the subject of pottery that could be seen in a photograph of Alto. Where did she get the clay? he asked. Lucas said that his mother had two favorite places, one southeast of Laguna Meadows, in a place he called Laguna Flats, and the other in the northern part of the Laguna Mountains. The clay was fine without rocks that could cause pottery to burst in the baking process. Often his mother mixed the clay with cactus juice, for the same reason that lime today is added to cement. After it was shaped, the clay would be placed in a hole at least 4 feet deep, and covered with oak bark which would be ignited. Rocks set around the circumference of the hole served as a windbreak. More of Carrico's step-by-step interview of Lucas may be read at http://www.sandiegohistory.org/journal/83spring/kumeyaay.htm.

For several years after the interview was completed, "Sylvia kept pestering me: 'When are you going to do an article in the Journal?'" Carrico remembered.

"She stayed on me, as she was supposed to do, and the result was not only the article. It got me to thinking in the mid to late 1970s that I really needed to find out if there were others out there besides Tom Lucas. That spurred me on to what became my career, doing a lot of anthropology rather than just archaeology. So I really owe her a lot."

Carrico, who is acknowledged as a leading living scholar of the Kumeyaay, is widely known for his 1987 book, *Strangers in a Stolen Land*, which covers the history of the indigenous people of San Diego County, including the Kumeyaay.

In 2015, some 30 years after his interview with Lucas, Carrico noted, "I have a contract to do an ethnography of the Kumeyaay Indians. I have been working on it for two years, and it's about a three-year project."

An "ethnography," he explained, takes "an anthropological approach rather than an historical approach." Carrico said he was told by Kumeyaay leaders that past studies of their people provided "good archaeology, but we are not there. Stone tools are, arrowheads are, broken pieces of pottery are, but where are we?"

Elaborating, Carrico said:

When a Kumeyaay looks up at the night sky, they don't see Orion as we do, they see a big horn sheep. A whole story goes with that. The Milky Way is the backbone of the universe, and a whole story goes with that. If you ask a Kumeyaay where knowledge comes from, it is through their songs, bird songs, and the things that go along with that. Archaeologists recorded trails out in the desert but didn't talk about why trails were important beyond trade and travel. Actually there is a whole cosmological, religious, spiritual thing that goes with these trails. Certain trails you would only use on spirit walks. That is what ethnography is about. When you look at broken pottery, talk about it as a science and an art form to the Kumeyaay. Or if you talk about ethno-zoology, an archaeologist would dig up a deer bones and say, 'well, gosh, the Kumeyaay had some deer,' and then talk about their diet. The Kumeyaay want us to know that these animals had spirits and their creator put them here, and they do different things. Some of them talk. If an owl comes around your house and makes a lot of noise, then someone is going to die in the near future. So, finding an owl bone on an archaeological site is one thing, but talking about the spirituality of this is completely another thing."

Sylvia Arden also was influential in the movie career of her son Daniel, who said he was "painfully shy" as a child. His mother decided he should "take a drama class at the JCC (then on 54th Street) and I loved it. It really did help me come out of my shell, at least to a degree, and that ended up being my passion all the way through my school years. I ended up going for a theater arts degree at the North Carolina School of the Arts, and then I was a professional actor for about five years in New York. Ultimately I ended up, through an acting job, involved with the production side, and I ended up switching careers into television and film production." Daniel is known primarily for documentaries, especially behind-the-scenes studies concerning the making of such famous film series as *Lord of the Rings* and *The Hobbit*.

Sylvia's older son, David, spent years touring Europe, South America, and Asia as a classical pianist who specialized in the works of contemporary *avante garde* and American composers. His goodwill tours were underwritten by the United States Information Agency, with his appearance at one all-Gershwin conference sponsored by the Crown Prince of Belgium, who later became King Albert II. In an interview, David recalled that when he first expressed interest in playing the piano, at perhaps the age of 5 or 6, his mother immediately signed herself up for night classes in which she too could learn the piano. Her idea was to teach her son whatever she learned, a process that came to its conclusion in about six months time, when the young pupil began outperforming his mom. David was signed up for a regular piano teacher. But Sylvia's interest, and desire to participate in the lives of her children, never abated. During the mid-1970s, when David was in Holland in a month-long music competition, Sylvia flew to Europe and sat in the audience every day, listening not only to David but to all his competitors. She took notes and correctly predicted that David would finish first. She also correctly predicted which two musicians would come in second and third in the competition.

Likewise, David recalled, when his brother Dan was studying in London for his junior year abroad, Sylvia not only attended his rehearsals and performances but volunteered as a secretary for the drama class, soon becoming a friend to all the students. She would regularly be invited out to dinner with Dan and the other drama students, and when the class finally mounted a production of *The Threepenny Opera*, their success and hers were one in the same.

As a motivator, Sylvia Arden won renown for her ability to recruit and train volunteers to conduct oral history interviews. At the San Diego Historical Society, her passion for conducting such forays into history inspired a corps of 25 to 30 people, some of whom were students, while others were retirees who themselves may have completed brilliant careers and were looking for productive ways to contribute their time. After Arden retired from the San Diego Historical Society, she remained active as an officer in various national and regional societies for archivists and oral historians. She also became a consultant who was hired by individuals and even by two counties in Nevada to conduct oral interviews and to teach others how to do them.

Recalling his own introduction to the field, Dennis Sharp said that he was hired by the society as an archivist a year or so after Arden's retirement. Asked to revive the oral history program, he attended a conference in Tempe, Arizona, of the Southwest Oral History Society. When Arden, who was an officer of the association, found out where he was from, she took him under her wing and made sure he met everyone in the society. She also shared with him contacts she had developed back home in San Diego. "She was all about promoting the historical society and San Diego's past; preserving its collections, records and documents; and sharing those with the community," he said. Arden for a while was the archive's only paid staff member and was remembered fondly as the "lone arranger," Sharp said.

Arden was a strong believer in the value of first-person history, her son Dan said. First-person accounts "are often in writing but often times, because they aren't writers, the people who played important roles or have knowledge of import-ant aspects of San Diego's history" only will have the opportunity to tell their sto-ries through the mechanism of an interview, Dan Arden said.

"She was very methodical about the oral history collection," Dan continued. "There were certain people who played very significant roles in culture, or the gov-ernment, or various other aspects of San Diego life. She was always looking for the important areas of San Diego history and who were the people who will be able through their oral history to shine a light on that."

Her approach to oral history "was very methodical," Dan said. "When she was going to interview someone, it could be a very long process. She would have been researching even before the first meeting with them. She might have been research-ing for six months to really prepare. And then the interview might be over 4, 8, or 12 sessions with a period of time in between. That was how in-depth it goes."

Sharp said oral interviews are designed largely to "fill in the gaps" of the his-torical record. In order to know what the gaps are, oral historians read extensively about their subjects, and then ask them questions that will add to the historical record.

Richard W. Crawford, Susan A. Painter, and Sarah B. West provided a sense of the scope of the historical society's oral history program in the Spring 1991 edi-tion of the *Journal of San Diego History*.

> The program was initiated in 1956 by a former county supervisor, Edgar Hastings. Supported by county funding, Hastings interviewed 309 pioneer residents of San Diego County in the next four years. The program lapsed after Hastings' death in 1961. In the late 1960s the program was revived by Historical Society librarian Sylvia Arden. Under Arden's direction, oral his-tory became a highly successful volunteer program.
>
> It is possible for the researcher to read, in a narrator's own words, a descrip-tion of the 1916 Hatfield flood in an interview with Dean Blake. An inter-view with Bert Shankland describes what it was like to "eat smoke" as a San Diego fireman in the 1920s. The Montague Brabazon interview details, step by step, the early methods of processing and shipping dried and fresh fruit in the beginning of an industry which became important to the San Diego economy.
>
> Little known aspects of 19th century life in San Diego are revealed in many of the interviews. The Alice Baldwin interview gives minute details of the mining industry in the back country. The social and economic conditions of Native Americans are described in interviews with Purl Willis and Tom Lucas, and rough frontier justice is depicted in an interview with Max J. Bowen.
>
> City politics is the subject of interviews with former San Diego mayors John Butler, Frank Curran, and Roger Hedgecock, Councilman William Cleator, and County Supervisor De Graff Austin. Work in the San Diego tuna industry of the 1930s is described by Edward Soltesz. Vincent Batta-

glia gives a detailed account of the tuna fleet commandeered for military service in World War II and cited by the President for its participation in such actions as the Battle of Guadalcanal...

Crawford, who today is an author and an expert in the San Diego Central Library's local history section, and Charles Hughes, a local history researcher, both trained under Arden at the Serra Museum, which they recalled as having only tiny quarters for researchers, accommodating no more than six at a time. (Today, the archives are housed in much larger quarters in the Casa de Balboa in Balboa Park.) Because of the Serra Museum's limited space, Arden required researchers to make reservations for seating, and she would bring to them material that they requested. Once she got to know a researcher, and what he or she wanted, she would greet the researcher with a mound of materials that she thought would be helpful.

Quite gregarious, Arden typically made it a point to get to know the researchers, learn about their families, and their interests. And she didn't hesitate talking about how proud she was of her sons David and Dan.

When she took the job, Arden had not been professionally trained as an archivist. In fact, having grown up the daughter of an impoverished single mother, she did not have the funds to go to college. But, after moving as a young woman to Los Angeles, she learned how to type, very fast and very accurately, and made money preparing the master's and doctoral theses of students at USC. Additionally, she was a very good copy reader, often saving students from mistakes in grammar or spelling.

After being hired as an assistant archivist at the San Diego Historical Society, and later being promoted to the top archival job, she became a trailblazer as an oral historian while continuing to follow the protocols that she had inherited in the archiving of written materials and in the treatment of photographs,

Some assistants chafed at her loyalty to the old traditions. For example, Crawford and Hughes recalled, Arden would break up collections donated by a family or an individual, filing individual papers in various subject folders. So, for example, if a paper in a collection donated by this or that family discussed the Kumeyaay, it would go into the Kumeyaay folder, and if another paper discussed the Old Town court house, that likewise would be filed by subject. Hughes and Crawford both subscribe to the theory that family collections should be kept intact. On the other hand, filing such papers by subject made it easier for specialized researchers such as Carrico to quickly find what they need.

Arden's former assistants also noted that she was protective of the San Diego Historical Society's archives, and would use a rubber stamp that said this or that document or photograph was the society's property. While this practice could potentially mar the face of documents, it also can help prevent theft, which is a problem at any archive. Clearly in both cases, there are good arguments on both sides. In any profession, practitioners are likely to differ on methods and procedures.

On one subject about which there was no argument--in fact, Hughes, Crawford and Carrico are unanimous about this--is that Arden deserves high praise for
her positive role in the development of the historical society's archives, particularly
its oral history collection.

Another important contribution Arden made to the history of San Diego
County was the annotation of a diary of a young Jewish girl, Victoria Jacobs, who
lived in the 1850s in what today is known as Old Town San Diego before marrying Maurice Franklin and moving to San Bernardino, where she died in child-
birth. Jacobs' diary, without annotations, would not have provided a casual reader with so nearly as rich a picture of early San Diego as it did after Arden added
footnotes that identified the people and places to which Jacobs casually referred.

The annotated diary was published by Jewish historian Norton Stern, and
won high praise from Professor Abraham Nasatir, the historian for whom one of
the buildings at San Diego State University is named.

Approximately in 2007, Arden moved from her home in Mission Hills to a
senior residence in La Jolla. The residence lacked facilities to care for her after she
developed symptoms of Alzheimer's disease, so Dan and his wife Ann arranged for
her relocation to another facility near their home in Studio City.

While her memory loss increased over the years, said Dan, her sociability did
not wane until the final few months before her death at age 92 on July 6, 2014. "She
would say 'Now, how do I know you?' and I would say, 'You're my mom; I'm your
son!' and she would smile and say 'You are!' and then a few moments she would
say, 'Now, who are you?' The great thing was that every time that I would tell her
that I was her son, she would be happy."

Having been divorced from her husband Ralph, who predeceased her and is
buried in San Diego, Sylvia Arden chose to be cremated with her ashes to be buried
in Whittier, where Dan and Ann have reserved space for themselves.

···

Take Sunrise Highway, Exit 47, north to Mount Laguna.

···

-San Diego Jewish World, June 23, 2016

64. Exit 51
Camp Lockett Buffalo Soldiers

John Finley at Camp Lockett

CAMPO, California — Like many Army installations, Camp Lockett was built for utility rather than for beauty. Rare would be the architectural student who would come to marvel at its buildings. But in the nation's memory, Camp Lockett nevertheless deserves an important place. It was one of those outposts where the time and talents of many black soldiers were squandered during much of World War II because white units, filled with the racial prejudice of the day, didn't want to fight alongside them. So instead of joining the nation's combat troops in the war against the Germans or the Japanese, the black enlisted men of the 10th and 28th Cavalry Regiments, under the watchful eyes of their white officers, patrolled the quiet Mexican border and languished in San Diego County's back country.

Such was not the fate of all black soldiers; other units such as the 92nd Infantry Division, though segregated, were sent in 1944 to Italy, where they fought the Germans in such locations as the Po Valley. Others such as the 761st Tank Battalion and 183rd Combat Engineers, were present in Germany and Austria at the time of, or just after, the liberation of such Nazi concentration camps as Dachau, Buchenwald, and Gunskirchen (a sub-camp of Mauthausen). As a Jew, aware of how my own people suffered during World War II, how they were segregated from other

Europeans, dehumanized, and finally mass murdered, I can't help but empathize with those black soldiers who wanted to prove themselves to be loyal and determined U.S. citizens and to rid the world of totalitarian, racist dictatorships. Although the Jewish connection to this story may be tenuous, it is nevertheless one of strong emotion.

Along with my grandson, Shor, 14, and longtime family friend, John Everett Finley, a former Navy enlisted man who is the third-generation of his African-American family to have served in the U.S. military, I recently visited Camp Lockett, named for Spanish-American War veteran Col. James R. Lockett and known to many as the home of the "Buffalo Soldiers" – a somewhat controversial term. According to the most-told story about the name's origin, during the American Indian wars of the late 19th century, Native Americans saw the dark skin and curly hair of Negro troops and likened them in that aspect to the buffalo of the plains. Another version suggests that the American Indians admired the black troops, even as they admired the buffalo, as fierce fighters who didn't go down, even after being wounded. Other versions say it was not the Indians, but white troops, who pinned the moniker on them.

Whatever the truth may have been, the "Buffalo Soldier" name stuck, and various all-black units came to identify with it proudly. Today there are Buffalo Soldier reunions and reenactments. Here in Campo, there are displays about the Buffalo Soldiers at the Gaskill Brothers Stone Store Museum operated by the Mountain Empire Historical Society. A far more extensive museum is planned by organizers of the 100-acre Camp Lockett Event and Equestrian Center (CLEEF). The organizers also anticipate setting up the kind of obstacle course for riders on which the mounted black troops of the 10th and 28th Cavalry Regiments trained.

John Finley's great uncle, Sgt. Everett Shankle, was a Buffalo Soldier, one of those who served with the 92nd Infantry Division in Italy. John's father, Garfield William Finley, Jr., so admired his Uncle Everett that he became a career soldier, rising in the Army to the rank of lieutenant colonel. Lt. Col. Finley's family cherishes stories of his childhood, when he would march around the house in Uncle Everett's cavalry boots. When John's turn came to serve, he enlisted in the Navy, spending a good deal of his eight years of military service on ships and on bases as an electronics technician. John said whereas his great-uncle Everett was segregated into an all-Negro unit; his father Garfield, serving in integrated units, suffered less discrimination than his Uncle Everett. Once, while traveling through Texas in the early 1960s in his Army officer's uniform, Garfield was denied service at a café, but that was the only incident that came to mind. As for John, himself, he said that during his Navy service, "race was rarely an issue for me, but when it was, it was more a nuisance than a major problem."

At the Gaskill Brothers Stone Store Museum, we learned that at the beginning of World War II, the all-white 11th Cavalry Regiment, as part of the Southern Land Defense Center, patrolled the U.S.-Mexico border against possible enemy invasion, and protected railroad bridges and tunnels as well as the Morena, Barnett and Otay reservoirs from potential sabotage. Six months after the Japanese surprise attack at Pearl Harbor on Dec. 7, 1941, the 11th transferred to Fort Benning, Georgia, trading in their horses for motor vehicles. The 10th was transferred meanwhile from Fort Leavenworth, Kansas, to Camp Lockett. With numerous non-commissioned officers from the 10th Cavalry chosen to serve as its cadre, the 28th Cavalry was created in late 1942.

In a video presented by the museum, Fred Jones, a retired master sergeant with the 28th Cavalry Regiment, said that unlike the troops of the 10th Regiment, which had a history extending back to the Indian Wars of the late 19th century, the men of the 28th Regiment had grown up in cities of the Midwest and for the most part were unfamiliar with horses. Nevertheless, he said, they were happy to be in the cavalry, charmed by the romance of the Buffalo Soldiers' history and their unique uniforms, "boots and spurs which made them look sort of glorious."

He recalled that when the 10th and 28th drilled together: "We all rode in formation… the first time we rode around at raised pistol at sort of a trot…went around again at a trot with rifles. The next time we rode around at a full gallop with pistols drawn." It was particularly difficult for cavalry members who had to carry machine guns or mortars on the backs of secondary horses. "If the pack was loose, the horse would rear up, or kick," he recalled. The most terrifying exercise of all was the full cavalry charge, as there was always "that worry that something could happen…. Your horse could fall and the rest of them would have to ride over you." He remembered that even while galloping, riders were expected to maintain "4 feet from your horse's nose to the hocks of the horse in front of you, and 6 inches from your boot to the boot of the man riding next to you. Holding it was practically impossible."

A total of 7,107 acres in the Campo area were purchased or leased by the U.S. Army for the housing and training of the two cavalry regiments. Camp Lockett covered an area of approximately 15 square miles – measuring five miles from east to west, and three miles from north to south, where it adjoined the U.S.-Mexico border. On the grounds of the former Camp Lockett is the southern terminus of the 2,663-mile-long Pacific Crest Trail, which hikers may follow from the Mexican border all the way to the Canadian border. Some of Camp Lockett's hundreds of buildings are being re-used today, such as by the headquarters of the Mountain Empire School District. Other buildings are abandoned, rat-infested, and awaiting demolition or refurbishment.

A former member of the Mountain Empire School District board, Cliff Northcote, who today serves as president of the Camp Lockett Event and Equestrian Facility, told us that the planned museum will be located within the refurbished home of Frank Ferguson, one of the designers of the binational San Diego & Eastern Railroad which was built through Campo in the early 1900s. During World War II, Camp Lockett's commander was billeted in Ferguson's old home.

Northcote said he would like to move one of the abandoned barracks buildings to a spot near the Ferguson House and re-create what a Buffalo Soldiers barracks would have looked like – everything from their beds to their personal belongings. He said a similar facility is on display at Fort Stockton, Texas, where other contingents of Buffalo soldiers had been stationed.

Elsewhere at the Camp Lockett Event and Equestrian Facility, there are plans to install a refurbished barracks near the terminus of the Pacific Crest Trail to provide hikers with a place to rest before or after the arduous hikes. Plans also call for demonstration areas where visitors could see leather working, saddle making. and blacksmithing.

Kathy Flores, a CLEEF board member, said the equestrian obstacle course would closely parallel the training members of the 10th and 28th did to familiarize their horses with various conditions they might encounter, so that the horses would not become frightened. For example on the new obstacle course, horse and rider will have to cross bodies of water and railroad tracks, go in and out of gated areas, and pass under low hanging tree branches.

The facility also will include RV and tent campsites. The primitive sites won't have water and electrical hookups at each spot, but will be equipped with two individual corrals for the horses, a picnic table and a fire ring. Along another ridge of the facility will be more fully equipped pull-through spots suitable for an RV and a horse trailer.

Before the 10th and 28th shipped out to Algeria in 1944, where their units were broken up, the cavalry men fought a forest fire in the adjoining Cleveland National Forest, and also had some opportunities for on-base entertainment. According to a historical report compiled for the County of San Diego in July 2007, the USO brought both black and white entertainers to Camp Lockett. These included, among others, Dinah Shore, Dale Evans, Betty Grable, Sammy Davis Jr., Ethel Waters, Hattie McDaniels, and heavyweight boxing champion Joe Louis. Of interest is the fact that Dinah Shore was a Jew, and Sammy Davis Jr. later in his life would convert to Judaism.

After the 10th and 28th were deactivated in Algeria, some of their members were reassigned to the 94th Infantry Division. It's possible that some of them met John Finley's great-uncle Everett!

••

From eastbound, Exit 51, turn right on Buckman Springs Road, go 10 miles to right turn on Highway 94, then 1.5 miles to left turn on Forest Gate Road. The address of the Camp Lockett Event and Equestrian Center is 799 Forest Gate Road, Campo.

••

-San Diego Jewish World, June 30, 2016

65. Exit 51
Gaskill Brothers Gun Battle

Gaskill Brothers store

CAMPO, California — During the 1870s, the San Diego mercantile firm owned by Abraham Klauber and Samuel Steiner supplied groceries and dry goods to general stores all over Southern California and Northern Baja California. One of their best customers was a fellow Jew, Louis Mendelsohn of Rancho San Rafael, Mexico. Sufficient trust developed between the two mercantile concerns that Mendelsohn arranged to send $600 in gold, which was an enormous amount on Nov. 30, 1875, to Abraham Klauber, who operated the San Diego headquarters of the partnership. Klauber's partner, Samuel Steiner, lived in San Francisco, where he purchased much of the company's stock from importers.

The buggy in which Mendelsohn's clerk, Henry A. Leclaire, and a former territorial governor of Baja California, Don Antonio Sosa, were traveling was intercepted, the gold stolen, and both men were murdered. The robbery and murders were part of a sinister plan by the bandit Cruz "Pancho" Lopez to acquire enough money, ammunition and supplies to enable his gang to attack and exploit the gold mines in the Mexican state of Sonora. Other customers of Steiner and Klauber— the brothers Silas and Lumen Gaskill who owned on the American side of the border in Campo a general store, blacksmith shop, post office, mill, and small hotel as well as apiaries and cattle—were the next intended targets of Lopez and his gang.

David Klauber, a great-great grandson of Abraham Klauber, recounted in *The Sounding*, a 2009 history of his family, that the Gaskill Brothers were no easy push-overs. In fact, he reported, they "had previously earned their living with firearms, hunting game for wagon trains and shooting literally hundreds of bear for north-ern California ranchers." Tipped off by a local worker that the Lopez gang planned to kill them and loot their store, the Gaskills made ready. They placed shotguns in strategic niches around their complex and went about their business. On Decem-ber 4, 1875, Lopez and five other heavily armed riders crossed the border, where two wagons drivers awaited instructions to haul away the Gaskill Brothers' goods.

As retold in Klauber's book, over the next six minutes the sequence of events went as follows: When the Lopez gang arrived, Lumen was in the general store and Silas was at the blacksmith shop. Gang member Rafael Martinez, who had been pretending to shop, stepped outside when his six cohorts arrived. Lopez en-tered the store joined by Jose Alvijo and Alonzo Cota. Then Alvijo and Cota pulled their guns on Lumen, who screamed "murder" and dropped behind the counter. He tried to get to his weapon but Cota pulled him up and Alvijo fired a six-shooter right into Lumen's chest, puncturing his lung. They left him behind the counter for dead, but somehow, although partially paralyzed, he survived, retrieved a shotgun, and crawled to a prone position just inside the door of the store.

Silas heard his brother's shout and grabbed a shotgun in the blacksmith shop. Gang member Teodoro Vazquez fired at Silas, nicking his inner arm, and Silas blasted his shotgun, killing Vazquez instantly. He then chased Martinez and gang member Pancho Alvitro around the building, wounding Martinez badly enough that he stayed down on the ground. Alvitro hid for a while be-hind a woodpile, then headed to the store, where he came into the sights of Lumen's shotgun. The subsequent blast severely wounded him.

Plaque commemorating historic gunfight

In the meantime, two passersby came upon the scene. One held Silas's shot-gun; the other, a Frenchman, used his horse as a shield, and wounded Lopez as he came out of the store. Cota and Alvijo then found Lopez and the three of them engaged the Frenchman and Silas in a gun battle, until the bandits broke off the engagement. Those who could ,rode back to Mexico, where apparently the wagon drivers also had fled. Lumen meanwhile crawled to a trapdoor and dropped to safety in the stream that ran below the house.

Once out of range, Lopez yanked the seriously wounded Alvitro off his horse and shot him in the head, killing him. Alvijo, who had been left behind with wounds, was arrested and placed under guard with Martinez. That night vigilante ranchers broke into the temporary jail and lynched the prisoners to-gether with the two ends of a single rope. About a month later, the Frenchman died of his wounds in San Francisco. Lopez subsequently also died from the in-fected wounds he had received from the Frenchman. Only Cota and another unnamed bandit got away.

In his book, David Klauber pointed out that the gunfight resulted in more deaths than Wyatt Earp's famous shootout at the OK Corral approximately four years later.

The wounded Gaskill Brothers worried that Lopez would assemble another gang to stage another raid, and Silas wrote to Abraham Klauber in San Diego that "it seems rather tough that we can't be protected in some way from being robbed and murdered here at home; minding our own business, does it not?"

He added: "I wish you would use what influence you can for us and see if we can't get some protection in some way. The government ought to protect the Post Office and Military Telegraph here. They will have to be discontinued; probably both officers will be killed in the next attack."

A ten-member committee of San Diego business leaders, including Klauber, persuaded the military to send troops to Campo. When a small military force ar-rived about a month later, tensions along the border somewhat eased. But, taking nothing for granted, the Gaskills decided to replace their frame store with a secure stone store, its walls four feet thick on the first floor and two feet thick on the sec-ond floor.

In 1898, The Klauber firm purchased the stone store from Ed Aiken, who was a successor of the Gaskill Brothers. The Klaubers sent among others, Abraham's son, Hugo Klauber, to run it for about two years. Aiken continued to work at the store for a brief period while Hugo familiarized himself with its operation. Campo, then, was cattle country, meaning that the ranchers only came into money once a year, after the cattle were driven to market. In the interim, they carried pass books on which the totals of their purchases at the store was noted on each occasion. A running total was shown for the year.

In a letter written June 26, 1898, Abraham gave his son some advice and spelled out the financial arrangements of their partnership.

I suppose it is unnecessary to say that the more rapidly you familiarize yourself with the details of the business, the better. Shall I send you my Spanish books? You will find them of great service when studied at the same time when you have a chance to put the theory into practical use. ... Our proposition to you is as follows: We will furnish the capital interest to be charged and paid quarterly as an expense of the business at 7% per annum. Losses, if any, to be divided equally. I don't see any chance whatever of a loss. The first $1200 per year (or 100 per month) of profit to go to you. Anything over 1200 and up to 2400 to go to us. If profits exceed 2400, they are to be equally divided. In other words if the profits were 3000 for the first year, you would get 1500 and we (K&LCo) 1500. All personal expense you will, of course, have to stand, such as board &c.

Melville Klauber joined his younger brother in Campo for the occasion of the store's grand opening, recalling later that "we gave a free dinner to the inhabitants of that section at the Campo Hotel. In order to make the affair as successful as possible, there being a large crowd to take care of, H.K. {Hugo} and M.K. {Melville} helped to wait on the table and did whatever else was necessary to make it a success." Hugo lodged at the same hotel, where the food was, frankly, awful.

A younger brother, Laurence M. Klauber, then 15 years old, came out to help in the summer of 1899. Sixty-one years later, he wrote an account for the *San Diego Historical Society Quarterly* detailing his impressions of the store.

At the left of the door, as one entered, there hung an olla of water. The olla was filled by carrying a bucket in from a nearby spring, in which resided the biggest goldfish you ever saw. Everyone entering the store paused for a drink from a dipper hanging by the olla, as a sort of greeting to those already within.

On three sides of the room there were counters. In front there were empty nail kegs intended for use as stools for the customers, but actually they were appropriated by philosophical cowboys resting from arguments with cows. At the right there was a wall rack containing rifles and shotguns, mostly museum pieces even for that day, although there were a few modern items, including an 1886 Winchester .38-55 that was Hugo's pet.

There was no cash register, but under the counters, at four locations, there were cash drawers of the kind then used. Each of these had four or five finger hooks out of sight on the underside. If you knew the combination, and pulled the right hooks, the drawer came open, otherwise a bell rang. Beside each cash drawer, on a small shelf hidden under the counter and open to the back, there was a loaded six-shooter. I may say in passing, that although every cowboy wore a .44, I never saw any shooting during the three months I was there.

Eventually, Hugo returned to San Diego, where in 1899, he was drafted by the San Diego team in a four-team league to play first base in what turned out to be a 15-inning championship game against San Bernardino. The regular first baseman,

Mike Donlin, had injured his finger so was sent to right field where he wasn't likely to field as many plays. The San Diegans won the contest 1-0 with the very rookie Hugo Klauber making 17 putouts with nary an error. Donlin, by the way, went on to play for the fabled John McGraw's New York Giants and later became a Broadway actor.

During Hugo's tenure, the Campo store later was operated as part of the Klauber & Levi-owned Mountain Commercial Company, which also included other general stores in far-flung locales. Eventually, Henry Marcus Johnson partnered with the firm, serving as its general manager through 1925. Later, philanthropist E.M. Statler purchased it for San Diego County for use as a museum.

Although Hugo had made quite a name for himself as a semi-professional baseball player, he remained loyal to the family business and eventually rose to the presidency of the company that, after Steiner's retirement, had been twice renamed, first as Klauber & Levi Company. After Simon Levi left to start his own grocery business, the firm became known as the Klauber-Wangenheim Company in honor of Julius Wangenheim, who married Abraham's daughter Laura and became a business partner.

Today, the old stone store houses the exhibits of the Mountain Empire Historical Society, with a re-creation of a 19th century general store on the first floor, and exhibits about the area's military history—including the story of the Buffalo Soldiers at Camp Lockett—retold on the second floor.

The townspeople of Campo periodically stage reenactments of the gun battle.

....

From eastbound, Exit 51, turn right on Buckman Springs Road, go 10 miles to right turn on Highway 94. Museum is at the intersection on the right.

....

-San Diego Jewish World, July 7, 2016

66. Exit 54
Pacific Crest Trail

Barney and Sandy Mann on the Pacific Crest Trail

CLEVELAND NATIONAL FOREST, California — The Pacific Crest Trail intersects with Kitchen Creek Road about 30 miles from where the trail begins on the U.S.-Mexico border and about 2,620 miles from where it ends on the U.S-Canada border.

Barney and Sandy Mann agreed to meet me there and answer some questions about the thrills and challenges of hiking a trail that is roughly equivalent to the driving distance between San Diego and New York via Interstate 40. Nothing about the Kitchen Creek Road crossing is extraordinary, except that it is easily reached by car. There is one part of the trail, up north, where one hikes some 200 miles without crossing a road.

The Manns are veterans of the Pacific Crest Trail, having hiked it in its entirety in 2007 on the occasion of their 30th wedding anniversary. As they tried to average between 20 and 25 miles per day on their hike, they reached Kitchen Creek on the second day of their five-month long backpacking adventure. They didn't go that distance every day; on some days they rested and those were called "zero" days. Other days, they walked fewer than ten miles, and those were called "nearo" days. "Nearo," it rhymes with "zero."

Since their 2007 odyssey, the Manns have been active in the protection, preservation, and promotion of the long, meandering pedestrian and equestrian trail that not only passes through the states of California, Oregon and Washington, but also traverses 25 national forests, 6 national parks, 5 California State Parks, and, 3 National Monuments in addition to other federal, state, local, and private lands.

The Manns are members of Temple Solel in Encinitas. Barney, a retired real estate attorney, sings bass in the temple's choir. Sandy, a PhD in molecular biology who taught advanced placement high school classes, has a brother who is a Presbyterian minister, while Barney, thanks to his sister, has a brother-in-law who is a rabbi. Sandy is a member with her husband of Reform congregation Solel's *chavurot* (friendship groups). She became a Jew by choice while pregnant with the first of their three children.

Together the Manns are known as "trail angels," who often pick up thru-hikers at San Diego's airport at Lindbergh Field, provide them with food and overnight lodging at their home in the University City neighborhood of San Diego, and drive them the next morning to the U.S.-Mexico border at Campo to begin their treks. Barney recently served for three years as president of the Pacific Crest Trail Association (PCTA) and still serves on its board of directors. Additionally, he frequently writes about the trail's history and customs in a variety of publications, including the quarterly of the Pacific Crest Trail Association, *The Communicator*. Remember the second word in the trail's name, it is the Pacific *Crest* Trail—so named because it goes over mountain ridges. It is not the Pacific "Coast" Trail; in fact it is considerably inland from the beaches.

The Manns, like many thru-hikers, have "trail names" by which they introduce themselves and are known by other hikers whom they meet along the way. Their fellow hikers call Barney "Scout" and Sandy "Frodo." There are stories behind each trail name, although Sandy's is more esoteric. Barney was a Boy Scout who completed his first 50-mile hike when he was 13. He reached the "Life" rank, forever regretting that he did not continue on to "Eagle," and later in life served for five years as a scoutmaster. As much as he loves the Boy Scouts, Mann credits Temple Akiba in Culver City, where he grew up, for entrusting him with leadership positions. The temple operated a summer camp, and while a college student, Barney was its head counselor. The temple's ruling board of directors trusted him to make decisions about the activities at the sleepover camp with little or no interference. Anyone familiar with temple or synagogue boards knows that is remarkable. Maybe someone should have given Barney the trail name "Akiba," which no doubt would have identified him quickly to fellow Jews. Akiba was a martyr in the Bar Kochba revolt who was executed by the Romans. Executed? Maybe "Scout" is a better name after all! Barney likes to slip fitting Yiddish words like *shlep* and *plotz* into his trail conversations, so you don't have to be an Einstein to figure out he's Jewish. Moreover, Barney wears a Magen David on a chain around his neck.

Sandy's brothers were Boy Scouts who also went on 50-mile hikes, but because she was a girl she didn't get to go. She resolved early in life she would do it anyway, and became a backpacker. It was serendipitous that Sandy was a counselor for a public school's outdoor school program that rented a San Gabriel Mountains camping facility at which Barney served as the director for three years between his college graduation and law school entry. Impressed by how well Sandy worked with youth, Barney hired her as a counselor for the upcoming summer camp session. Eventually, they fell in love and were married in 1977.

Before the Manns began their 2007 journey, Barney had a gold ring fashioned for Sandy on which were engraved the logo of the Pacific Crest Trail as well as depictions of some of the sights they were bound to see along the way. People who have seen or read J. R.R. Tolkien's *Lord of the Rings* trilogy would instantly get the joke of Sandy's trail name. Frodo was the inheritor of the One Ring who traveled to Mount Doom to destroy it. There, of course, the analogy breaks down. Notwithstanding her trail identity as "Frodo," there's no way that Sandy would destroy her keepsake ring – ever!

While Sandy good-naturedly accepted the Frodo name, she wished she would have been offered "Fleet Foot" or some other honorific. She explained that during a vacation from teaching duties, she read a lot of trail journals that thru-hikers had posted on line. Some of the people whom she read were of the opposite gender than what their names implied. "Girl Scout" and "Hot Sister" turned out to be guys, and "Cucumber Boy" was a girl. Annoyed, Sandy hoped for a trail name that wouldn't cause gender confusion. But then came her ring, and "I said 'no, Frodo is a guy' but it didn't work. ... I was not thrilled but it made sense, so I accepted it."

What were some of the more interesting trail names that they have encountered along the Pacific Crest Trail?

Barney told of a professional cellist, who was a first chair with his symphony, who one day was sitting around with other hikers and didn't yet have a trail name. "He started a sentence with 'wouldn't it be awful if you got a trail name like' – and here the creative side of his brain kicked in, but the other side was still resting –'like Cuddles?' And he is still 'Cuddles' today.

Sandy recalled the story of two male hikers who were resting at Warner Hot Springs, when the resort was open and welcoming to hikers. "There was a little 5-year-old girl birthday party going on and the girls were arguing: 'I want to be Rainbow Sparkles,' said one. 'No, I want to be Rainbow Sparkles' and one of the fellows turns to his buddy and says, 'No, I am Rainbow Sparkles' and he still is.

Warming to the subject, Barney told of a journalist who thru-hiked the trail in 2006. "One of the first places where you can go and get non-trail food is the Mount Laguna store, which is at PCT Mile 43, and the best he could do there was microwaved burritos." In a scene reminiscent of the campfire scene in *Blazing Saddles*, the hiker felt the burrito gas roaring through him. A gal asked "what was that?" and he responded "that would be rolling thunder." The man today remains "Rolling Thunder."

For a thru-hiker, matters that are taken for granted in day-to-day life at home--drinking, eating, going to the bathroom, what clothing to wear, what supplies to keep near--all have to be thought about anew. In response to the trail, thru-hikers dramatically must change their life styles, so why not their names too? It's not only the physical challenge and the ever-changing scenery that attract the Manns and other thru-hikers; the opportunity to experience a kind of metamorphosis on the trail also beckons to them.

For Sandy, one call of the trail is "the community, the people. We have lots of friends that we still stay in touch with, who help us help hikers, and whom we go to visit." At the stage of life when their children are grown and they are hoping they soon will have grandchildren, the Manns delight in serving as mentors to young hikers. "We have some 'trail children,' a couple of trail daughters, a couple of trail sons," Sandy said. "We get to hang out with young people. It's a different kind of hanging out than in class; on the trail, you are peers."

"I am my best self when I am outdoors," Barney says. Agreeing, Sandy says. "I tell people that it feeds my soul. It meets a need inside of me, just a real primal need. In science, we call it 'biophilia,' a love of nature."

Comments Barney: "There are so many things about it I love. I am around people who are feeling the same thing. If I love one thing in the world it is being kind. The default position on the trail is that in every interaction you are going to be looking out for each other. When I am out there at any time a small miracle can happen. They happen in our lives daily but we don't see them because we are so busy, and out there we have the time. I might be at a pass, and an eagle might swoop by within touching distance and I can feel the displacement of air. That doesn't happen in the city. I am walking in a place with no guard rails; there is something primal about that. I walk 25 miles a day and I can look back and see something in the far distance and the only thing that brought me from there to here was my feet. I look at objects in the distance, and my first thought is to approximate how long it will take to get there: two hours, half day, a full day. You get a sense of tremendous accomplishment. I feel special and important out there in a way that is entirely different than in the city. How often in your life do you get to do something that is extraordinary? By the mere fact of walking, twice now (the Pacific Crest Trail and the Continental Divide Trail), I have gotten to do something that is extraordinary."

Sandy adds that on the trail "everyone is looking out for everyone else, everyone is eager to meet other hikers; they are wonderful people and that is a big part of it. A lot of it is you come to the top of a pass and there is new stuff ahead. It is amazing. I love seeing the trail snaking out ahead, and knowing that I am going to walk that and see what is around that bend. I am going to meet that challenge."

While the trail can carry its lovers to the sublime, it also makes many a gritty demand upon them. Water, for example. The first 20 miles of the northbound trail has no water; hikers must carry their own, through a semi-desert climate. Water is heavy; the more you carry, the greater your load. The less you carry, the greater the risk of dehydration, maybe even sickness and death. Where is the balance? Barney carries on his back two 2-liter bladders, from which he can straw-sip while he is walking, and another two or three 1-liter plastic bottles in the side netting of his ultra-light backpack. "It is one thing to say 5-7 liters, but what that means is 10 to 15 pounds of water," Barney cautions.

Besides for drinking, water is used for rehydrating lighter-to-carry dehydrated foods. Sandy says after she eats she will add water to her cup or tin, swirl it around, and then drink the remainder. Water must not be wasted! Most thru-hikers don't carry soap; it requires water to lather and can be detrimental to the ecology. Instead they used alcohol-based cleansers like Purell to sanitize their hands.

Hiking 20-25 miles per day will burn 5,000-plus calories, and trail food will replenish about 1,500 to 2,000 calories of that, according to Barney. One result is that thru-hikers can burn off a lot of body fat. Another is that in those places where the Pacific Crest Trail passes near a restaurant, hikers tend to eat ravenously.

Bears eliminate their body waste in the woods and so do thru-hikers. Following the maxim of "leave no trace," the hikers pack out their used toilet paper, carrying it in a Zip-Loc bag until they can safely dispose of it in a trash can. This may not sound pleasant, but even more unpleasant would be to find the trail strewn with used toilet paper. Some 1,800 thru-hikers registered for the Pacific Crest Trail in 2015; imagine how disgusting it would be if they all just left the paper where they pooped. Even burying it doesn't solve the problem; animals will dig it up. So packing it out is the solution.

In their role as trail angels, Barney and Sandy sometimes pick up at the airport hikers whom they can tell are not properly prepared for the journey. Sometimes they come wearing jeans and cotton shirts, neither of which will dry easily after a rain. Polyester clothing is recommended. There was one hiker who didn't bring a sleeping bag; she figured she'd just sleep on the ground. Sandy told her she wouldn't drive her to the starting point unless she borrowed a sleeping bag from the Manns. It can get freezing cold in the mountains, especially toward the northern end of the trail. Whenever they see a would-be hiker who is ill-prepared, the Manns quietly pass the word to other hikers: "Keep an eye on so-and-so; don't let him (or her) get into trouble." The beauty of the hiking community is that they will take the admonition to heart.

Although they had joined the Pacific Crest Trail Association before their 2007 hike, it was during their odyssey that Barney decided that he would become more active in the association. He became the association's fundraising chair, and in 2008, he was invited to join the board. Eventually, he became the board chairman, carefully developing in association with the PCTA's executive director a comprehensive strategic plan.

About 90 percent of the trail is in public land, with the other 10 percent in easements across private land. To protect the trail for posterity, Barney and the Association would like to eventually have as much of that private land as possible to be acquired by the public. Financed with public funds and private donations, the trail needs continuous maintenance, additional signage, and the benefit of educational outreach. With fewer than a score of paid staff, but with some 1,500 volunteers and 10,000 members, many of them drawn to the Pacific Crest Trail as the result of Reese Witherspoon's portrayal of Cheryl Strayed in the 2014 film *Wild*, the PCTA is made up of people who like nothing better than to overcome challenges.

....

From Kitchen Creek, Exit 54, head north about 5 miles to where the trail crosses the road.

....

-San Diego Jewish World, July 14, 2016

67. Exit 61

Golden Acorn Casino

Entrance of Golden Acorn Casino

CAMPO, California — The Golden Acorn Casino participates in a multimillion dollar progressive slot machine jackpot fed by the losing bets of players not only here, but also located in numerous other casinos served by International Gaming Technologies (IGT)—a manufacturer and distributor of slot machines and other gaming devices. When I last looked, the possible pot was over $3 million.

For most of the people who gamble in casinos, winning that much money would be the stuff of dreams. It could pay off a mortgage, finance an Ivy League college education, fuel a luxury vacation, and even, perhaps, serve as seed money for starting one's own business.

The psychological rush that someone might feel from winning that jackpot may resemble, to a tiny degree, the feelings of elation experienced by the investors in the gaming industry when they successfully stage a takeover or a buy-out. Such a rush might approximate how Jason Ader could have felt had he been successful in his effort to win three seats for his designees on the IGT board.

Or, even headier, it might approximate how Wall Street tycoon Ronald Perelman feels whenever he wins control of an important company such as the Revlon cosmetics company or Scientific Games Corporation (SGC), which manufactures slot machines and lottery ticket dispensers, among other products.

Perelman, whom Comic Con fans may remember as the man who won control, then lost it of Marvel Comics and its related enterprises, is famous for buying companies that have expanded into ancillary and unrelated businesses and then selling off those divisions to return the companies to their core specialties. In some cases, the billionaire Perelman has made nearly as much money from selling off the other divisions than the initial purchases cost him.

Ader, who spent many years on Wall Street as a gaming industry analyst, left the sidelines in order to be able to play in the investment arena. He formed Ader Investment Management, which focused on gaming industry opportunities throughout the world. In 2013, Ader owned over 3 percent of the common shares of IGT, and notified the company that he wanted to replace three members of the board of directors, whom he felt did not have the requisite knowledge for their positions. He criticized IGT for purchasing for $500 million the online gaming company Double Down. He said IGT could have provided its own similar product for a fraction of the cost.

Beyond that, he contended that the management and board of directors really didn't have an economic stake in the success of the company. His 3 percent ownership, he said, amounted to six times as much as the holdings of all the company's officers and board of directors combined. Clearly, he argued, he had a reason for being more concerned than they that the company's stock had fallen over the years by 30 percent.

Among the three people whom Ader had proposed for membership on the board was IGT's former chairman Charles Mathewson, a 17-year-veteran of the industry, who was immediately attacked by the company's current management for having enriched himself during his tenure with too many company perks. That prompted Steve Wynn, owner of the Wynn Hotels, to come to Mathewson's defense, and eventually to back Ader's attempt to repopulate the board.

Following a proxie fight, Ader was able to put only one new member--Daniel Silvers, the Managing Member at Matthews Lane Capital Partners--on the board, thereby increasing the IGT board's size from 9 to 10. However, within eight months, Silvers resigned, and Ader and IGT announced that their differences had been settled. Ader agreed not to initiate any other action against IGT for at least four years, and IGT agreed to refund over $2 million that Ader had spent for the proxie fight. Both sides said their agreement had put the company in a stronger position, and the board membership was once again put at 9.

Perelman's Scientific Games Corporation recently purchased Bally, the oldest and perhaps in the public's eyes the best-known manufacturer of slot machines. Scientific Games Corporation previously had acquired WMS, another manufacturer of gaming devices, so the company is now beefed up for head-to-head competition with IGT. Golden Acorn Casino utilizes slot machines of WMS and IGT manufacture, but not Bally.

Our "Jewish story" in all this is that Ader, Silvers, and Perelman are members of the Jewish community.

In many cases, IGT slot machines and video devices are named after popular television shows. For example, some of the slot machine products offered to casinos such as The Golden Acorn include "Wheel of Fortune," "The Price is Right," "Jeopardy," "Family Feud," "Let's Make a Deal," "The Newlywed Game," "Sex and the City," "The Amazing Race," "Star Wars," and "Elvis."

The Golden Acorn Casino, on its website, has been advertising that among its 750 slot machines and video games are such other IGT games as "Cleopatra," "Kitty Glitter," "Wolf Run," "Texas Hold 'Em," "Davinci Diamonds," and "Siberian Storm."

Had Golden Acorn chosen the Bally division of Scientific Games Corporation as its provider, the lights and bells ringing on its casino floor would be from such games as "Pawn Stars," "Midnight Diamonds," "Quick Hit Pro," "Shadow Diamond," "Quick Hit Las Vegas," "Sumo Kitty;" Hand of the Devil," "Moon Goddess;" "Double Dragon," and "Aloha Island" to name just a few.

Slot machines have come a long way from their beginnings. No longer are payouts simply based on the three symbols that show up after a spin on the center line; now one may bet many different lines, horizontal, diagonal, and even zig zag simultaneously. To win the loyalty of younger consumers, some slot machines also have been combined with video games, requiring a certain level of skill in addition to chance.

For the Campo Kumeyaay Nation, which counts 365 tribal members and spouses and dependents, the casino is but one effort to bring prosperity to the historically impoverished 16,512-acre reservation in San Diego's back country. With three major Indian casinos—Viejas, Sycuan, and Barona—situated between Campo and San Diego, large crowds of gamblers never even see the Golden Acorn Casino. It does have the advantage, however, of being the first casino in San Diego County that is accessible to westbound traffic on the Interstate 8.

With more and more states permitting forms of off-reservation gambling, there always is the chance that the gaming market will become saturated, and that operations such as the Golden Acorn will suffer even more adversely from the competition.

Both to diversify and to supplement the reservation's income, the Campo Kumeyaay nation has built a combination gas station and travel center to accommodate passing motorists and truckers. It offers laundry facilities, hot showers, a quick-serve delicatessen, and packaged snacks in addition to gasoline.

More visually striking are the 25 wind turbines of Kumeyaay Wind for which the Campo band has provided the land for a share of the revenues. Since 2006, Kumeyaay Wind has been producing 50 megawatts of clean energy, which is carried via the Sunrise Power Link to a substation of San Diego Gas & Electric Co. Kumeyaay Wind helps to assure that the utility meets its goal of utilizing clean energy sources for 33 percent of the power delivered to customers. Kumeyaay Wind and other wind and solar sources, mostly in the Imperial Valley, enable the Sunrise Power Link to consistently supply 1,000 megawatts of sustainable energy to customers, according to SDG&E spokesman Hanan Eisenman.

As imposing as these wind turbines are, and as important as they are towards the goal of decreasing California's reliance on fossil fuels, the turbines are not a panacea for the reservation's economic problems. Falling energy prices have decreased the amount of money that they generate for the tribe. Property taxes charged by the county decrease the tribe's net revenues even further.

The Campo Kumeyaay Nation had proposed building a three-story hotel near the casino, but this met opposition during the county's planning process, and to date no groundbreaking has occurred.

Gambling is risky, and so too are investments in casinos and energy resources. But what else is a small reservation in a relatively remote location to do?

From Crestwood, Exit 61, turn right onto Old Highway 80. Casino entrance is on the left.

-*San Diego Jewish World, July 21, 2016*

68. Exit 65

Rough Acres Ranch

Rough Acres Ranch where San Diego Chargers trained in 1963

BOULEVARD, California — Whatever developers may someday build on the Rough Acres Ranch, it will be remembered by pro football fans as the place where San Diego Chargers Head Coach Sid Gillman decided to conduct the team's 1963 summer training camp. Gillman ordered his team, which had compiled a miserable record of 4 wins and 10 losses in the 1962 season, to report to what was then a rural and primitive dude ranch for the express purposes of toughening up. The coach wanted his players to be far from the distractions of coastal La Jolla, where in the previous pre-season the team had trained on the UCSD campus.

In the preceding 29 years of his football coaching, Gillman had been celebrated as the father of the modern passing game. In 1963, the Jewish coach decided to pioneer at least two additional modifications to classic football. In what was then the era of the Civil Rights Movement, he committed himself to thoroughly integrating his team with seven black players, who bunked with their white counterparts according to field position.

Additionally, he introduced a rigorous weight training program, especially for linemen. For this purpose, he brought aboard Alvin Roy, who had been the coach to the 1960 U.S. Olympics weightlifting team. To bulk the football team up, Roy prescribed not only lifting weights but also eating three hefty meals a day, each meal accompanied by 5 milligrams of a pink pill known by the brand name Dinabol and by the generic name methandrostenolone. The pills contained an artificial form of testosterone. Today, they would be known and understood as steroids, illegal in professional sports. But that was the dawn of the steroid era, when they were legal and their effects little understood. Roy said the Soviet Union's men's weightlifting team used the pink pills for the 1960 Olympics in which they took a gold medal in six of the seven events. Bulking up the Chargers, he figured, would enable them to outmuscle opponents at the line of scrimmage.

Some critics have said that because the Chargers linemen were "doped" by Roy, that was why the team would go on to win the 1963 American Football League (AFL) championship with a thrilling 51-10 victory over the Boston Patriots. One who disagrees is Ron Mix, who was later inducted into the pro football hall of fame and the International Jewish Sports Hall of Fame. He played on that team and led a player's revolt against use of the pills.

In an e-mail exchange with *San Diego Jewish World*, the former offensive tackle said the Chargers' 1963 championship was attributable to superior coaching and to on-the-field talent. Mix related that the team had only been taking the pills for approximately five weeks when he learned of their possible harmful side effects. He called a team meeting and informed the players and the vast majority of them stopped taking the pills. Mix said he could recall only a couple of players who continued and none of them were starters on the team. He said any benefit to taking Dianabol would have worn off long before the regular season started.

Mix said his fellow Jew, Gillman, who died in 2003, "had a group of assistant coaches who were stars in their own right: (1) Chuck Noll, later a Hall of Fame coach of the Pittsburgh Steelers; (2) Al Davis, later a Hall of Fame owner-coach, general manager of the Oakland Raiders; (3) Bum Phillips, later Head Coach of the Houston Oilers; and (4) Jack Faulkner, later Head Coach of the Denver Broncos. In addition, the Chargers had one of the top directors of player personnel, Don Klosterman. All these men were hired by Sid Gillman."

Furthermore, said Mix, an attorney now residing in San Diego, the talented Chargers squad included Tobin Rote; Hall of Famer Lance Allworth; All-Pro quarterback John Hadl; offensive tackle Ernie Right, who was "340 pounds of mean;" defensive end Earl Fasion who was also "mean," 280 pounds worth; and Mix himself as an offensive tackle. Mix declared that "Earle Ladd and Earl Fasion played their positions as well as anyone ever played and would both be in the Hall of Fame if injuries had not shortened their effective careers." Additionally, he said, no one should forget "two of the best running backs of all time, Paul Lowe and Keith Lincoln."

In Mix's view, although Gillman believed the team's success was due to "isolating the team in Rough Acres, the truth is we won despite Rough Acres."

He said that the Rough Acres Ranch consisted of "a mess hall, about 40 one-room shacks (yes 'shacks.') It would be an exaggeration to call these facilities 'ranch houses.' They were small, made of wood, no air conditioning, so small that players were assigned two to each shack and slept in bunk beds. (no misprint bunk beds!)

"The practice field was so rough and hard that grass could barely grow and the entire field had to be covered in sawdust," wrote Mix, apparently living the nightmare all over again. "There were no indoor showers—a slab of cement was laid, surrounded by a mid-sized fence and players showered outdoors.

"During our eight weeks there, a total of between 15 and 20 rattlesnakes were killed.

"The food was perhaps the worst I have ever had at a training camp. Wait I need to change that: it was the worst I have ever had before or since.

"Sleep was difficult because, as I said, there was no air conditioning in the shacks but there were enough holes in the wooden walls to admit mosquitos and the desert heat did not seem to diminish much in the evening. Bad food and lack of sleep do not present ideal conditions to mold a team.

"To me, Rough Acres was a negative. The players took things into their hands by causing enough damage to the ranch that the owner sued the team and declined to rent the ranch again to the team."

Summarizing, Mix said, "the positives, however, outweighed the negatives. And the positives were that we were a team that because of weight-training was the strongest team in professional football; we had the smartest coaches, and we had superior talent."

ESPN writer T.J. Quinn wrote in 2009 about the use of steroids by the 1963 Chargers, quoting Mix extensively. He noted that Mix was then the team captain and a four-year veteran of the AFL. Mix said a doctor was shocked to learn what the players were taking, and showed them the literature about the pills. Said Mix:

> I still remember what it says. It was in big red letters. It said, 'Dangerous. Not to be taken over extended periods of time, will cause permanent bone damage, liver damage, heart damage, testicle shrinkage.' Now comes the obligatory joke," Mix says. "The other three we could live with. But the last — no!"
>
> ...[Roy] was a very knowledgeable guy. Unfortunately, apparently, he had a major character flaw," Mix says. "And that character flaw was [that] he wanted results. He didn't care how you got the outcome of the results. And, if the outcome of the results included using something that had the potential of being dangerous, he endorsed it. Hence the Dianabol.

Mix spoke up against mandatory use of Dinabol during a team meeting prior to the regular season. Thereafter players no longer were required to take them, although some did–at least until 1970, according to Quinn.

Steroids were banned by the NFL in 1983, two decades after the experiments at Rough Acres Ranch.

....

From Exit 65, take CA-94/Ribbonwood Road toward Campo Boulevard, then turn right onto CA 94, turn left onto Old Hway 80, turn left onto McCain Valley Road, slight left to stay on McCain Valley Road, then a left, and a right at 2750 McCain Valley Road in Boulevard.

....

69. Exit 73
Jacumba Hot Springs

The faded town of Jacumba Hot Springs

JACUMBA HOT SPRINGS, California — At one point, Henry LaZare owned practically the entire town of Jacumba, including its water company and the storied Jacumba Hotel, where legend has it that such Hollywood stars as Clark Gable and Marlene Dietrich liked to hang out in the 1930s.

Located near the border of Baja California, Mexico, and the boundary line between San Diego County and Imperial County, Jacumba's 2,800 foot elevation also drew Imperial Valley residents seeking to escape the summer heat in the days before homes were air conditioned.

Longtime Jacumba resident Beverly Woodward, in a 2015 interview, remembered LaZare quite kindly. In 1947 when she was about to be married to James Woodward, the water to her home was limited because pipes were being replaced. LaZare offered her a room at the hotel to prepare for her wedding, which was conducted in the old Community Church. Like the hotel that church is no longer standing.

Asked to describe the old four-story hotel, Woodward said: "You stepped in the front door off the veranda into a huge room that had a huge, beautiful rock fireplace... When you first stepped in, to the right there was an alcove where you would check in. The receptionist also served as the secretary for the LaZare Water Company, and you paid your water bills there. The secretary also helped alert people when we had a fire. My husband was the fire chief for many years and when there would be a fire, I would call the hotel, and she would go through the list and notify all the volunteers. Past her desk was a stairway that went straight up to the guest rooms. There was a bar adjacent to the dining room, east of the front door. It was a well-lit room."

Another longtime resident, Shirley Fisher, said at a time when she was experiencing trouble walking, LaZare invited her to stay at the hotel, and "it was lovely, a great place, homey and nice. It wasn't elegant, just nice and homey. Everyone ate at the same time in the dining room. He was kind. In the old country, he was a chiropractor, specializing in rehabilitation."

As for the guest rooms, "the one I stayed in was very nice; it was old fashioned, not fancy, kind of sparse like a Motel 6. Since they had movie stars who'd come there, they probably had fancier rooms. I think mine cost $20 per day" back in the 1950s.

All this was during Jacumba's golden era, when the major route between San Diego and points east—Highway 80—passed through the heart of town. But time worked reverse alchemy on Jacumba, turning gold to dross. In April 1967, a new highway, Interstate 8, bypassed downtown Jacumba, and although the town lay only three miles from Exit 73, most motorists kept right on driving. Eventually, many businesses were boarded up, but dreams of revitalizing the town, and bringing it back to its former glory, refused to die.

LaZare eventually sold the hotel—which previously had been known as the Vaughn Hotel after the town's founder Bert Vaughn—to an investment group. After that, the hotel changed hands more than once. San Diego investor Morris Slayen was among a group that purchased the hotel with plans to capitalize on the area's hot springs and market Jacumba to working class travelers.

Slayen's son, Ron, recalled that "he saw it as a spot where working class people, who couldn't afford places like the Golden Door or Rancho La Puerta, might enjoy the hot springs, which were located right across the street."

He wanted to provide something for working class people, Ron Slayen added, because "that was in his DNA." One of eight children born to a working class, immigrant family, Morrie Slayen's first business was the California Upholstery and Hobby Shop on 7th Avenue, between F and G Streets, in San Diego.

"He did whatever he needed to do to make a living, Ron recalled." It usually had something to do with interiors. He started off in upholstery, then he added window coverings, carpets, whatever it was.

"When I was in high school, he traded with the famous tennis coach Ben Press (whose students included tennis star Maureen "Little Mo" Connolly) for lessons for me and my brother Larry in return for window coverings."

Slayen's business grew little by little: he did interior work for military housing in the Kearny Mesa area of San Diego and the City of Twentynine Palms, and also for the interiors of ships built at local shipyards. All the while, he remained in downtown, even as other businesses, following the trend, moved to suburban shopping centers.

"He believed in downtown," said Ron. Little by little he bought properties in the downtown area, and was among the local business leaders who successfully pitched developer Ernest Hahn to build the downtown Horton Plaza Shopping Center. Once the shopping center was built, property values started to climb back, and eventually surpassed the pre-shopping center levels. Slayen found himself counted among the rich men in the city.

Usually he would buy properties on his own, fix them up, and then rent them out. He didn't believe in any fancy renovations, often snorting that his purpose in life wasn't to make architects rich and famous; he just wanted the buildings rehabbed to make them serviceable.

Friends seeing his success would ask Slayen whether they could invest with him. For the Jacumba Hotel, he put together small group of investors and after purchasing the property put his sister Sylvia behind the hotel's front desk. Work began on the guest rooms, but, Ron recalled, "the rest of the building was in need of elbow grease. It was an old building, with an old electrical system."

In 1983, fire possibly of electrical origin, destroyed the old hotel. Today, only the chimney stands as a grim reminder of what once was.

Slayen was elected as a president of the United Jewish Federation of San Diego County (today simply called "The Jewish Federation"). There were stories about how Slayen would ask people to pledge money to that communal organization and kept the doors locked until they said yes. While the stories probably are exaggerations, Slayen was one of the Federation's best fundraisers. He was very enamored with Israel and did whatever he could to help the Jewish state.

Ron said his father, who died in 2009 at age 87, was generous in other ways. While he didn't have the patience to sit through a symphony, he was a supporter of music. One favorite story concerned a parking lot attendant whom Morrie heard playing the violin. In answer to Morrie's queries, the musician said he was studying at a conservatory, but needed to work at the parking lot to pay for his upkeep. Morrie asked him how much he made a week and arranged to pay him the same amount, if he would stop working at the parking lot and concentrate on his music.

Ron said he would love to know if the musician ever experienced great success, but he lost track of him.

Slayen also was a supporter of actress and producer Kit Goldman, whose Gaslamp Quarter Theatre was important to bringing culture back to the Gaslamp Quarter. Ron said his father donated all the space for the theatre's offices and for their set designs. "They were there for a number of years, and he was a major supporter."

Although the Jacumba Hotel was destroyed, the hope of the town for revitalization were not.

Dave Landman, who once worked as a mortgage broker in Northern California, purchased many of the properties in Jacumba and step by step, little by little, he has been attempting to revitalize the town.

While the grand Jacumba Hotel still is but a memory, within a short walking distance down and across Highway 80 is the southwestern themed Jacumba Hot Springs Spa and Resort, which offers guests the opportunity to dip and lounge by a hot-springs-filled pool and Jacuzzi. The resort has 24 rooms, the Raven's Bar, and the Tepary Southwest Grill. The spa started life as a café--before the pool and Jacuzzi were added--so there is a long tradition there of appeasing people's appetites.

More famous, a couple miles out of town, is the De Anza Springs Resort, which Landman, a nudist himself operates with his wife Helen, as a clothing optional facility. Additionally, Landman owns the small Lake Jacumba, previously known as Lake LaZare, which sometime in the future he hopes to restore as well. The name "Jacumba" is reported to stem from a Kumeyaay word meaning "hut by the water." On the Mexican side of the border fence is a small town, "Jacume," inspired by the same Kumeyaay word. Although there was once a border crossing between the two towns, post 9-11 the way has been blocked by a tall fence.

Symbolic of his hopes for the future, Landman recently had the name of the town officially changed from Jacumba to Jacumba Hot Springs. He said the latter was its original name, but somehow people shortened it to Jacumba.

LaZare and Slayen were both Jews. Landman is the son of a Jewish father and Baptist mother.

....

From Exit 73, follow Carrizo Gorge Road south to Olde Highway 80 and turn right. Follow this road into town.

....

-San Diego Jewish World, August 4, 2016

70. Exit 77
Desert View Tower

Merle Ratcliffe sculptures and Desert View Tower

JACUMBA HOT SPRINGS, California — The dogs that greet visitors at the entrance to the venerable Desert View Tower are alive, if sleepy in the hot sun, but there are many other animals nearby that never drew a breath of life since they were whimsically created in the 1930s by sculptor Merle Ratcliffe.

Climbing with my grandson Shor amidst the boulder patch facing the Desert View Tower, I couldn't help but imagine what would have happened if Mount Ararat, the supposed resting place of Noah's Ark, had been situated in the climate found here at the border of San Diego and Imperial Counties, where mountains littered with igneous outcroppings descend quickly to the desert floor.

Would the passengers of the Ark--both animals and people--somehow have become calcified, or transformed to pillars of stone, only to be discovered later by indigenous explorers and latter-day picnickers? The Desert View Tower's owner and curator, Ben Schultz, says the topography here, with its plenteous La Posta pluton, is duplicated in only one other place in the world--the rocky descent from the Judaean Mountains down to the Dead Sea in Israel.

Really, your imagination can run wild up here in the cliffs west of the Imperial Desert floor--as apparently Ratcliff's did. Not much is known about the sculptor, except that he was an out of work engineer during the Great Depression years, and that he spent at least two years carving his fantasy, which today shares honors with the Desert View Tower as a state historic monument and a stellar example of folk art. An historic marker at the site misidentifies him, calling him W. T. Ratcliff, instead of the correct M.T. Ratcliff, according to Schultz.

Schultz suggests that the crannies amid the boulders have been used for thousands of years by Native American peoples seeking protection from the winds, which occasionally can be "horrific." It is likely, he said, that Yuman Indians were the first to find potable water seepage in this pass through the mountains. In the 20th century, they were followed first by Highway 80 road builders and later by Interstate 8 construction teams. "Going down from here to the desert floor is a terrible way through, but it is the best for 100 miles," Schultz said. "The pluton makes a strong wall, and this is the best place in the wall to get through."

Construction of the Desert View Tower preceded the carving of the boulders. Bert L. Vaughn, who owned the resort at nearby Jacumba Hot Springs, began the rock tower in the 1920s, but left it unfinished. After World War II, an American flyer, Dennis Newman, purchased and renovated the tower before opening it to the public as a roadside tourist attraction in 1950. On land of 3,000 foot elevation, it stands an additional 70 feet tall. Visitors winding up its staircases to the top floor lookout can find eclectic collections of weapons, curios, and relics at different landings.

Ownership of the structure passed through several hands until 2003, when Schultz purchased it. Having grown up in San Diego--near the now demolished 54th Street Jewish Community Center, where he picked up Jewish expressions while swimming regularly in the Olympic-size pool--Schultz said the Desert View Tower always was one of his favorite places to hang out. He said he can remember when many cars couldn't make it up the mountain without overheating unless they stopped at the Desert View Tower.

It's a good place to buy a soft drink and perhaps a curio, and to scan the descent to the desert floor. For kids, the adjoining Boulder Park is a delightful playground, filled with surprises.

Is that a skeleton's skull up there?

....

Take In-Ko-Pah Park Road, Exit 77, turn left to north side of freeway and turn right onto In-Ko-Pah Park Road, which leads to the Desert View Tower.

....

-San Diego Jewish World, August 11, 2016

Index by chapter

-H-

-N-

-Y-

-Z-

57341489R00193

Made in the USA
San Bernardino, CA
19 November 2017